BEST OF TIMES

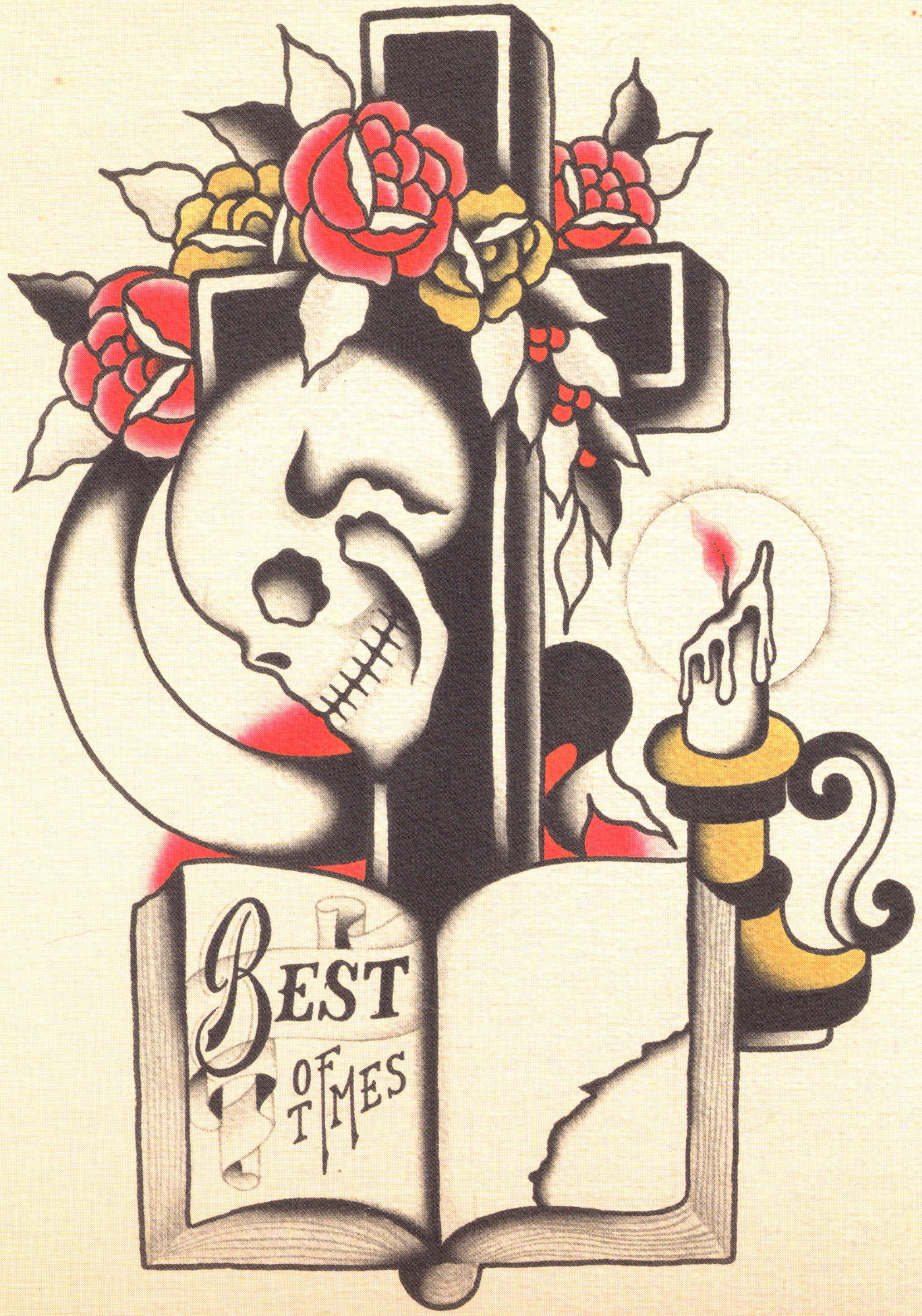

ITALIAN TATTOO FLASH

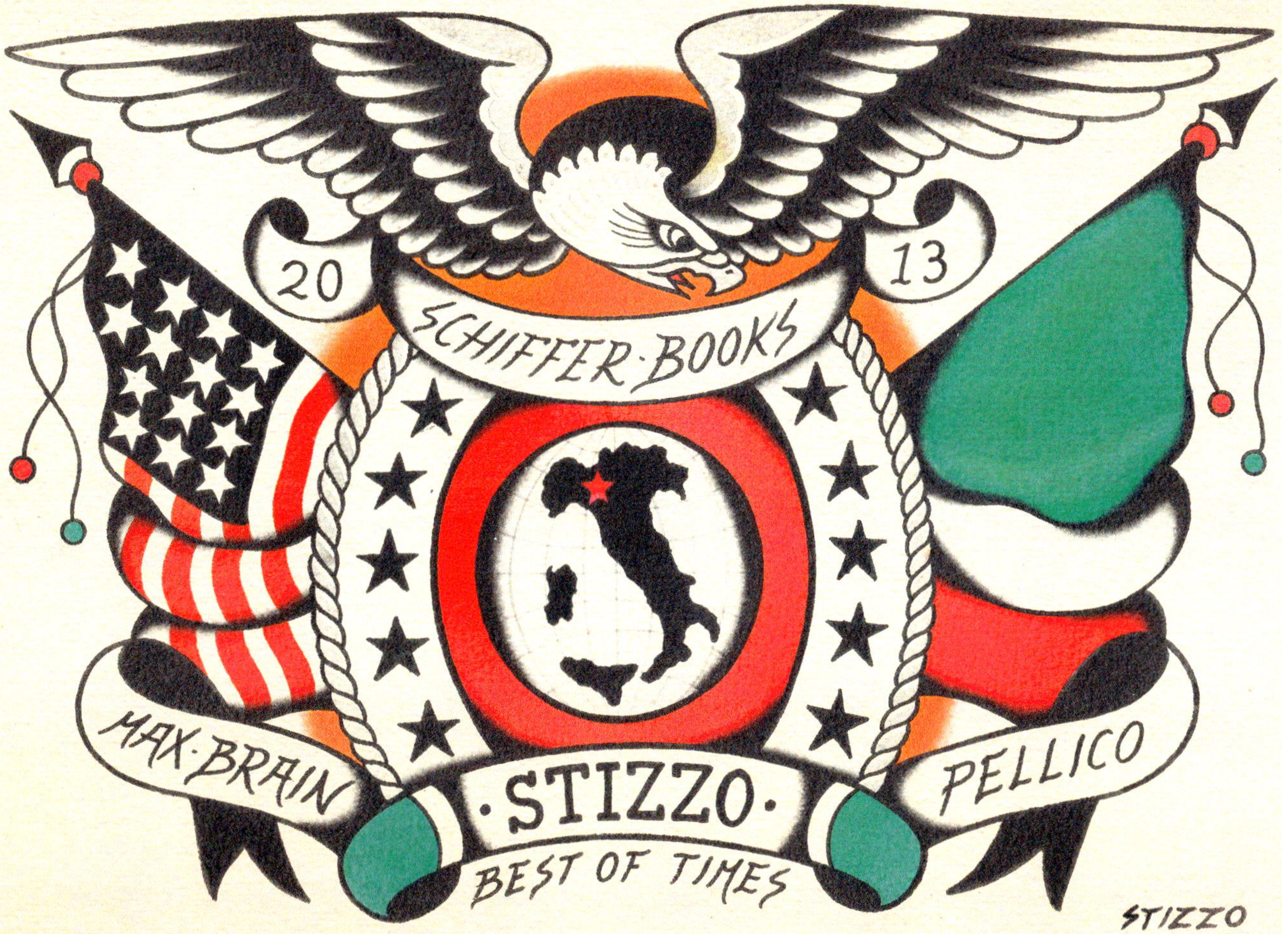

20 13
SCHIFFER·BOOKS
MAX·BRAIN
·STIZZO·
PELLICO
BEST OF TIMES
STIZZO

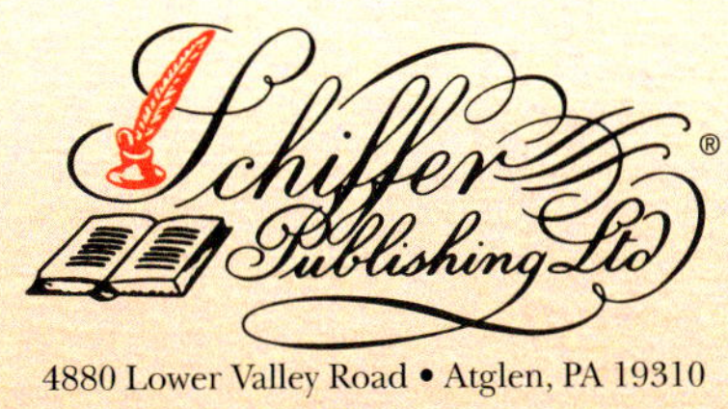

4880 Lower Valley Road • Atglen, PA 19310

Other Schiffer Books on Related Subjects:

Flash from the Bowery: Classic American Tattoos, 1900-1950. Cliff White. ISBN: 978-0-7643-3928-8.

Life & Death in Tattoo Flash. Christopher Norrell. ISBN: 978-0-7643-4205-9.

Classic Flash in Five Bold Colors. Jeromey "Tilt" McCulloch. ISBN: 978-0-7643-3165-7.

Library of Congress Control Number: 2014930797

Designed by Justin Watkinson
Type set in URWWoodTypD/Aachen BT/Zurich BT

ISBN: 978-0-7643-4626-2
Printed in India

Published by Schiffer Publishing, Ltd.
4880 Lower Valley Road
Atglen, PA 19310
Phone: (610) 593-1777; Fax: (610) 593-2002
E-mail: Info@schifferbooks.com
Web: www.schifferbooks.com

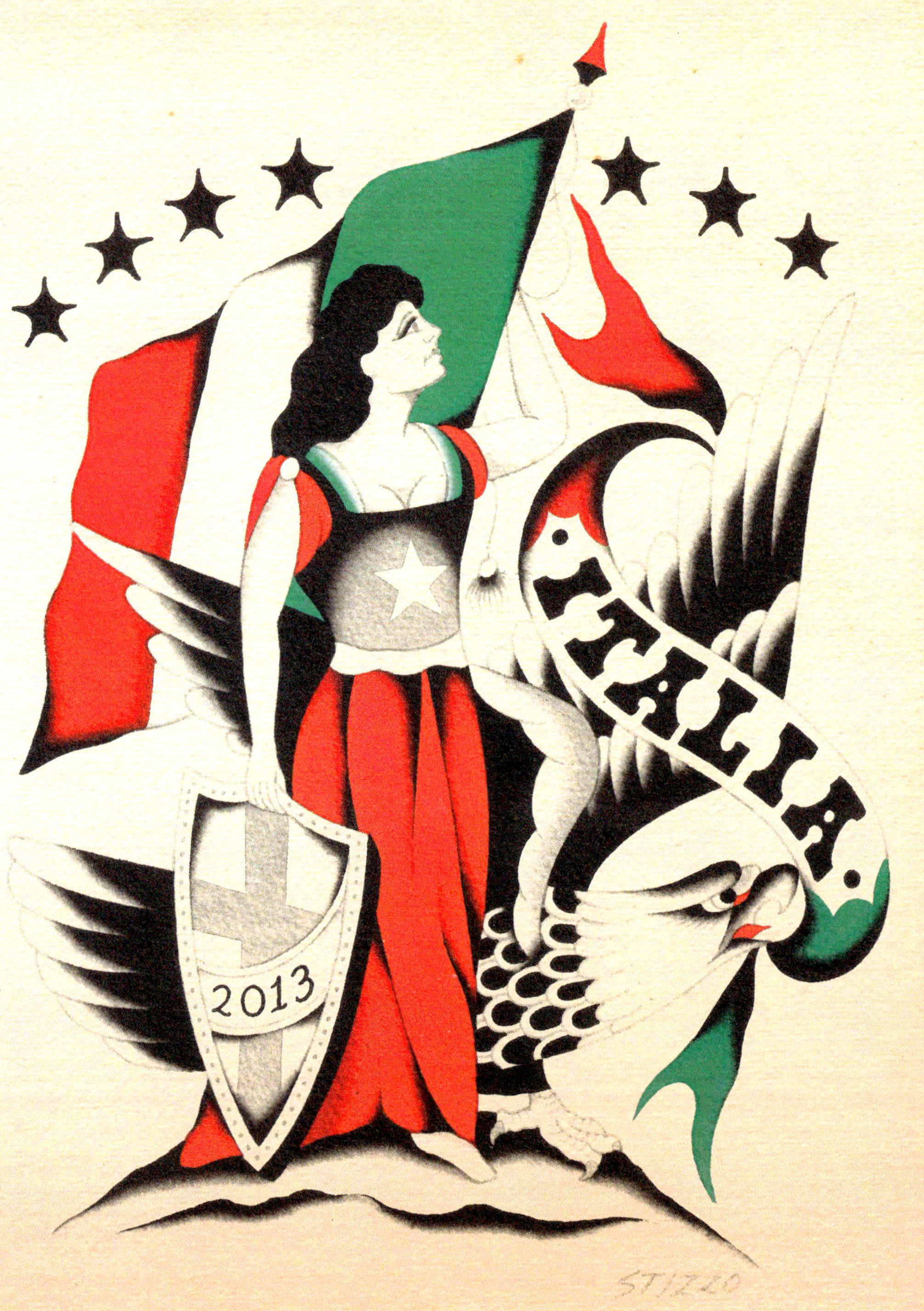

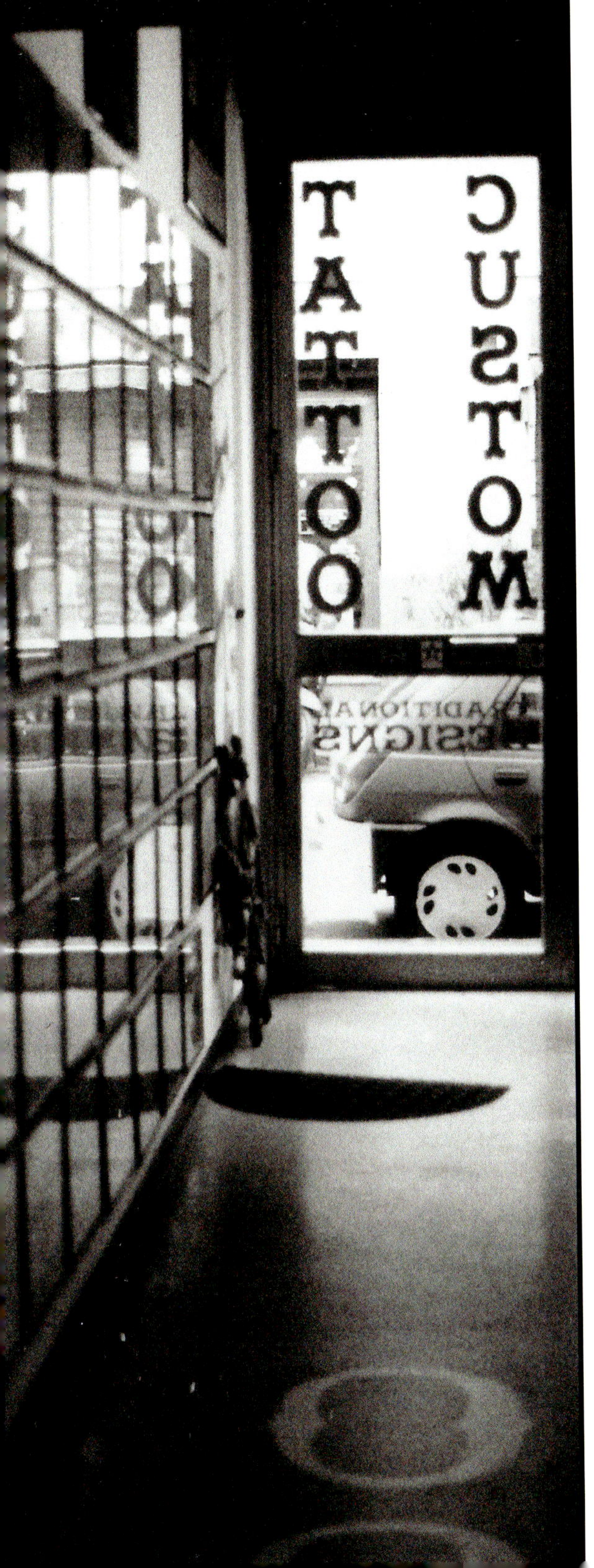

CONTENTS

INTRODUCTION

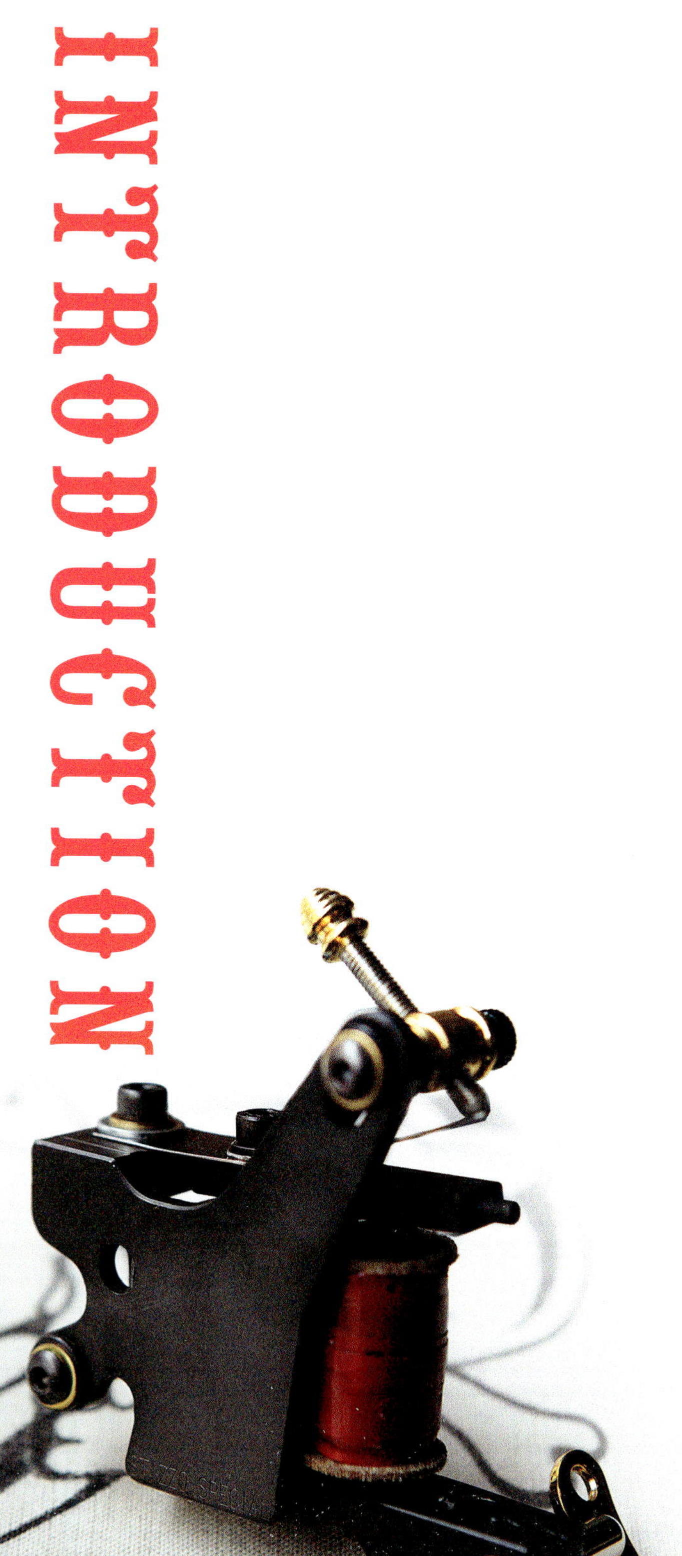

The fulfillment of this book represents a very important goal in my artistic and working career. Flipping through the pages, I hope you can get and almost touch by hand what painting means to me, even if in this case it is limited to tattoo flash sheets.

The continuous research of a style, a character, a mark: this is the idea that accompanied me and still follows me through my artistic life, giving me so many satisfactions. At the beginning, this clearly concerned just me; but then the idea expanded when the "Best of Times" was born. I soon realized, with pride and satisfaction, that my thoughts, my style, and my dedication to work are an inspiration and an example for all the people around me and for all those who try to "read" my works carefully. In these pages, I think I succeeded in really expressing what I wanted to, hands on. It's hard to express in words, but a few years ago I couldn't even imagine improving the artistic reputation of a team in such a way. And now the works of Max Brain and Silvio Pellico are the demonstration of all these things.

All that I feel when I'm painting and tattooing, I can see in the eyes of the people to whom I've handed down all my knowledge about "this world." I hope I have been successful in communicating to everybody the power and the mark of our work. Commitment, dedication, and perseverance are essential for the career of an artist, and they must be pursued daily. I've tried particularly to draw attention to the genuine side of this work, addressing specifically those who are starting to move closer to the world of tattoo. The sheets that compose the book have been painted within a year—you can indeed notice the improvement and evolution of the style in a such short time.

The research and study of european tattoo artists, above all from England, gave me the starting point for the painting of these sheets, in which it is possible to find many references to these artists. Also, the history of Italian and European art served as a huge inspiration to all three of us. As an Italian, I effectively tried to give to my work a traditional and classical mark, with constant references to the city of Milan, where I was born and I still work, a city to which I'm truly bound up with memories. Milan is a city with an important history and I really hope, with this book, to contribute to the writing of a chapter of this amazing story, too.

Stizzo, June 2013

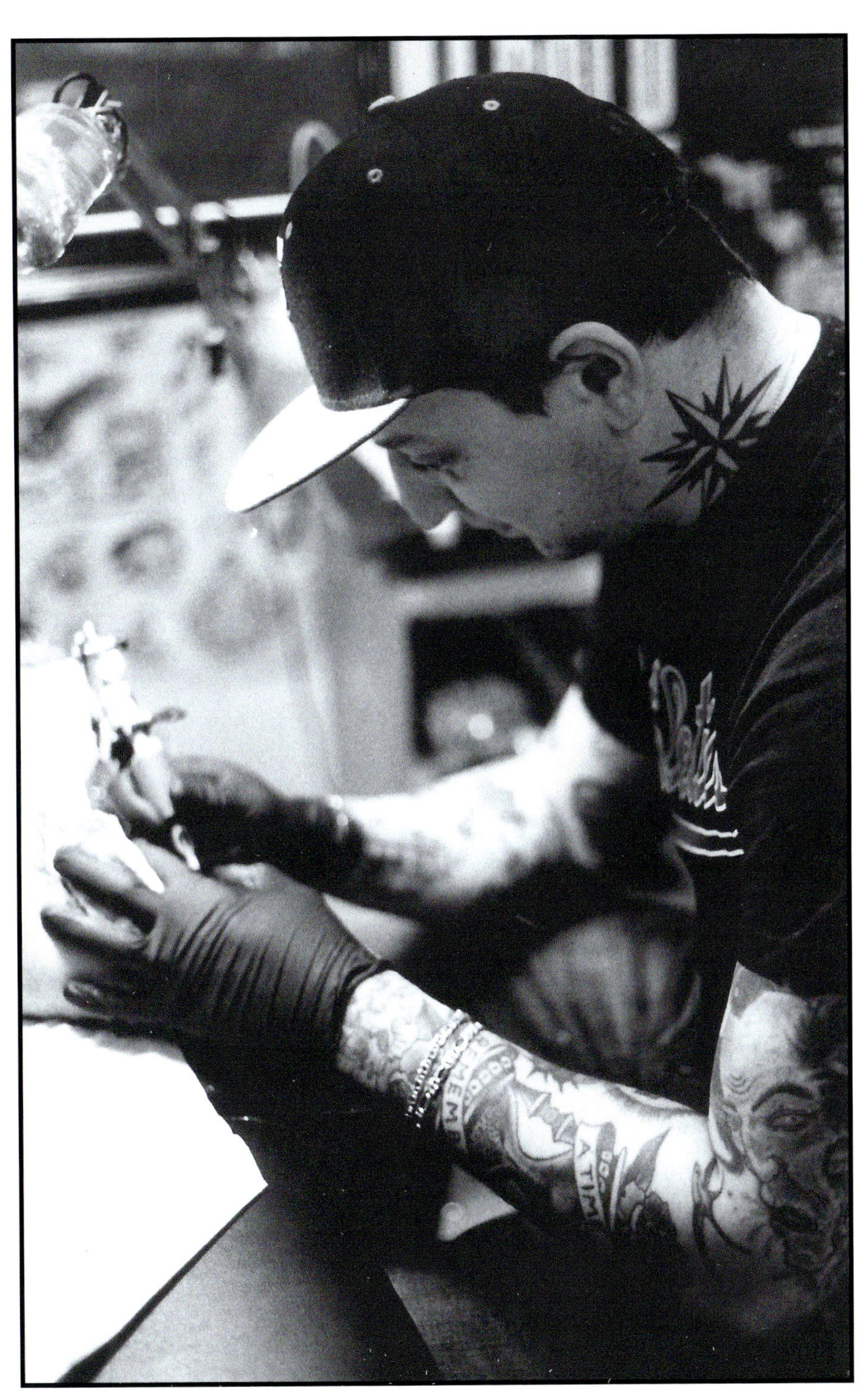

STIZZO

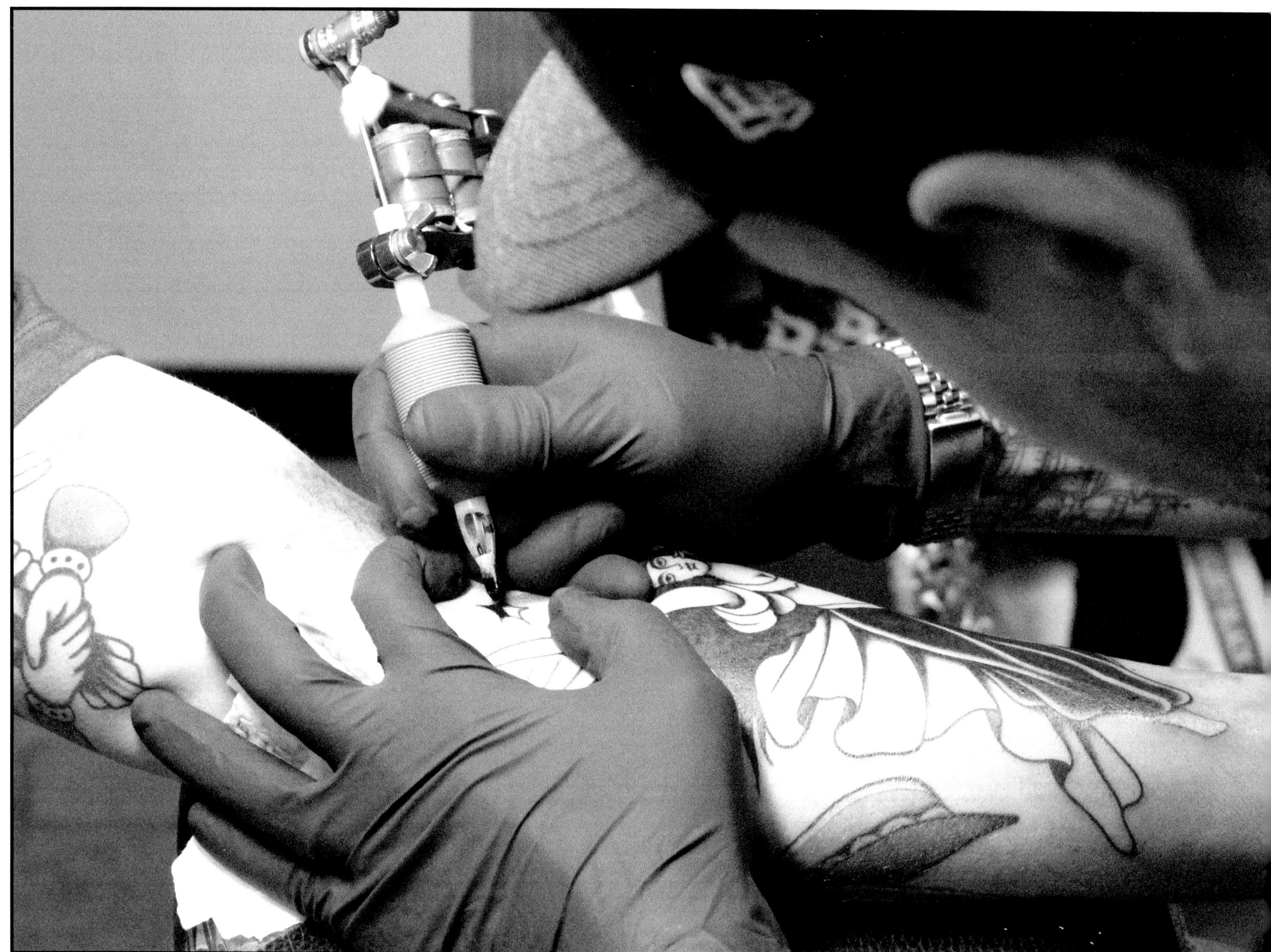

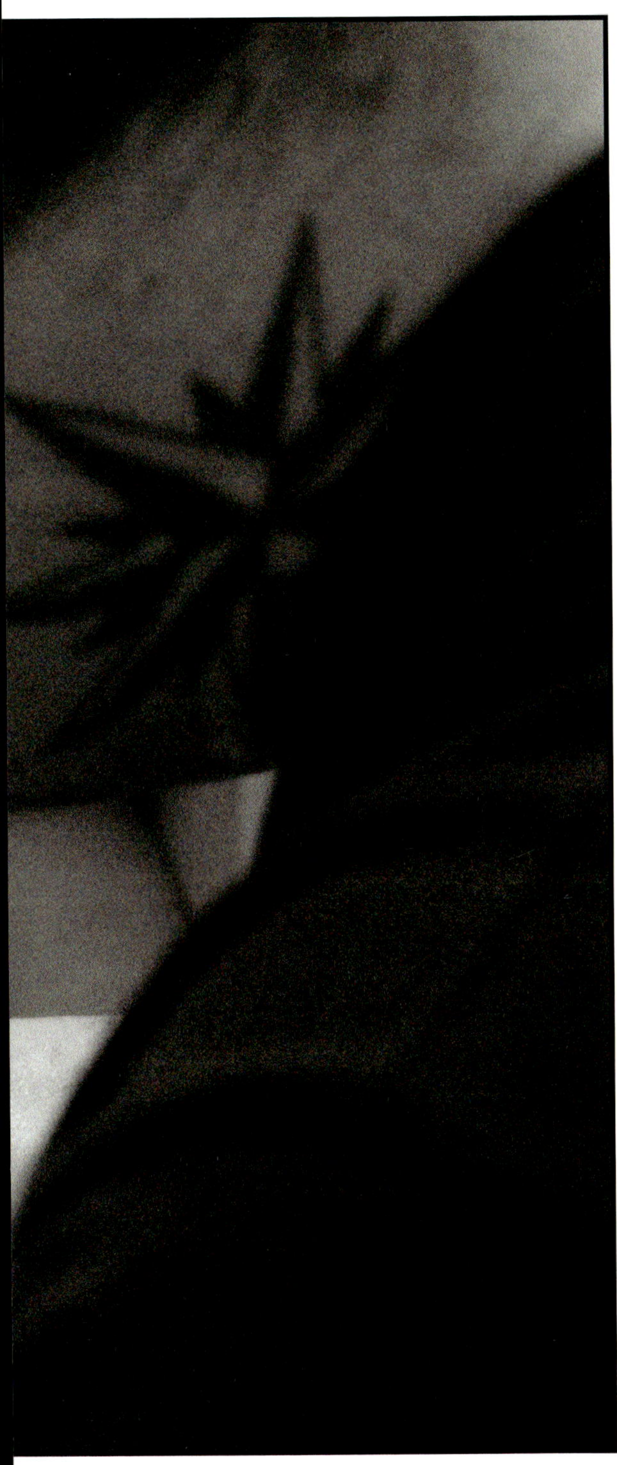

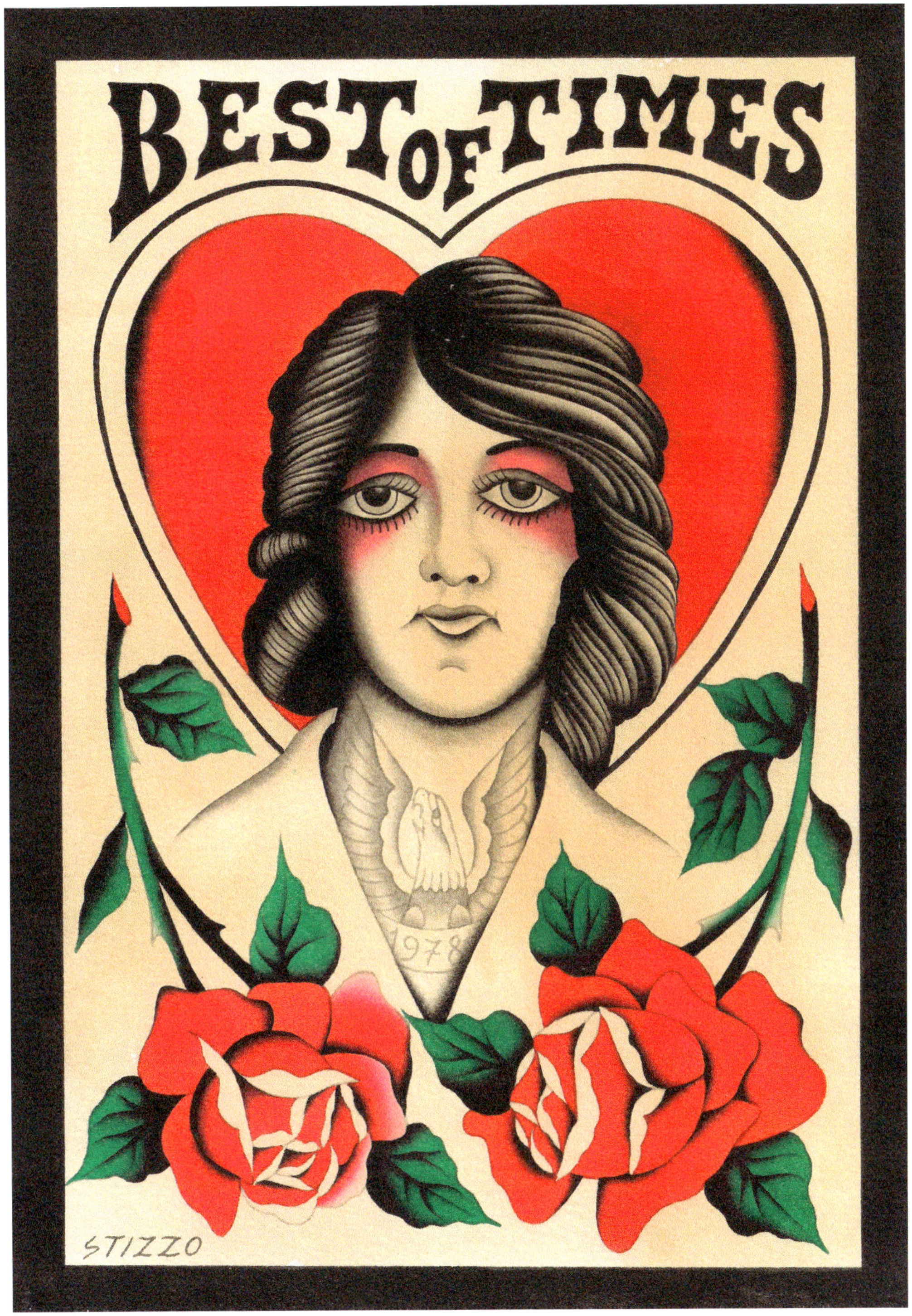

BEST OF TIMES

1978

STIZZO

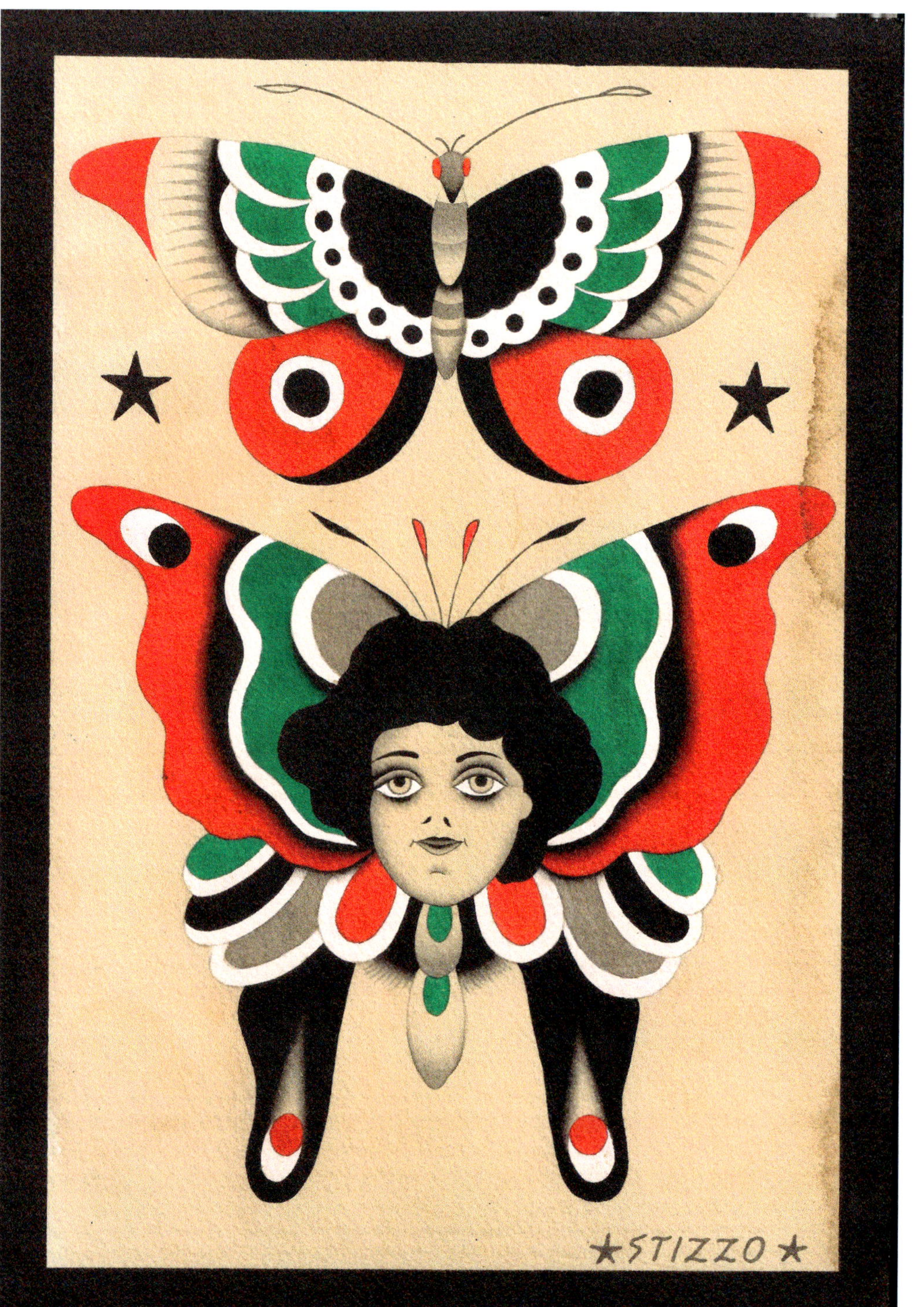
★STIZZO★

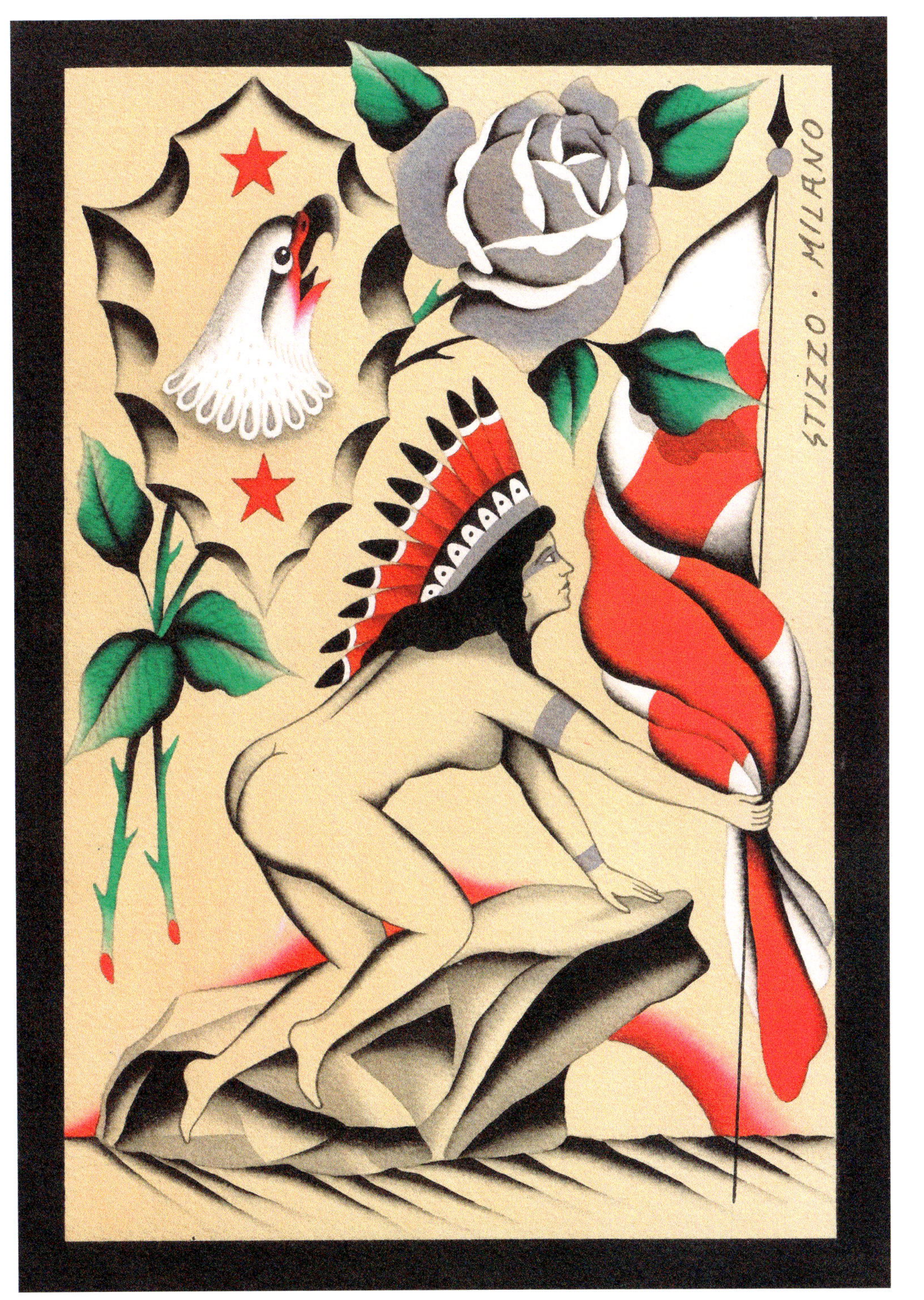
STIZZO · MILANO

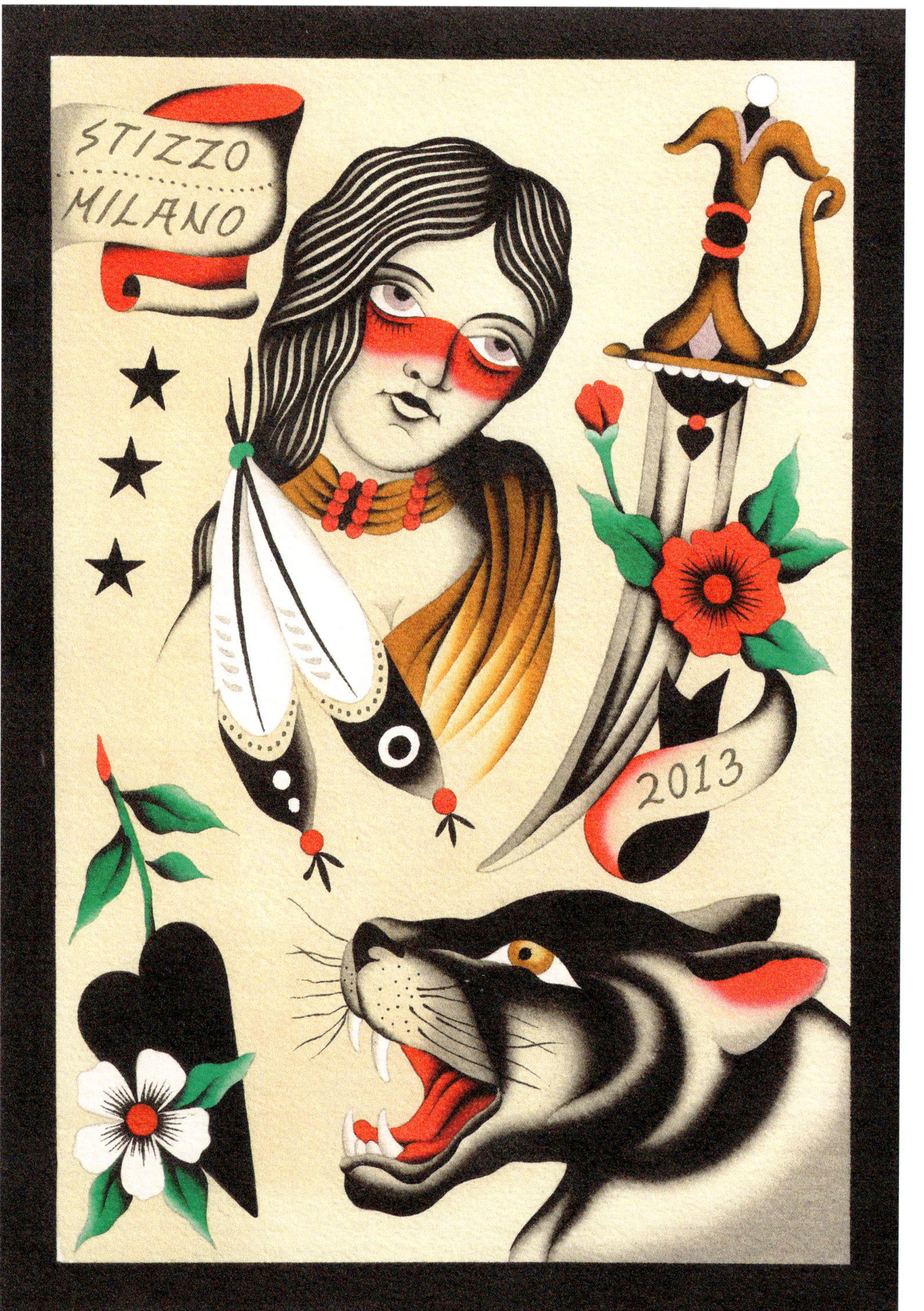
STIZZO
MILANO
2013

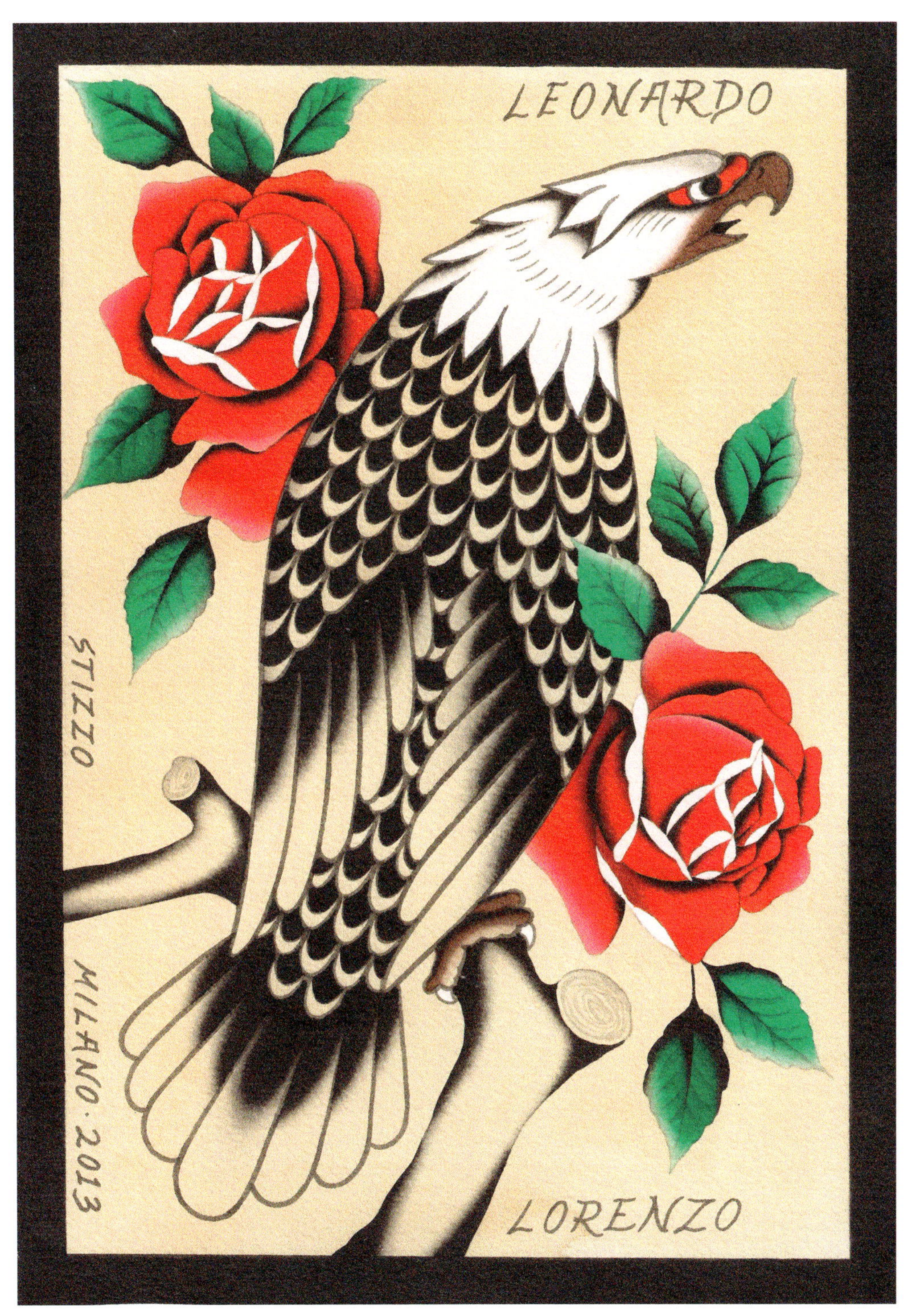
LEONARDO
STIZZO
MILANO · 2013
LORENZO

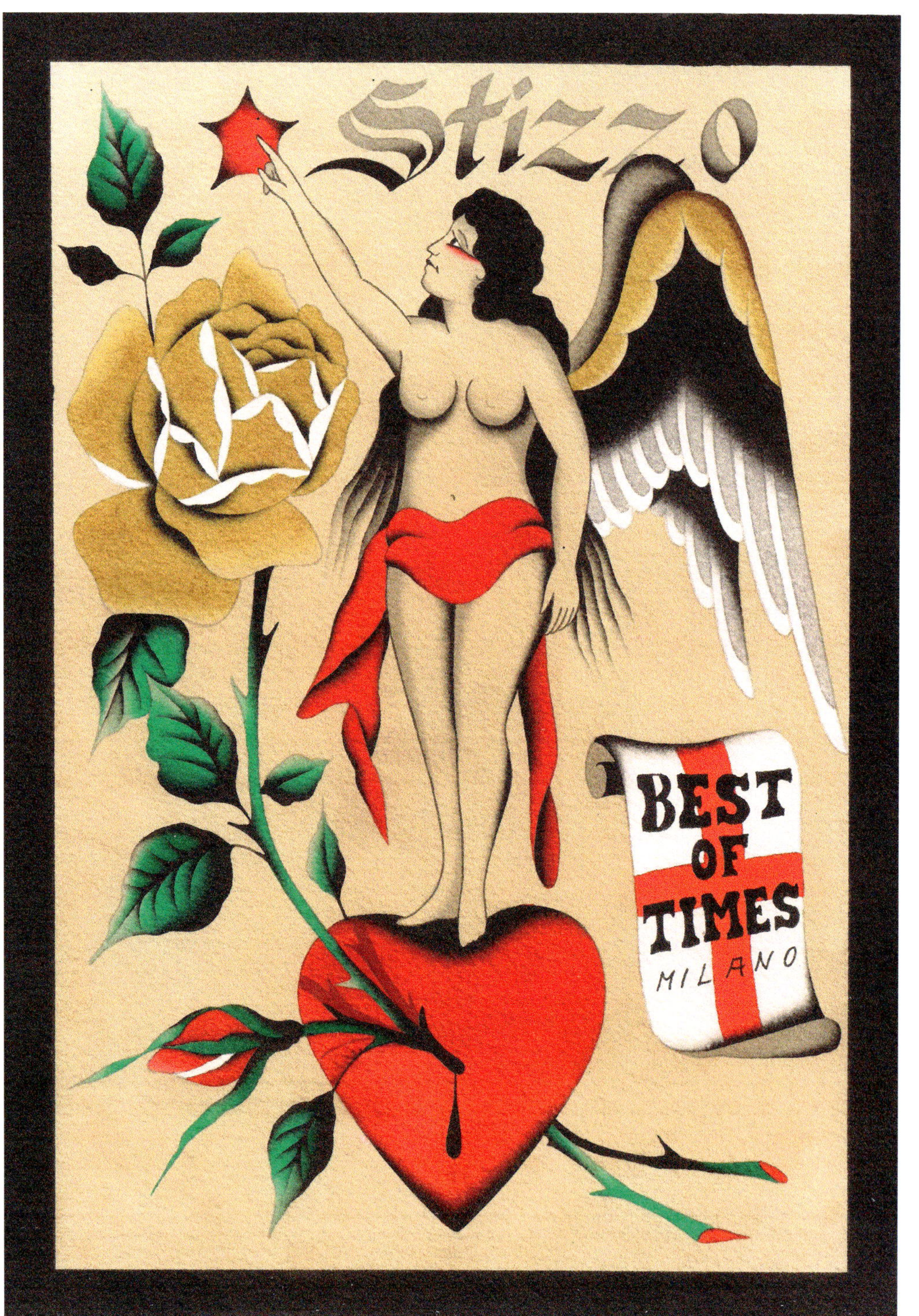
Stizzo
BEST OF TIMES
MILANO

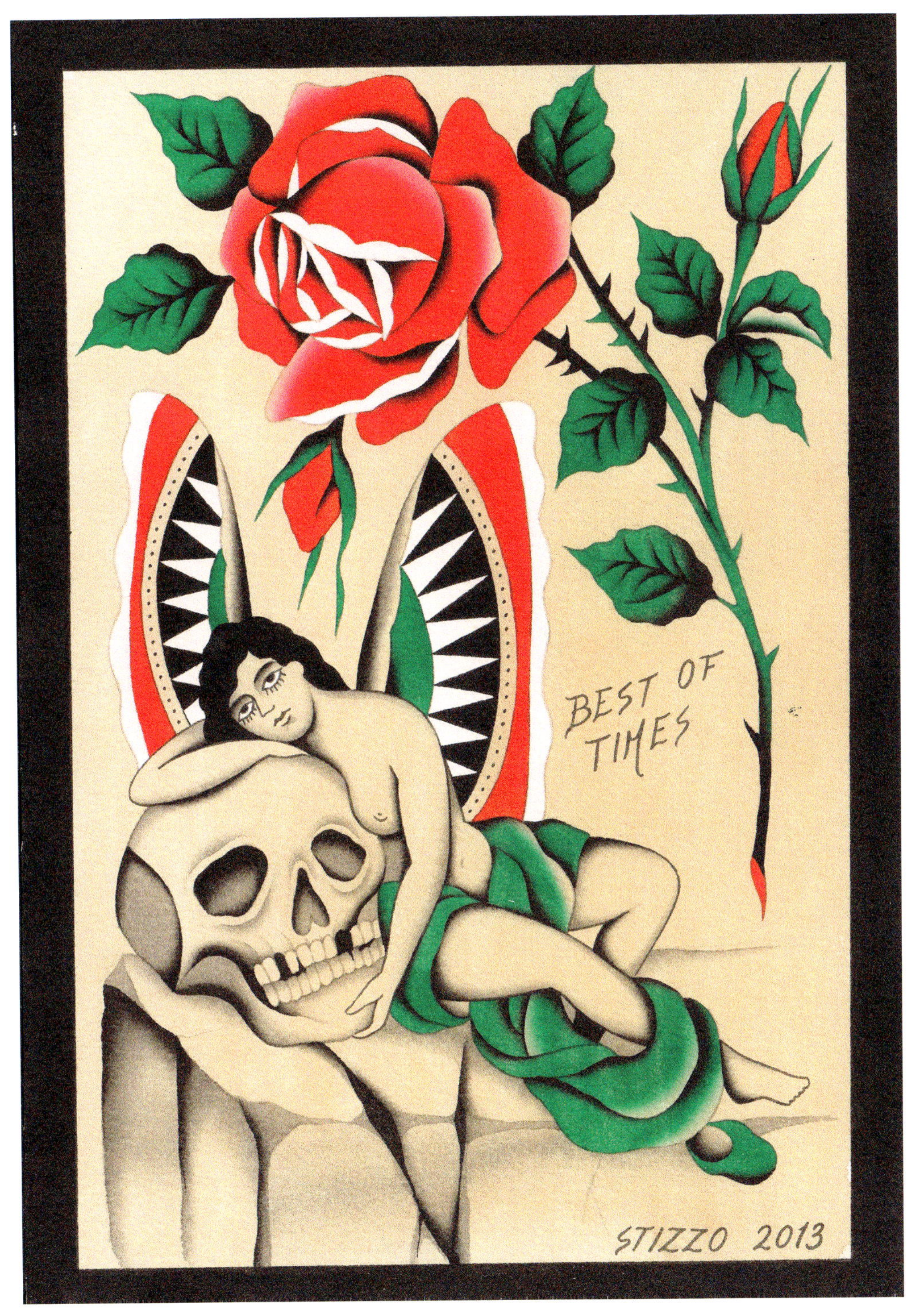
BEST OF
TIMES
STIZZO 2013

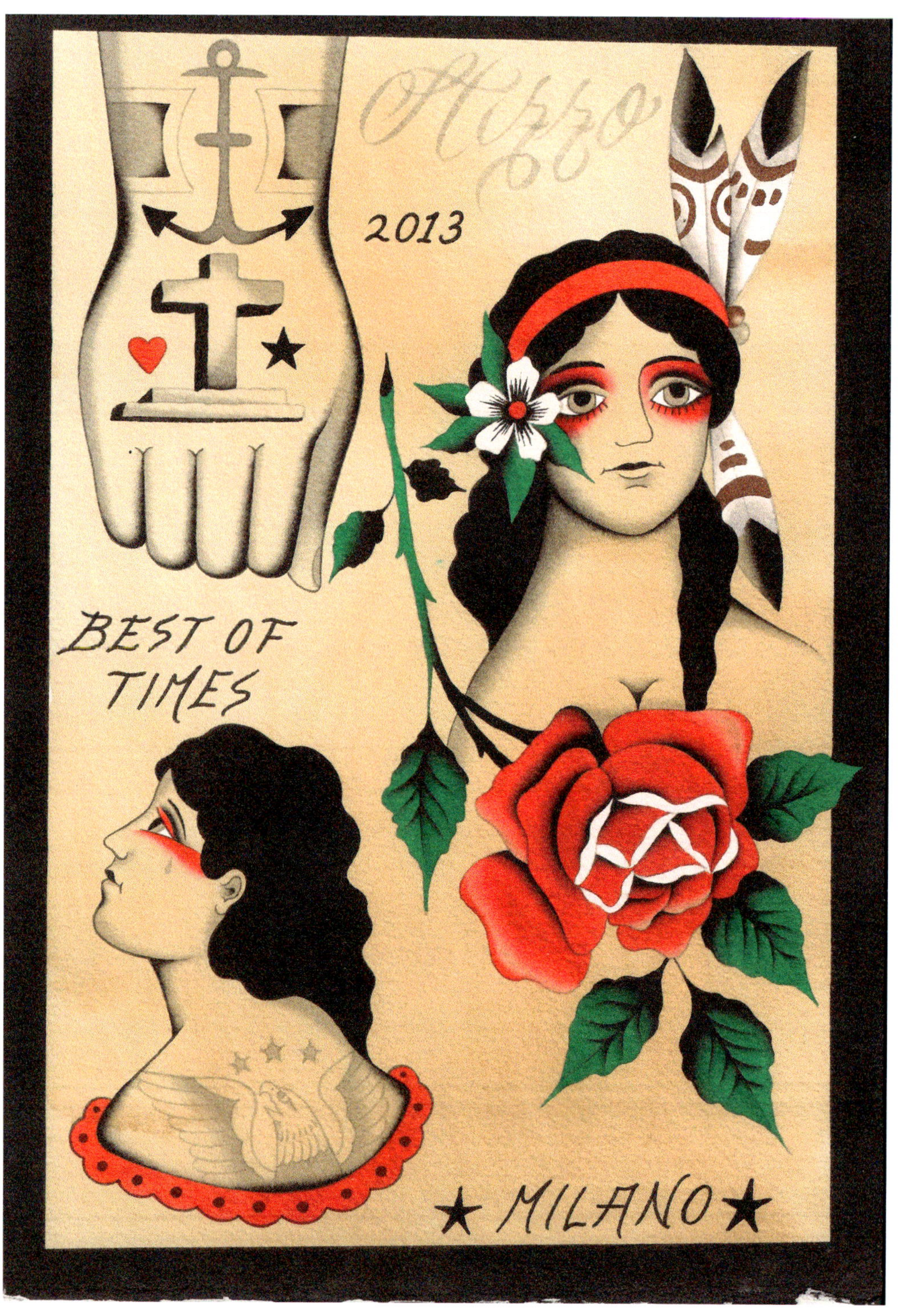

2013
BEST OF
TIMES
★ MILANO ★

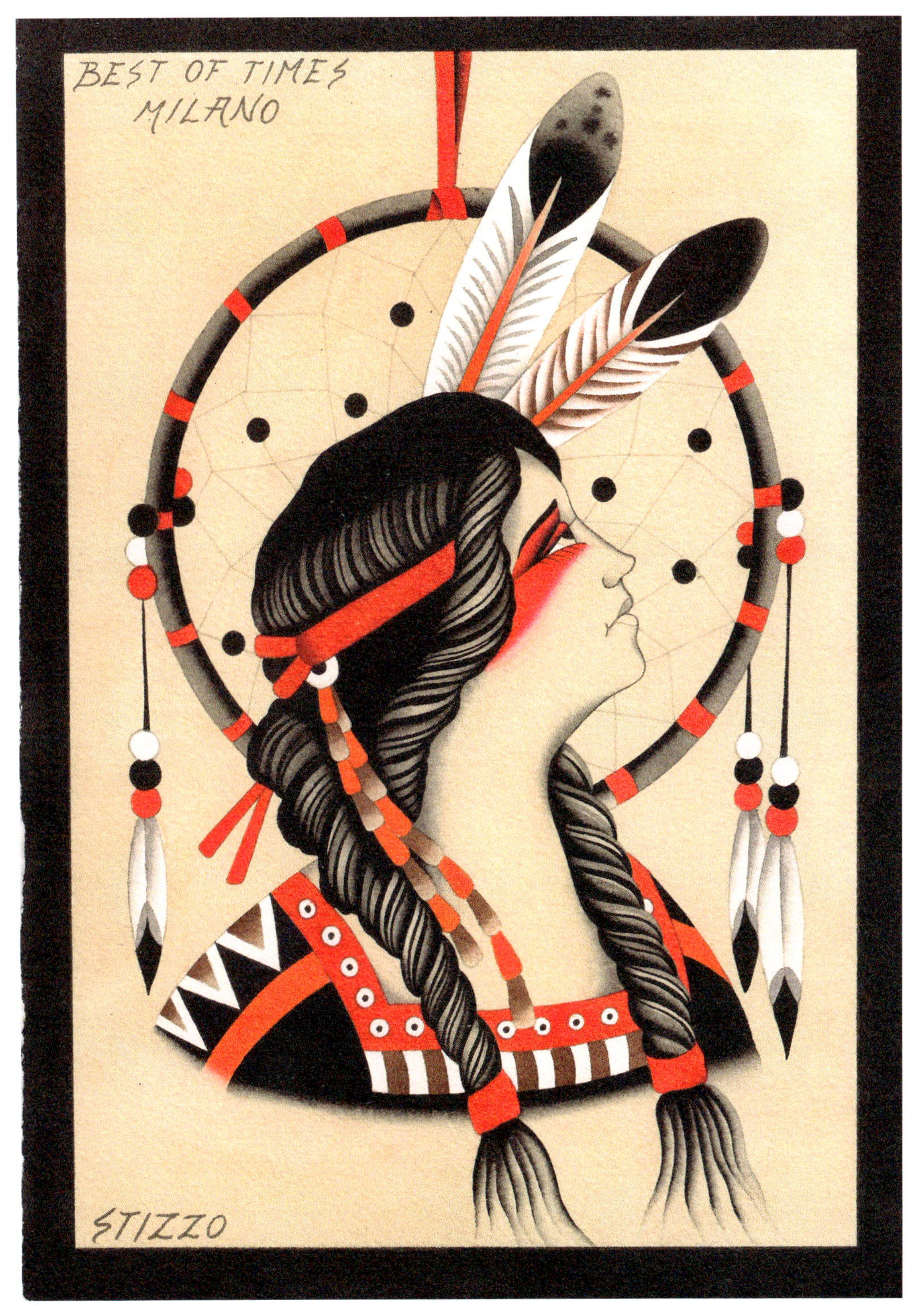
BEST OF TIMES
MILANO
STIZZO

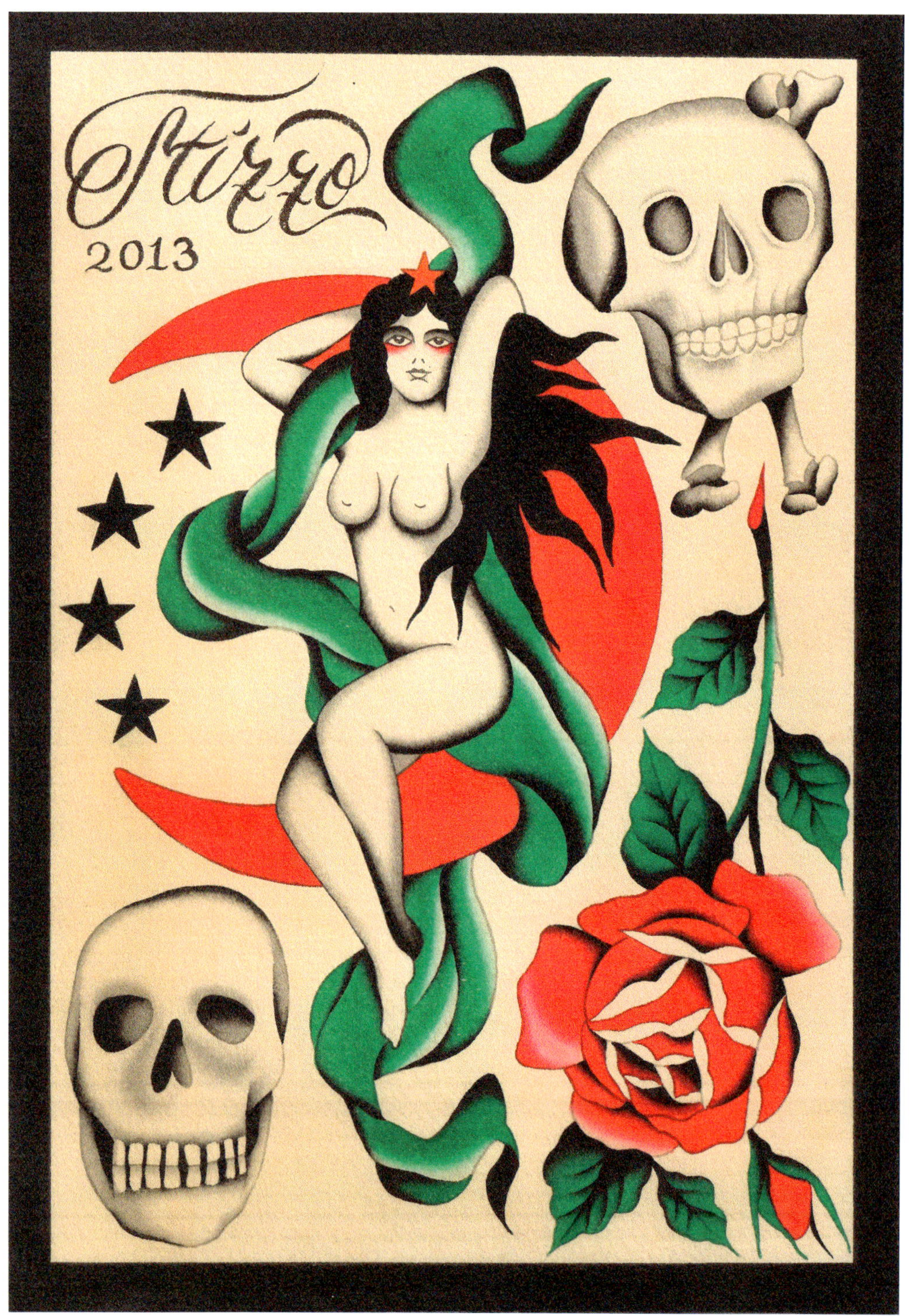
Stizzo
2013

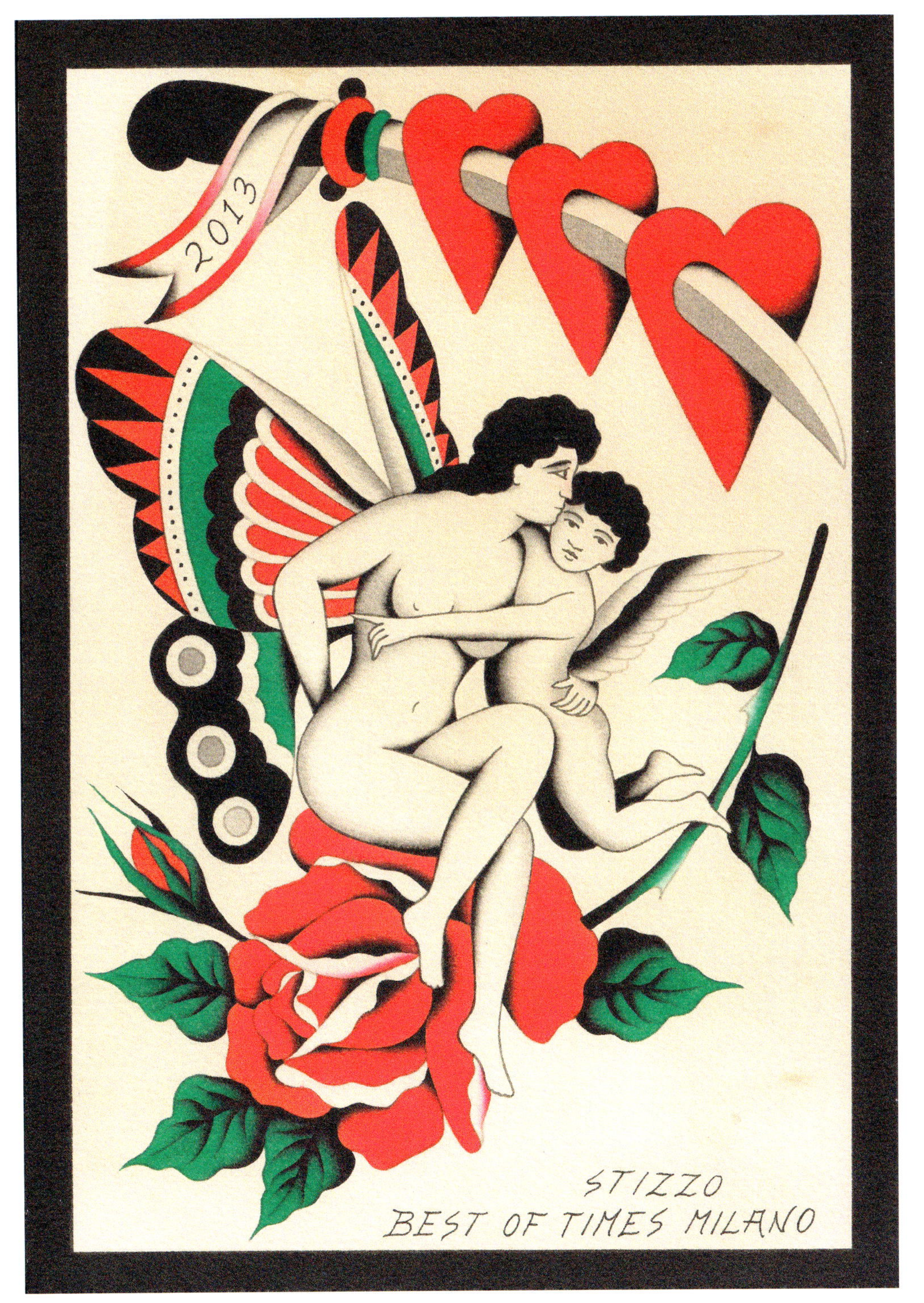
2013
STIZZO
BEST OF TIMES MILANO

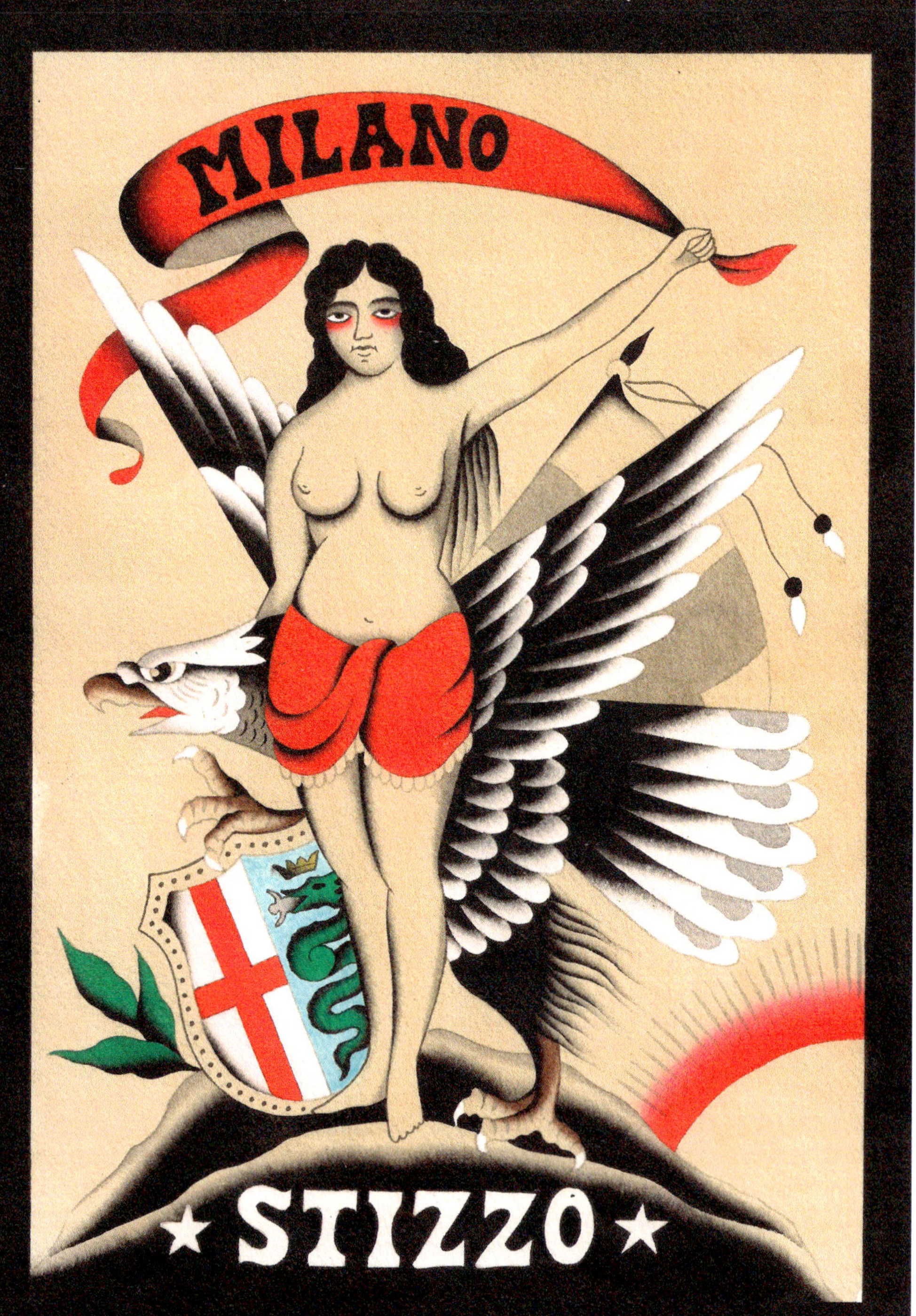
MILANO
★ STIZZO ★

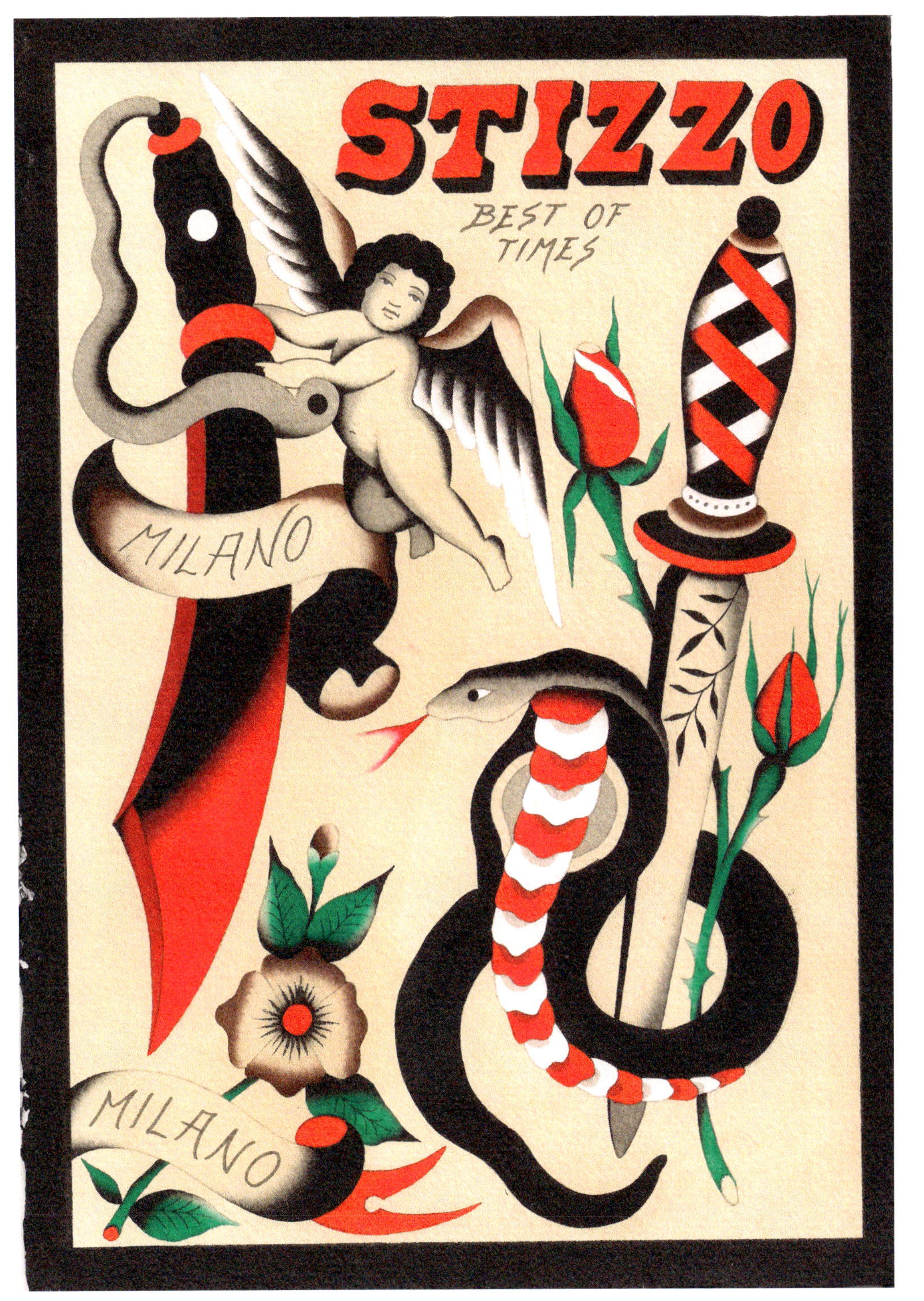
STIZZO
BEST OF
TIMES
MILANO
MILANO

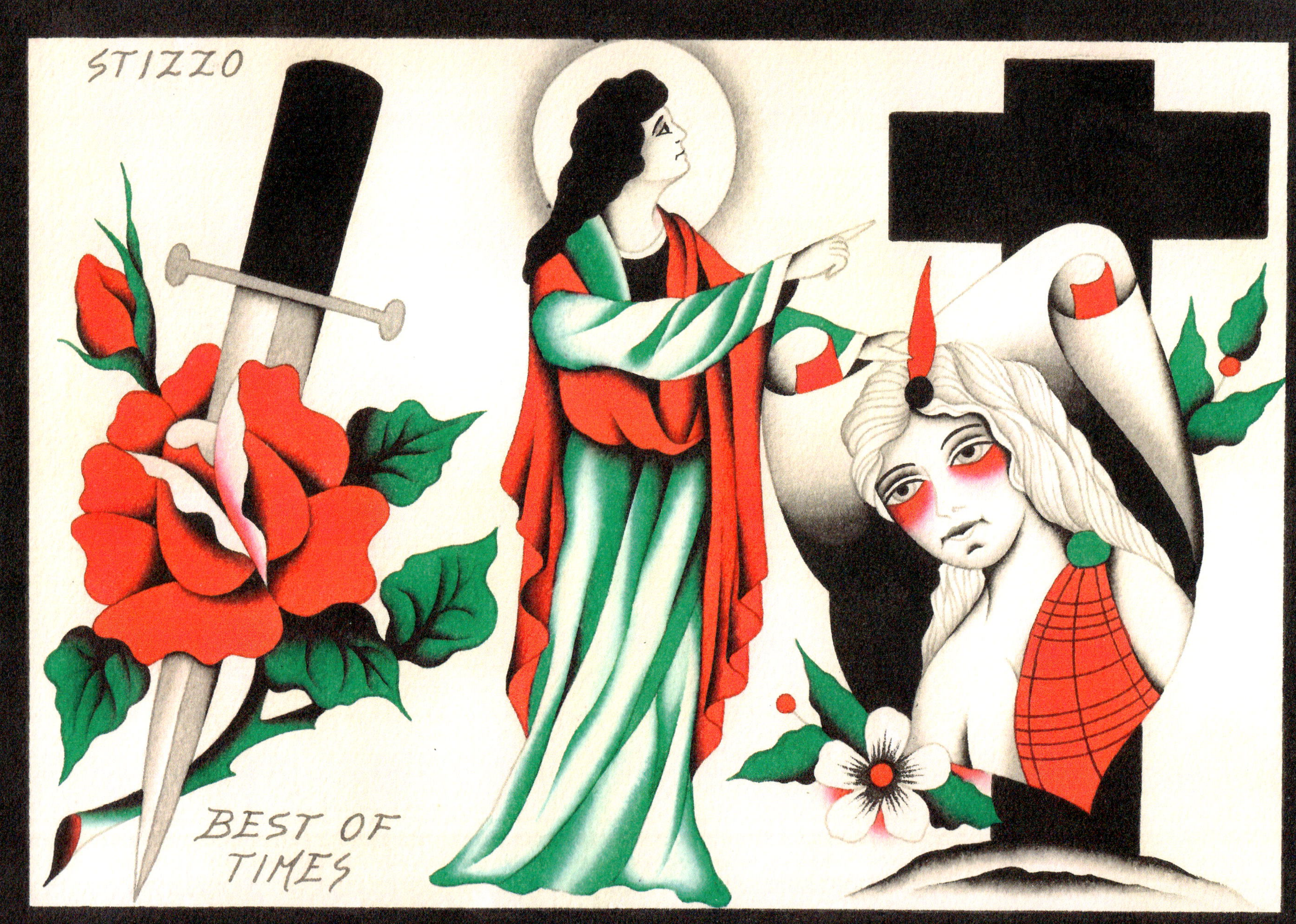
STIZZO
BEST OF TIMES

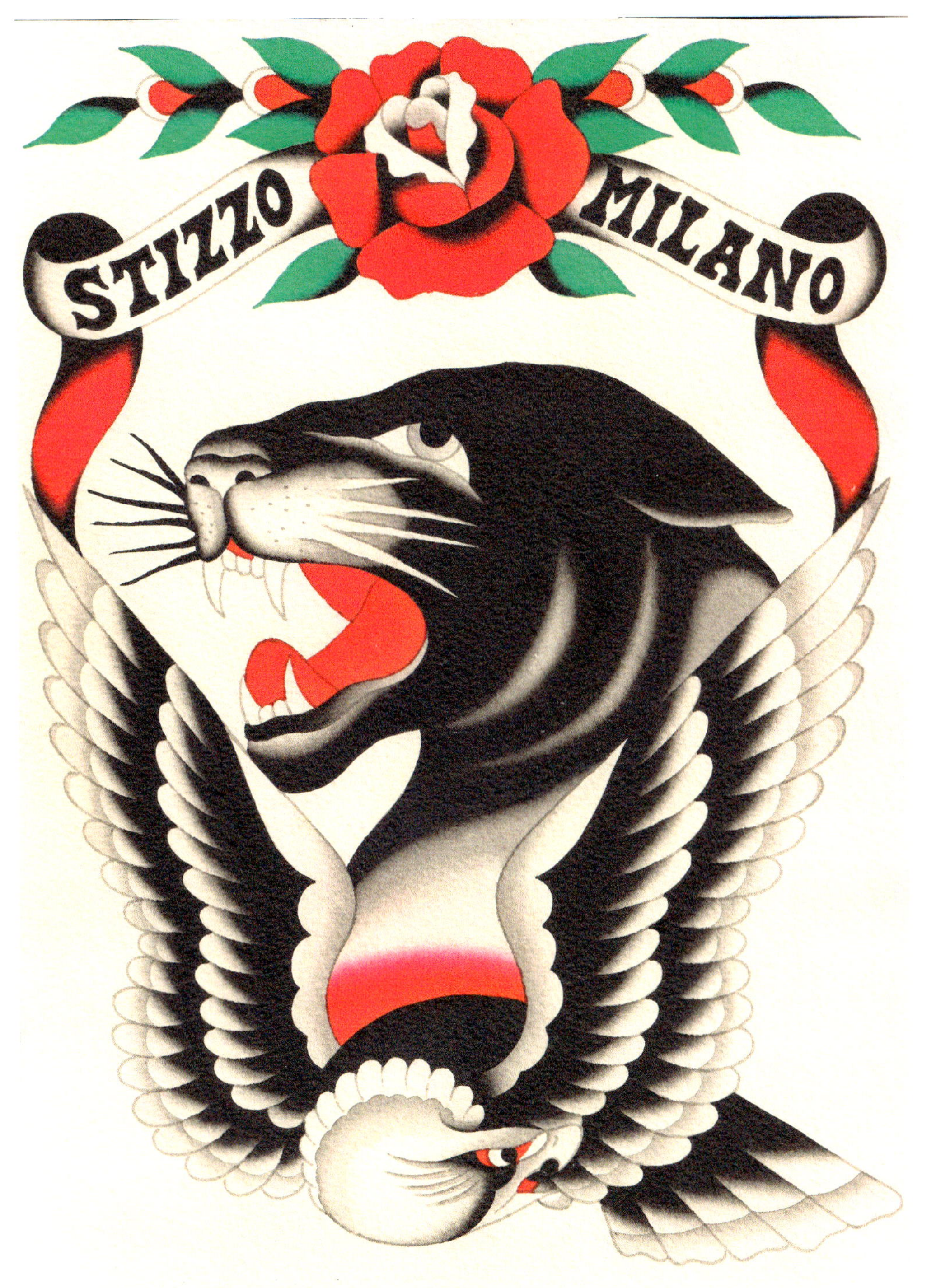
STIZZO
MILANO

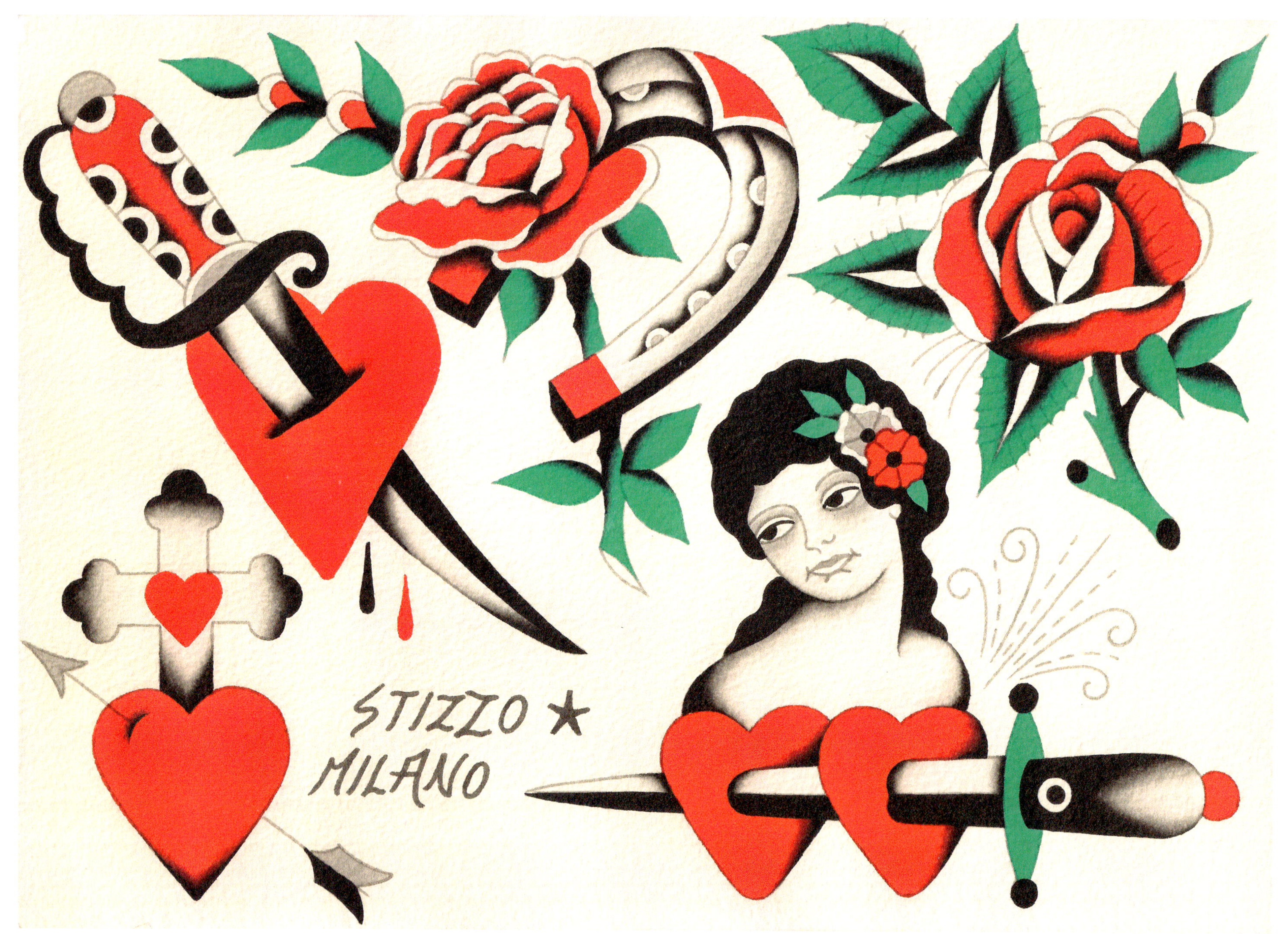
STIZZO ★
MILANO

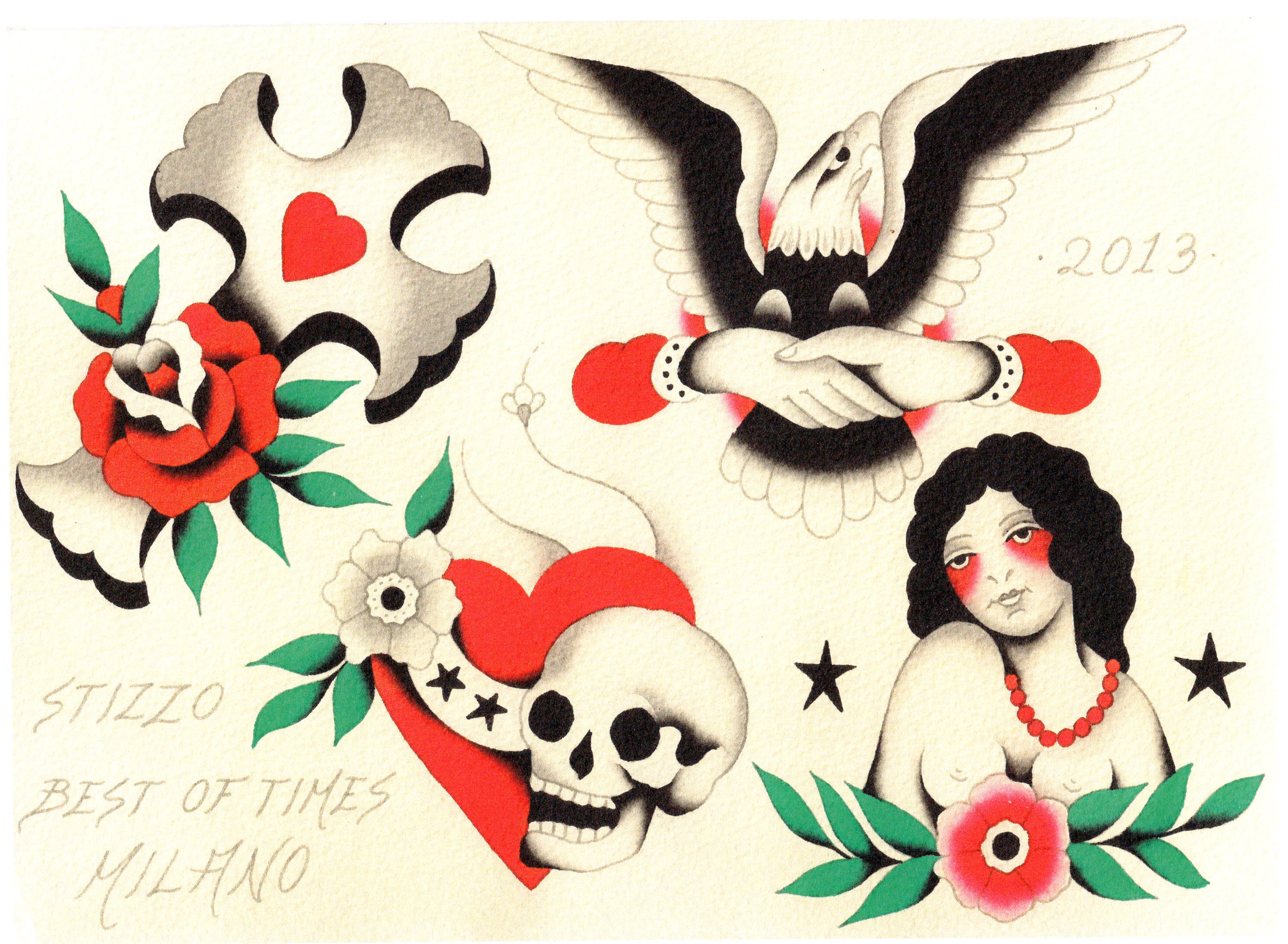

·2013·
STIZZO
BEST OF TIMES
MILANO

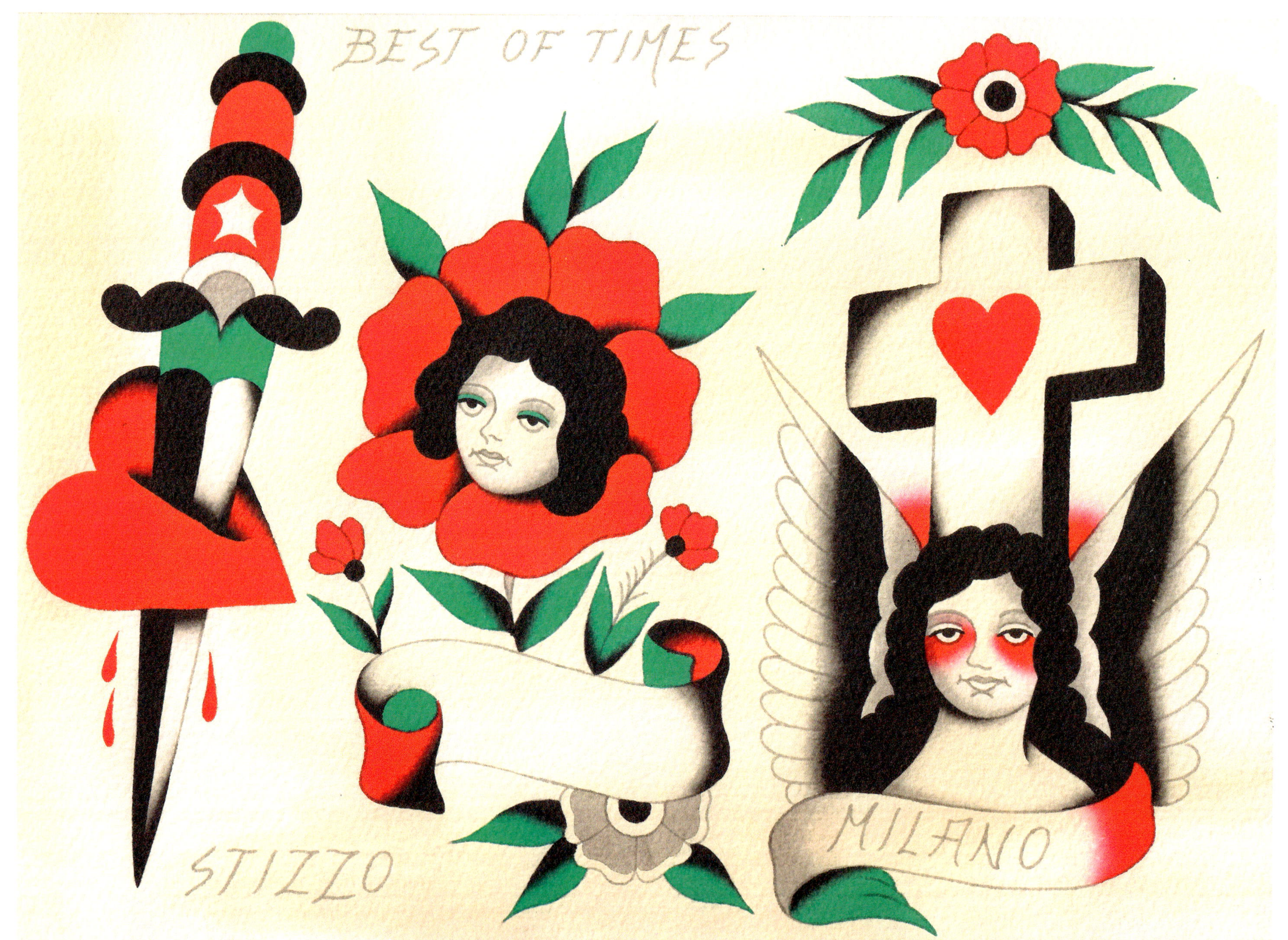
BEST OF TIMES
STIZZO
MILANO

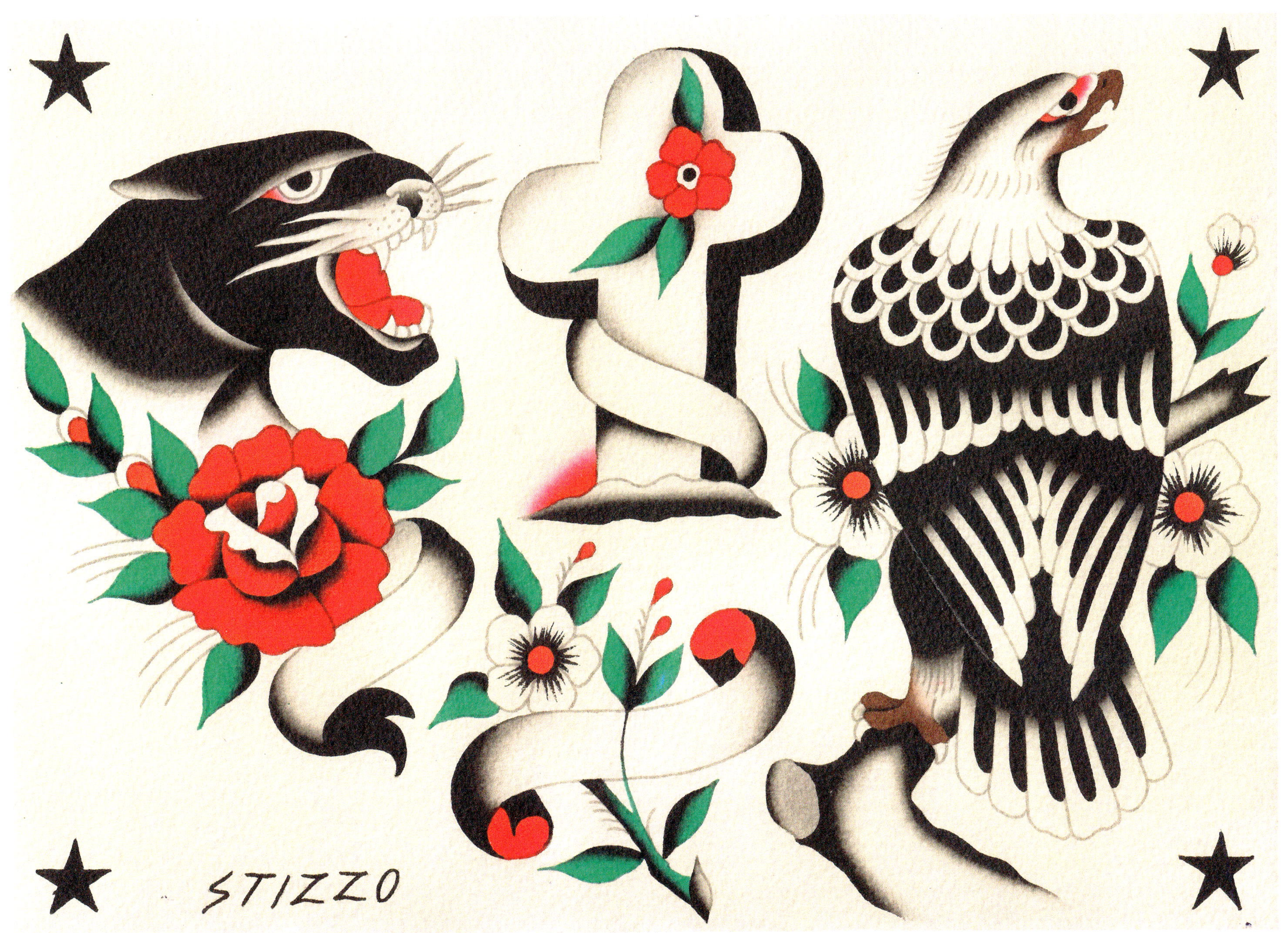
STIZZO

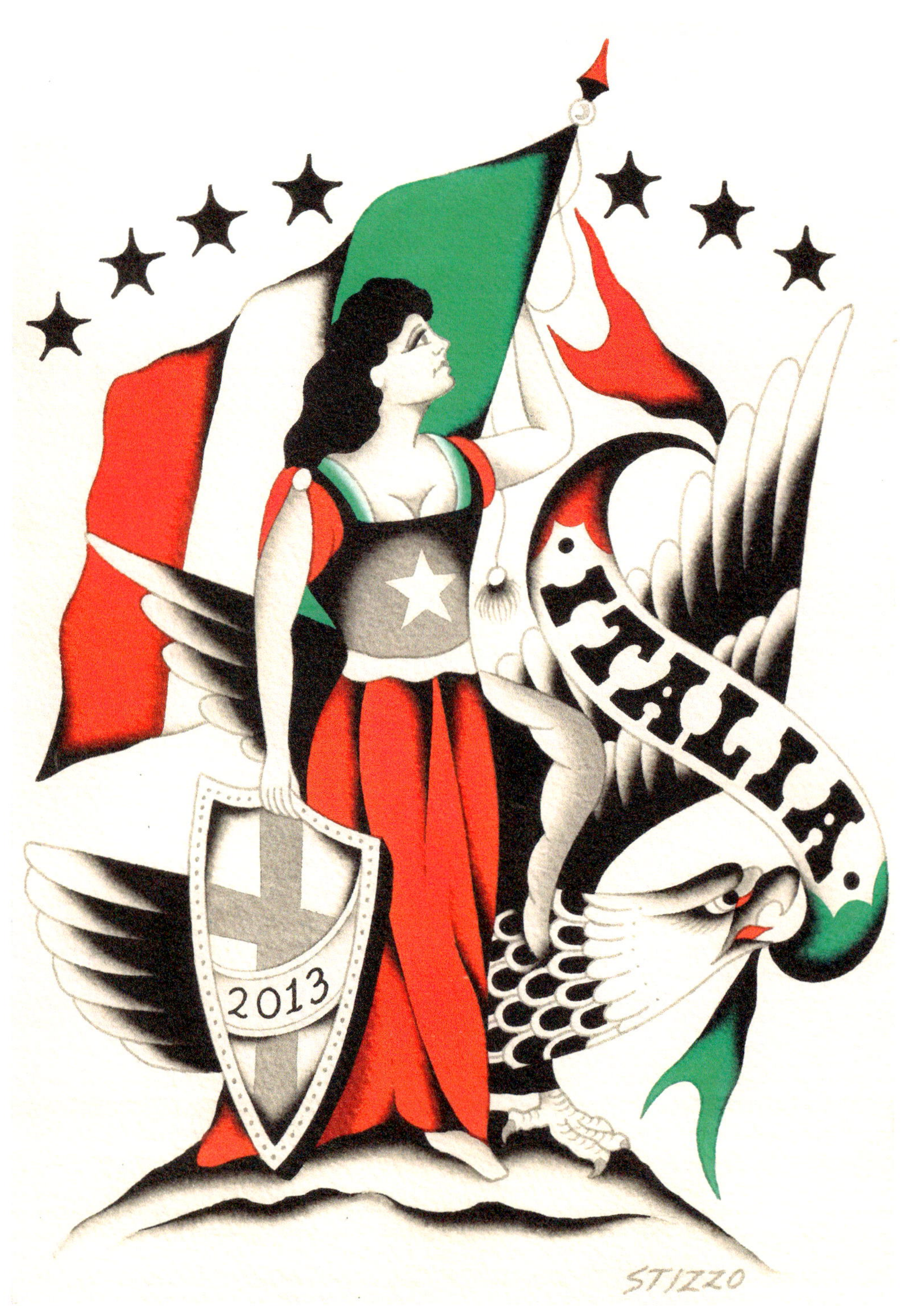

ITALIA.
2013
STIZZO

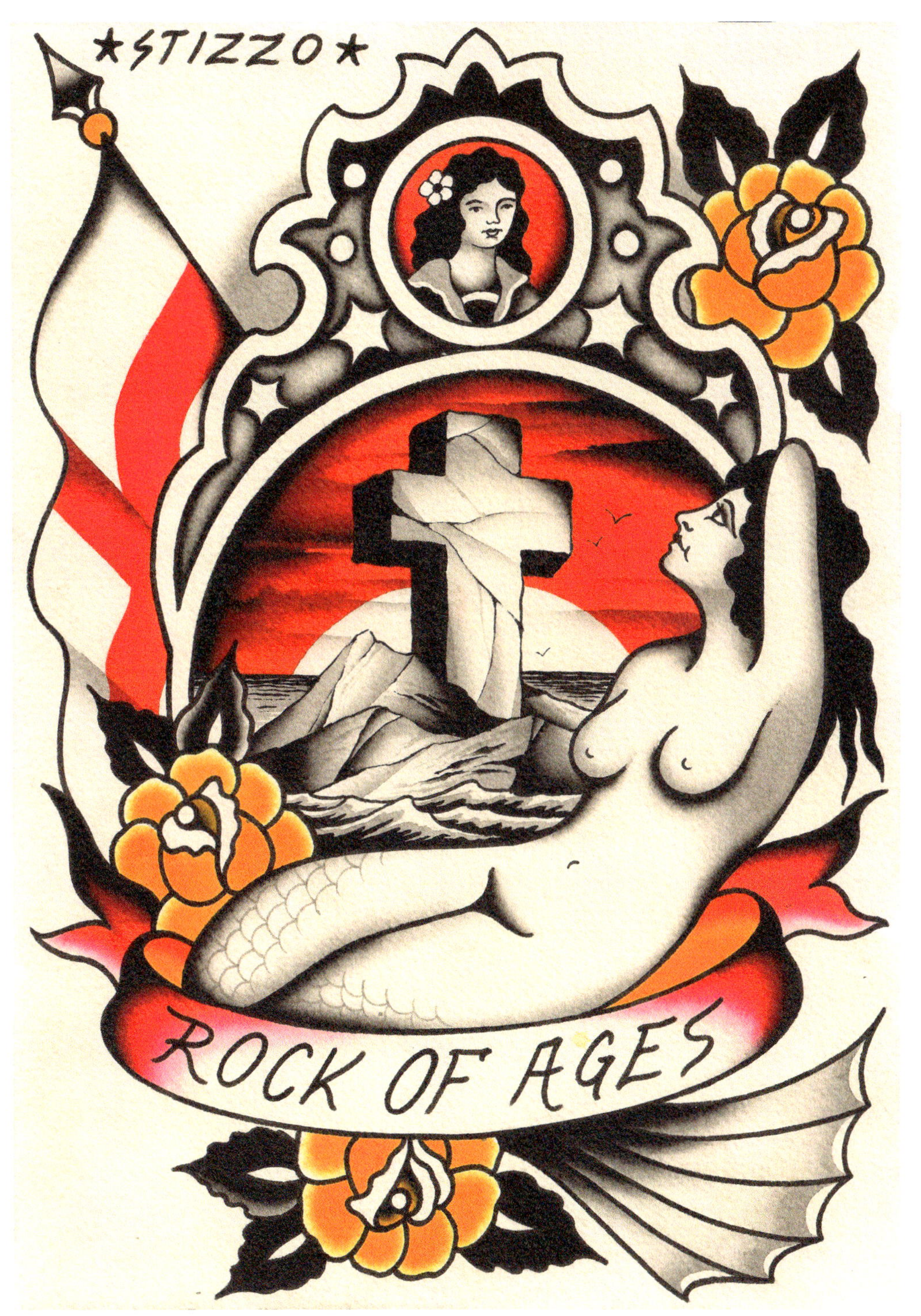
★STIZZO★
ROCK OF AGES

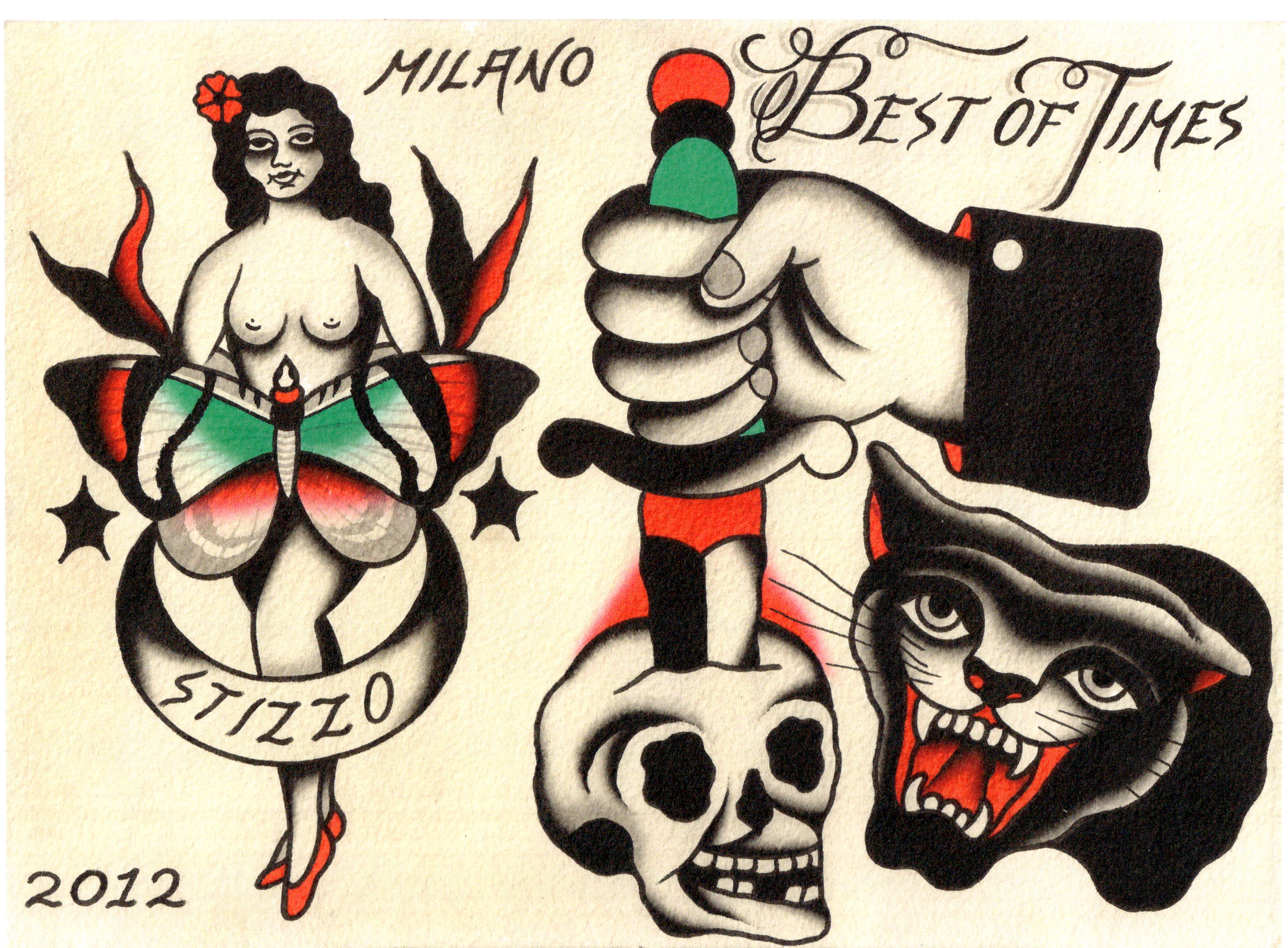
MILANO
Best of Times
STIZZO
2012

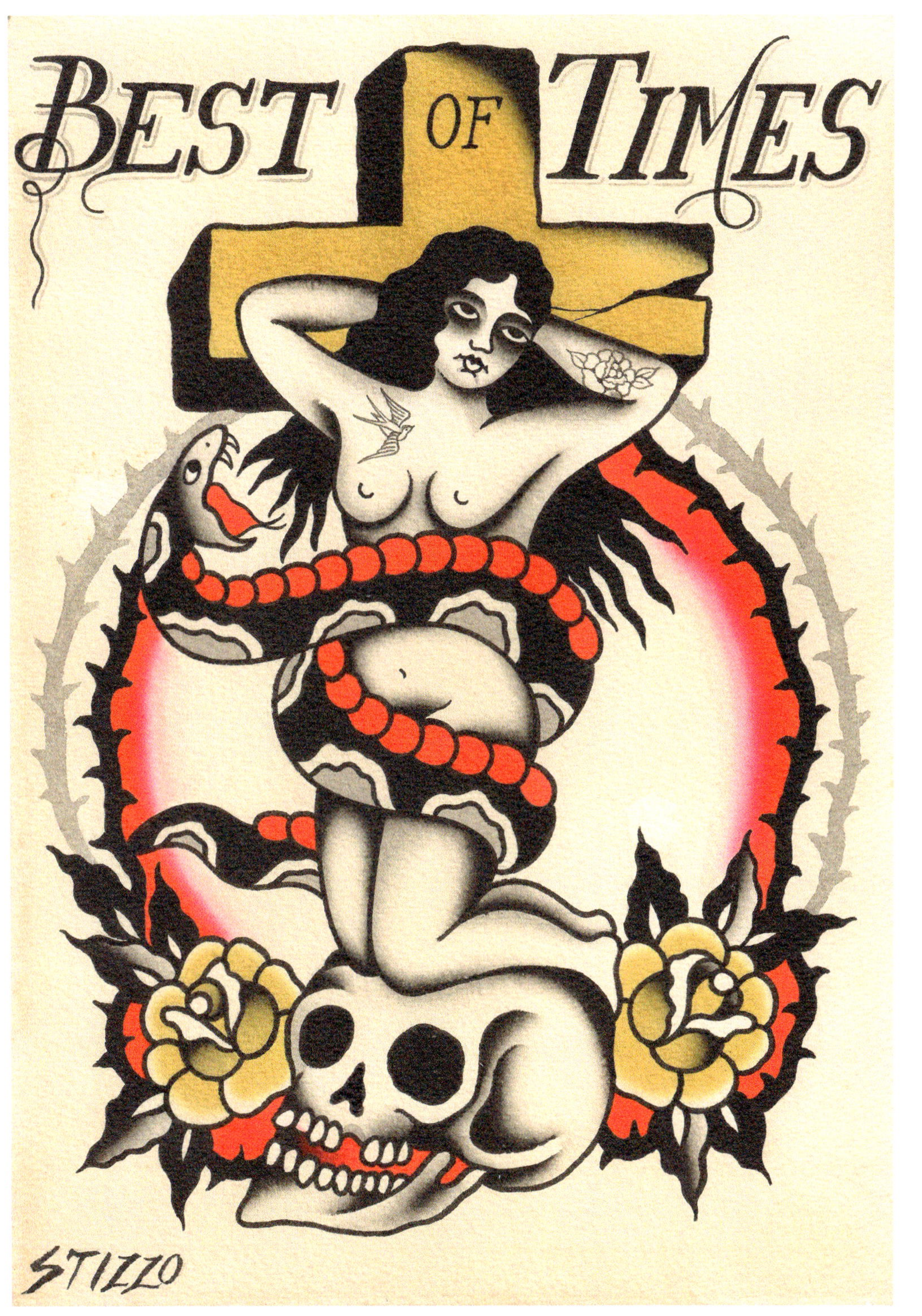
BEST OF TIMES
STIZZO

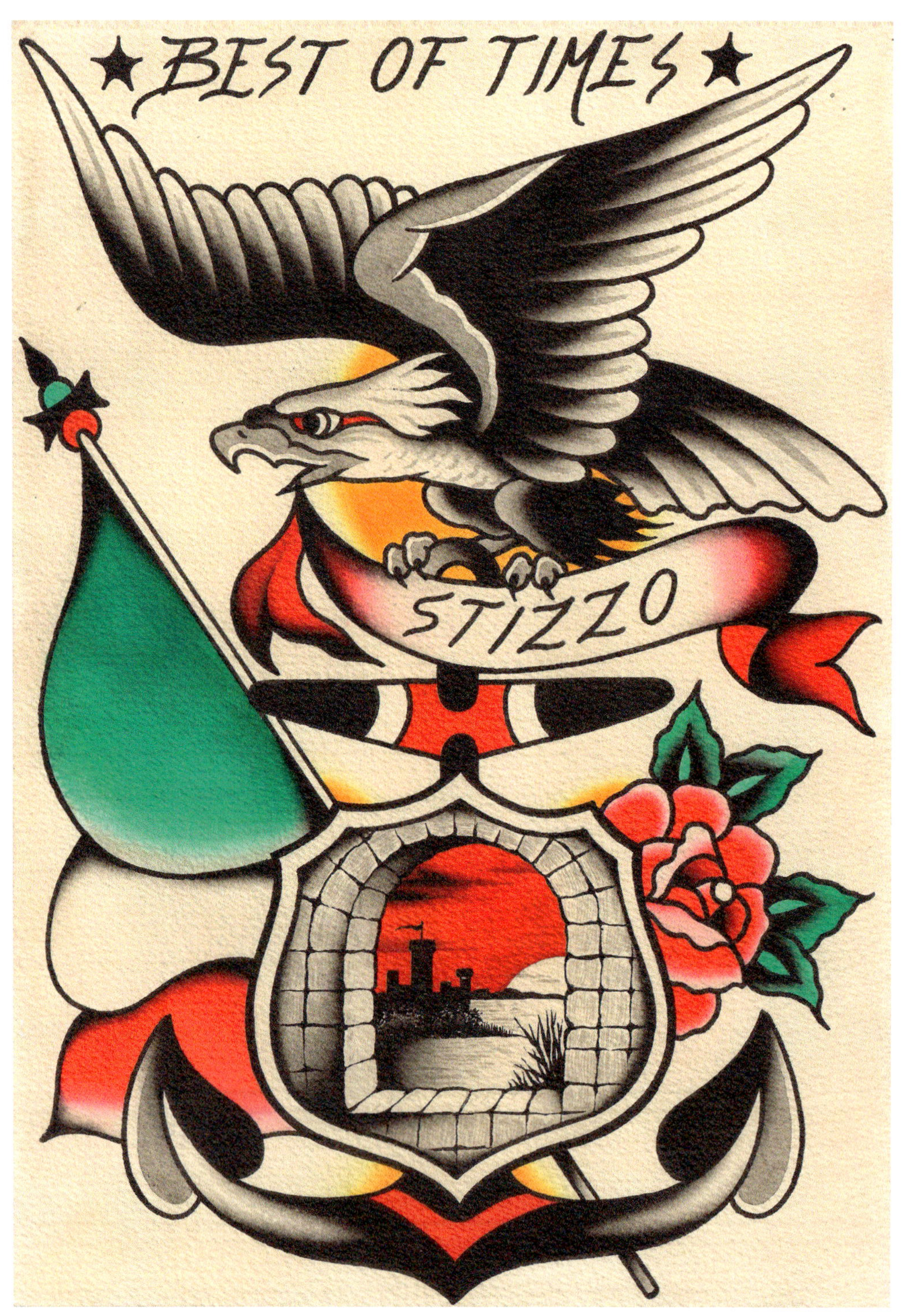
BEST OF TIMES
STIZZO

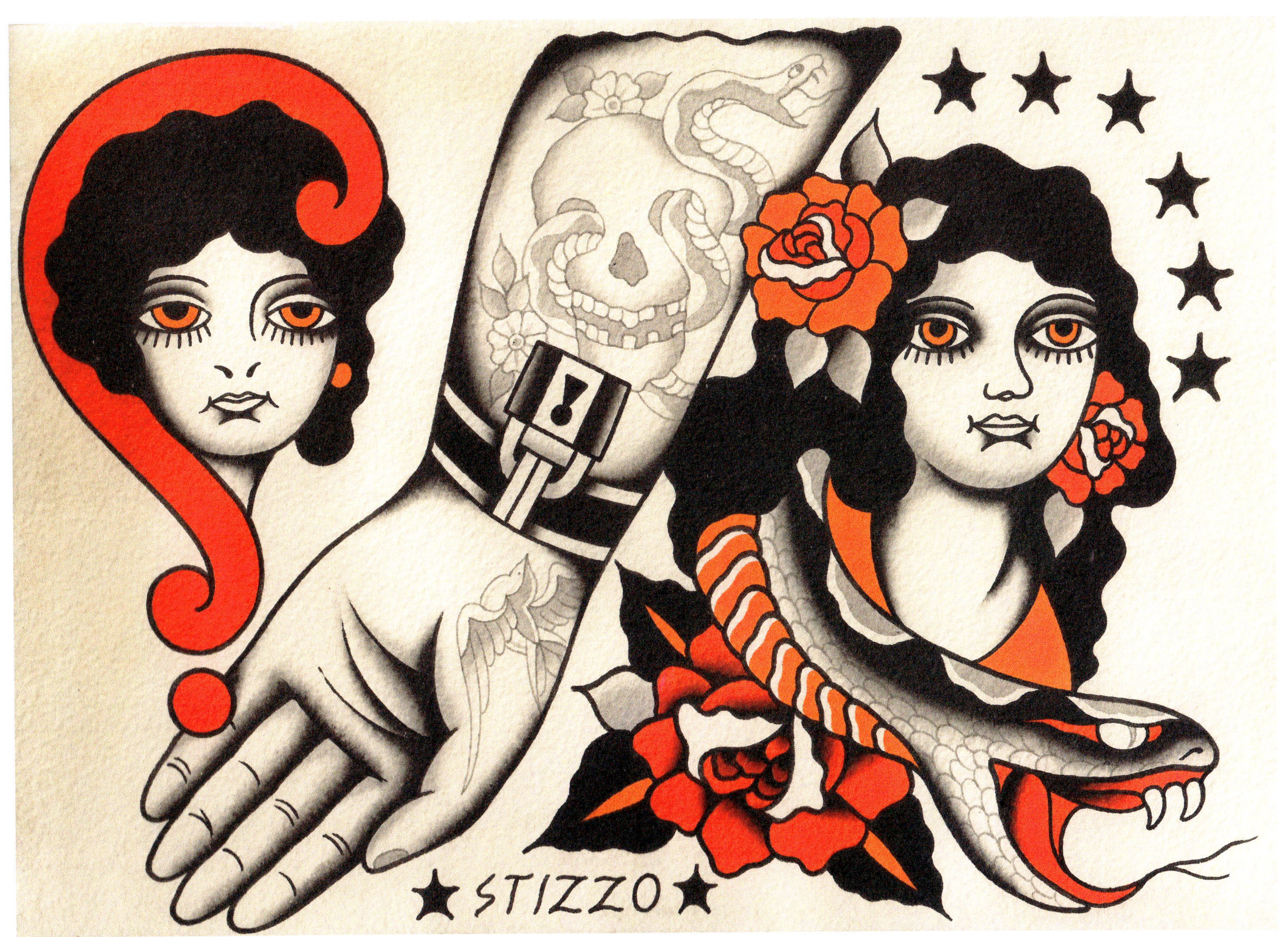
★STIZZO★

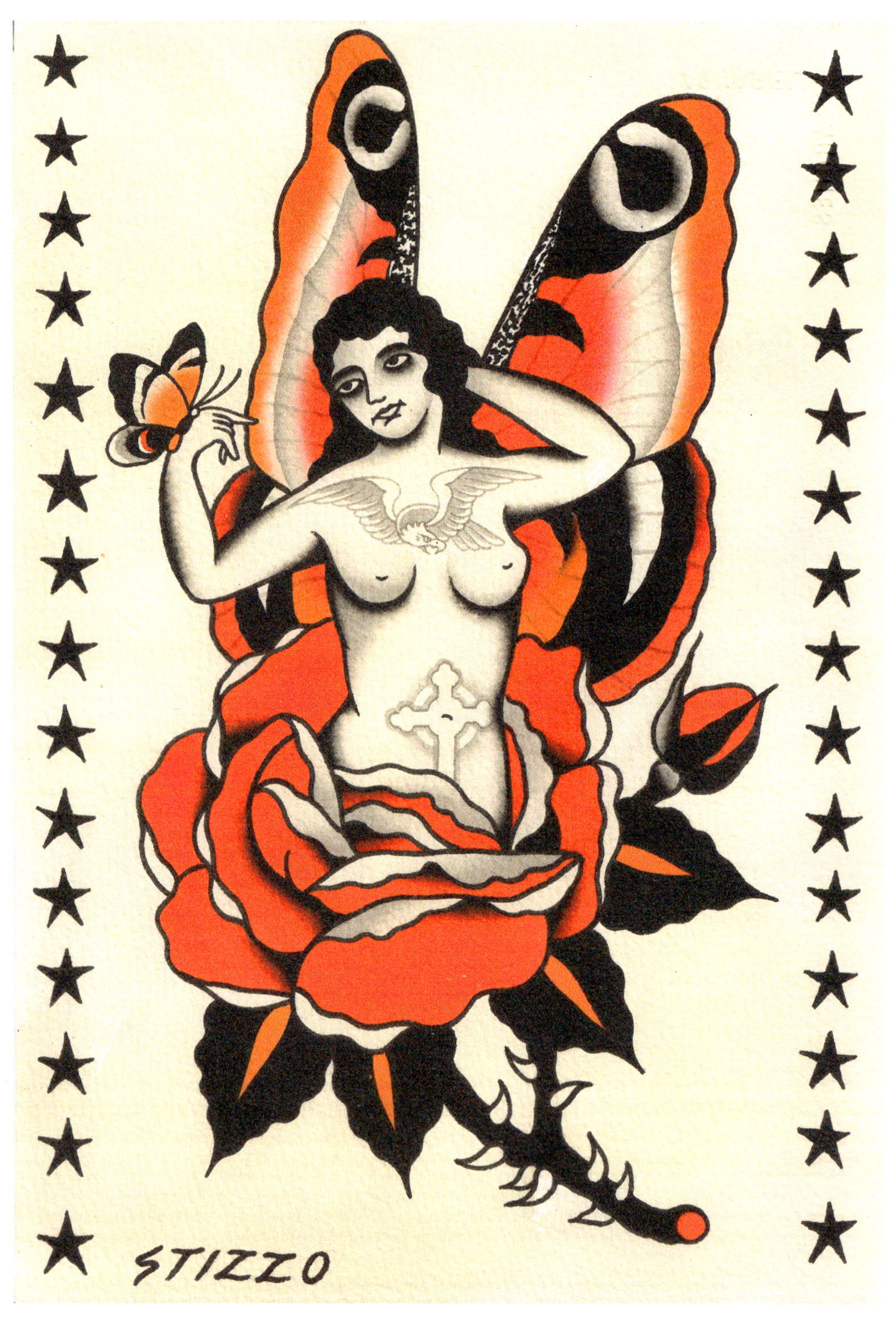
STIZZO

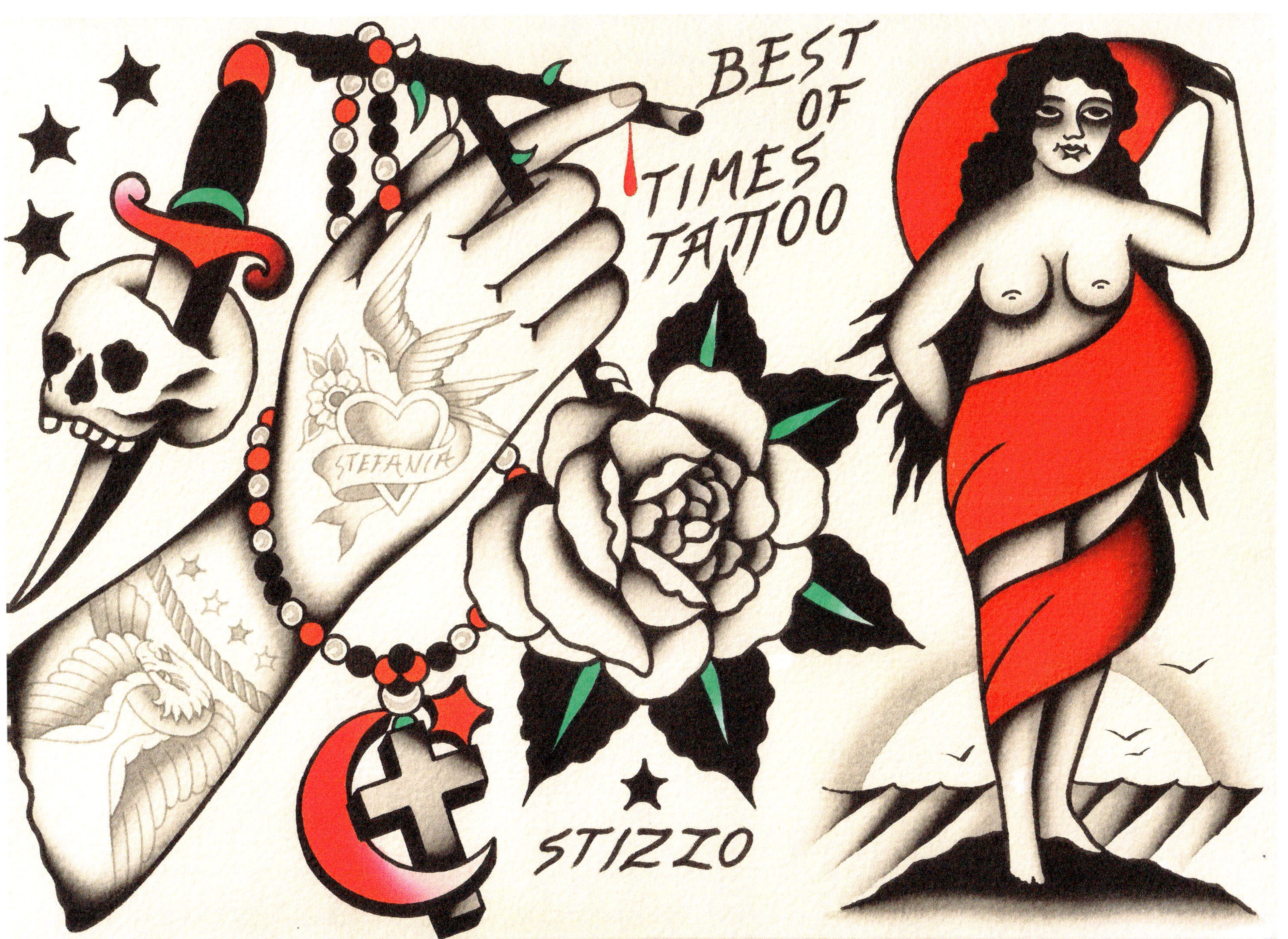
BEST
OF
TIMES
TATTOO
STEFANIA
STIZZO

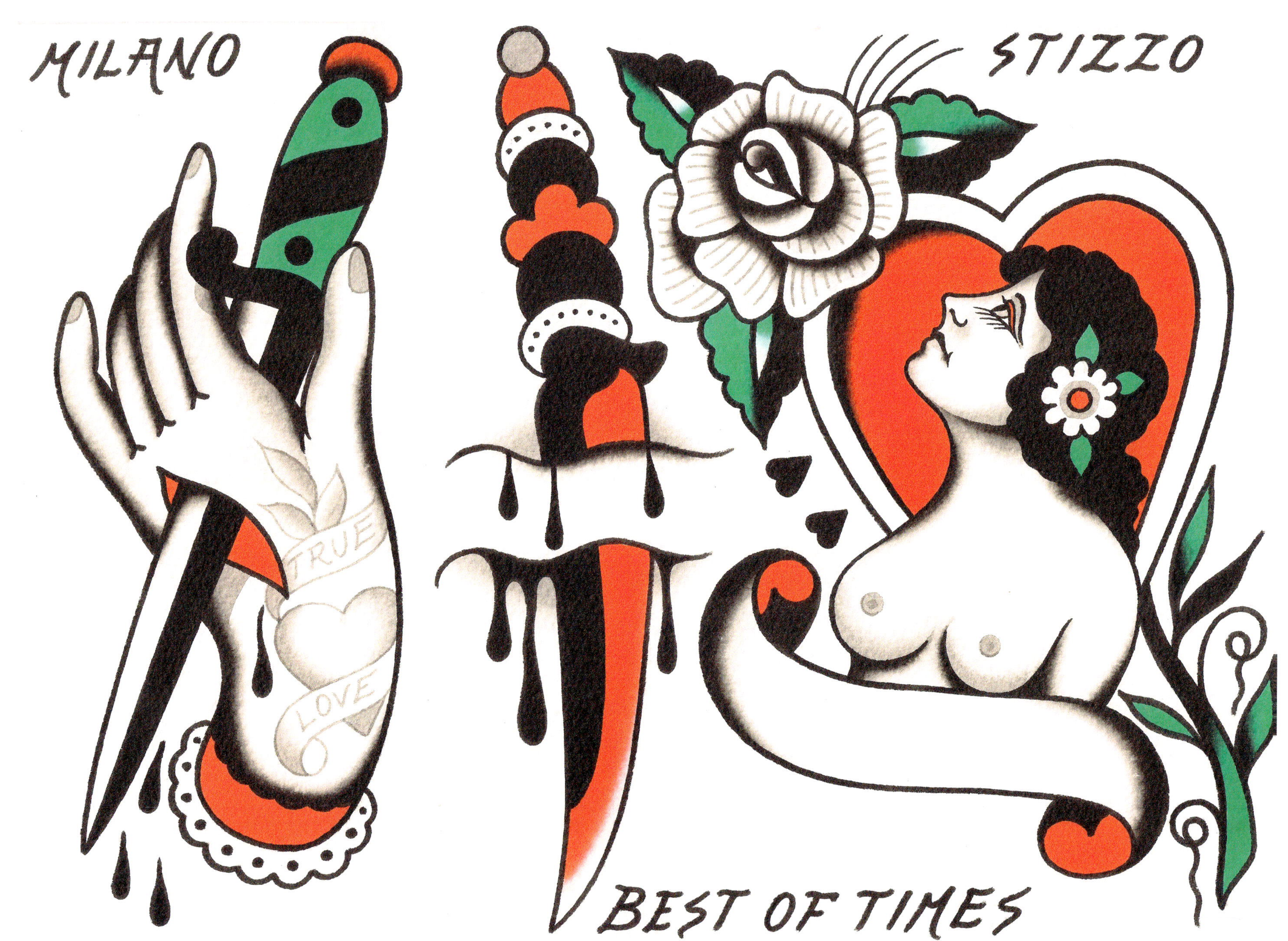
MILANO
STIZZO
TRUE
LOVE
BEST OF TIMES

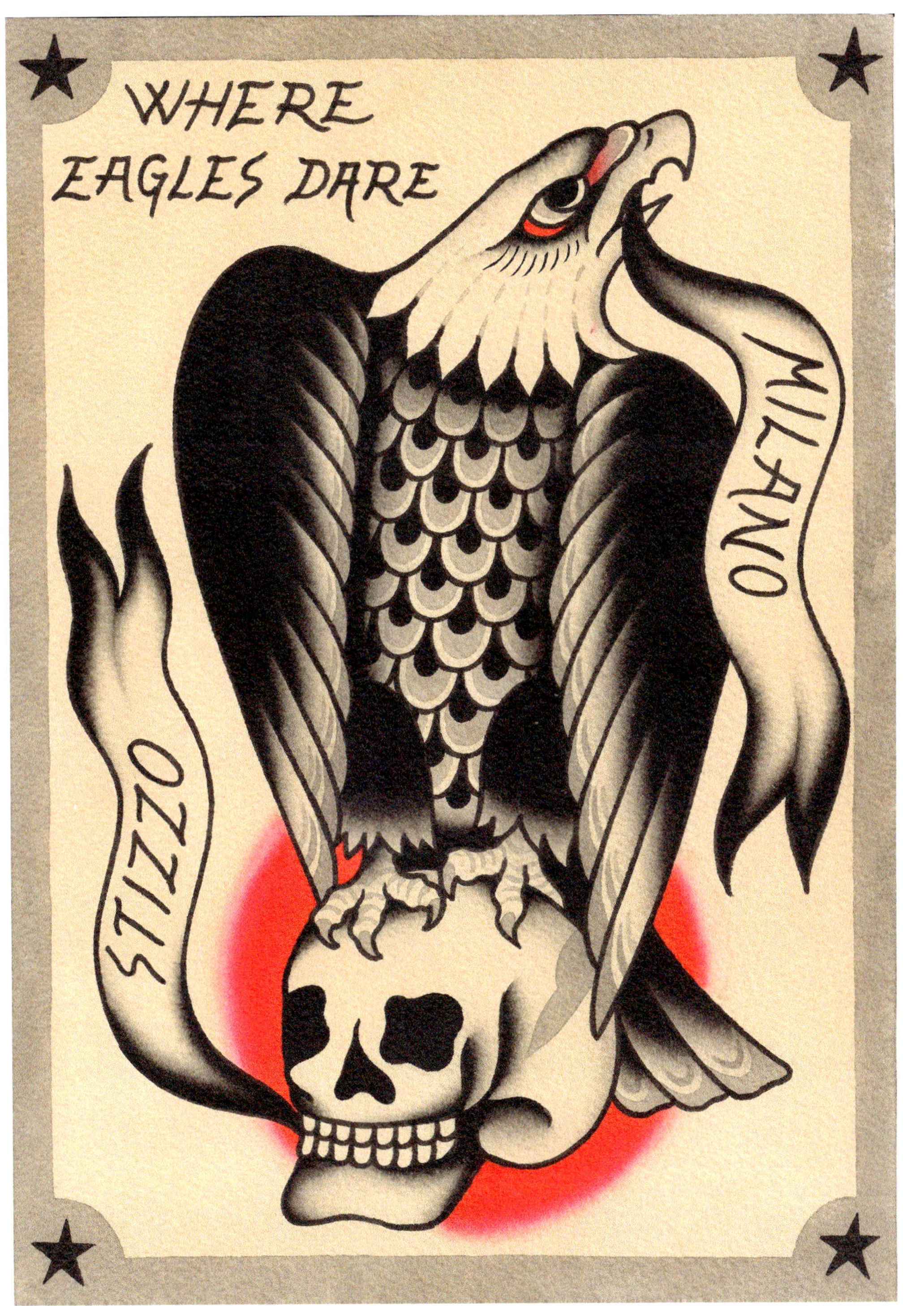
WHERE
EAGLES DARE
MILANO
STIZZO

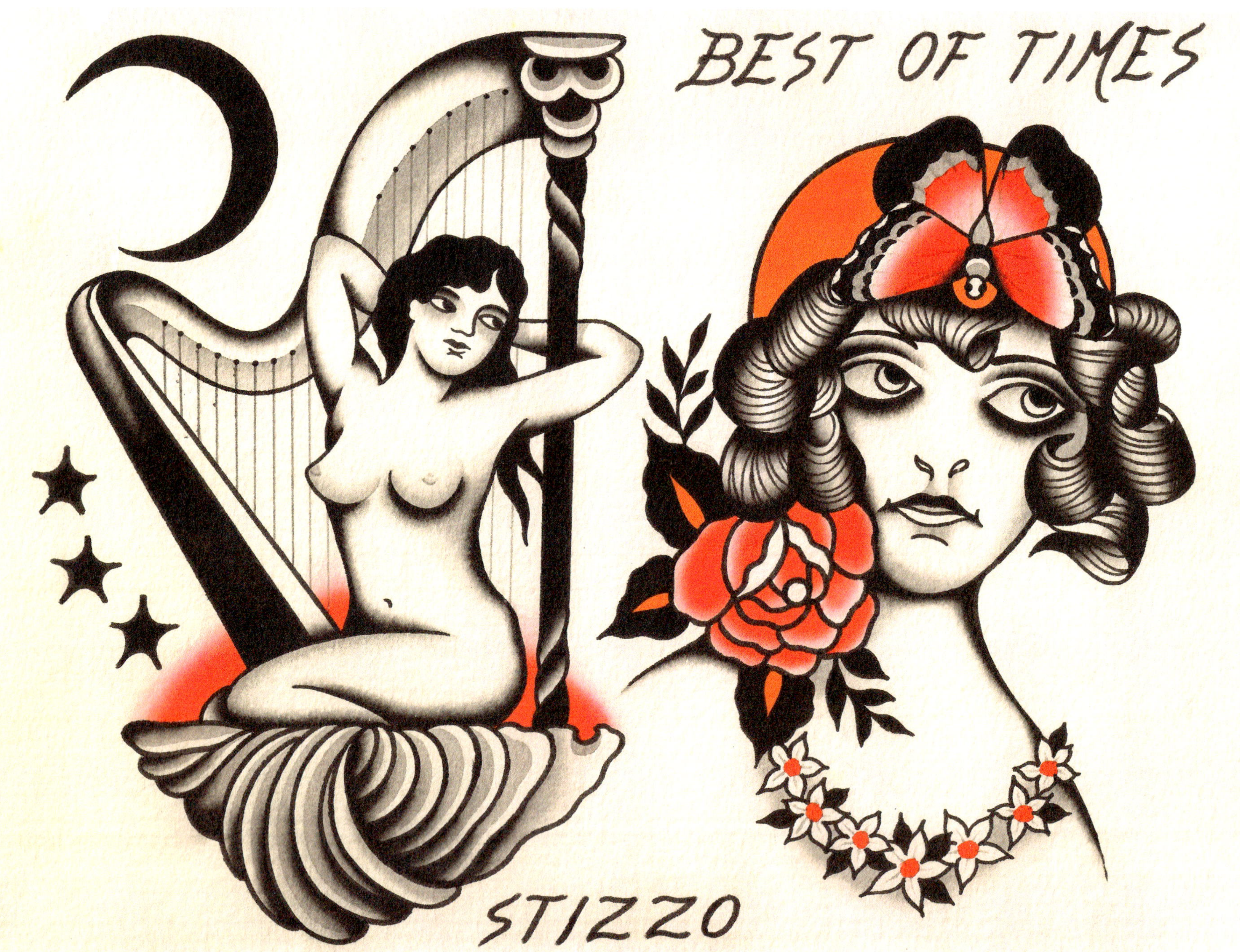
BEST OF TIMES
STIZZO

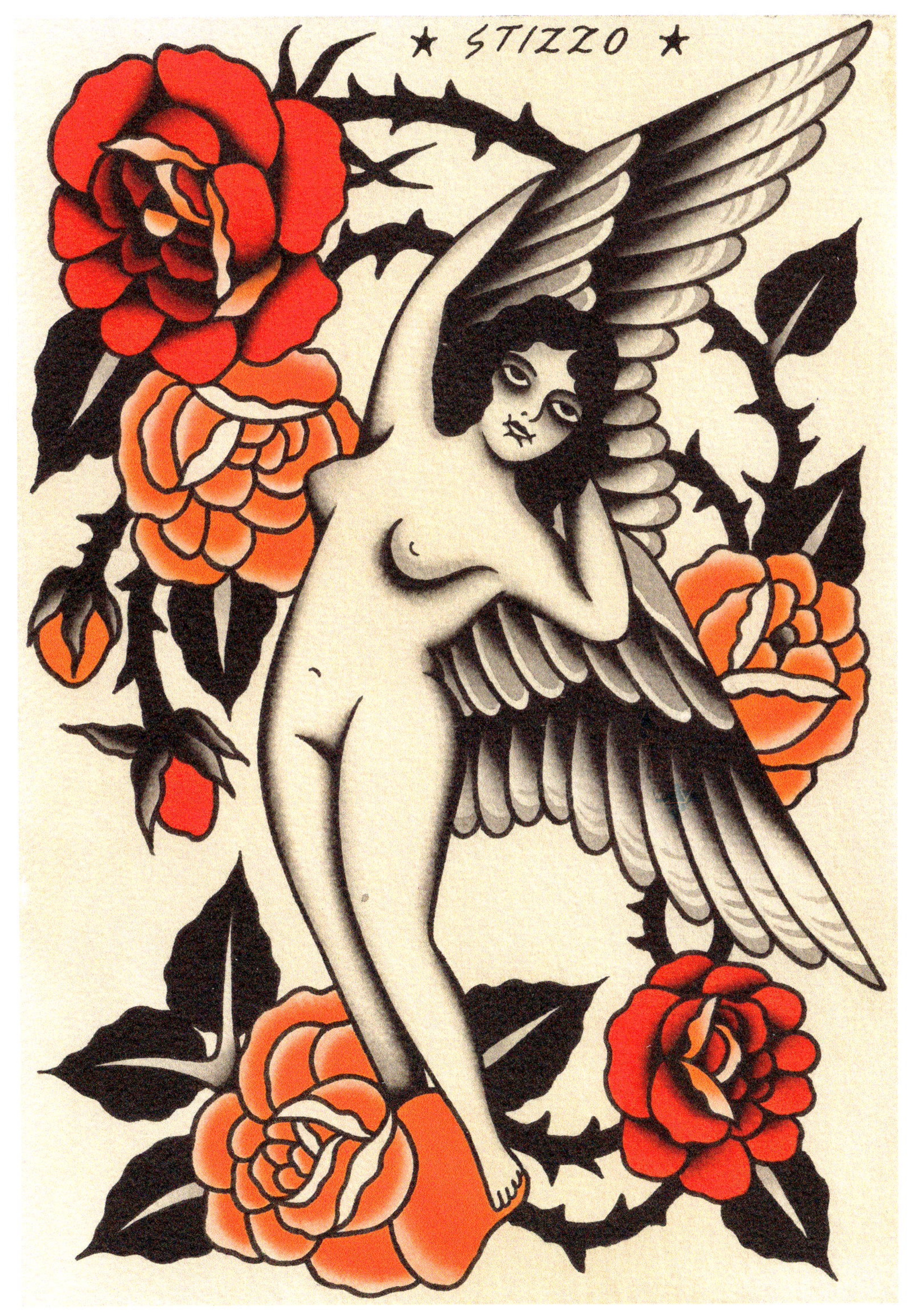
★ STIZZO ★

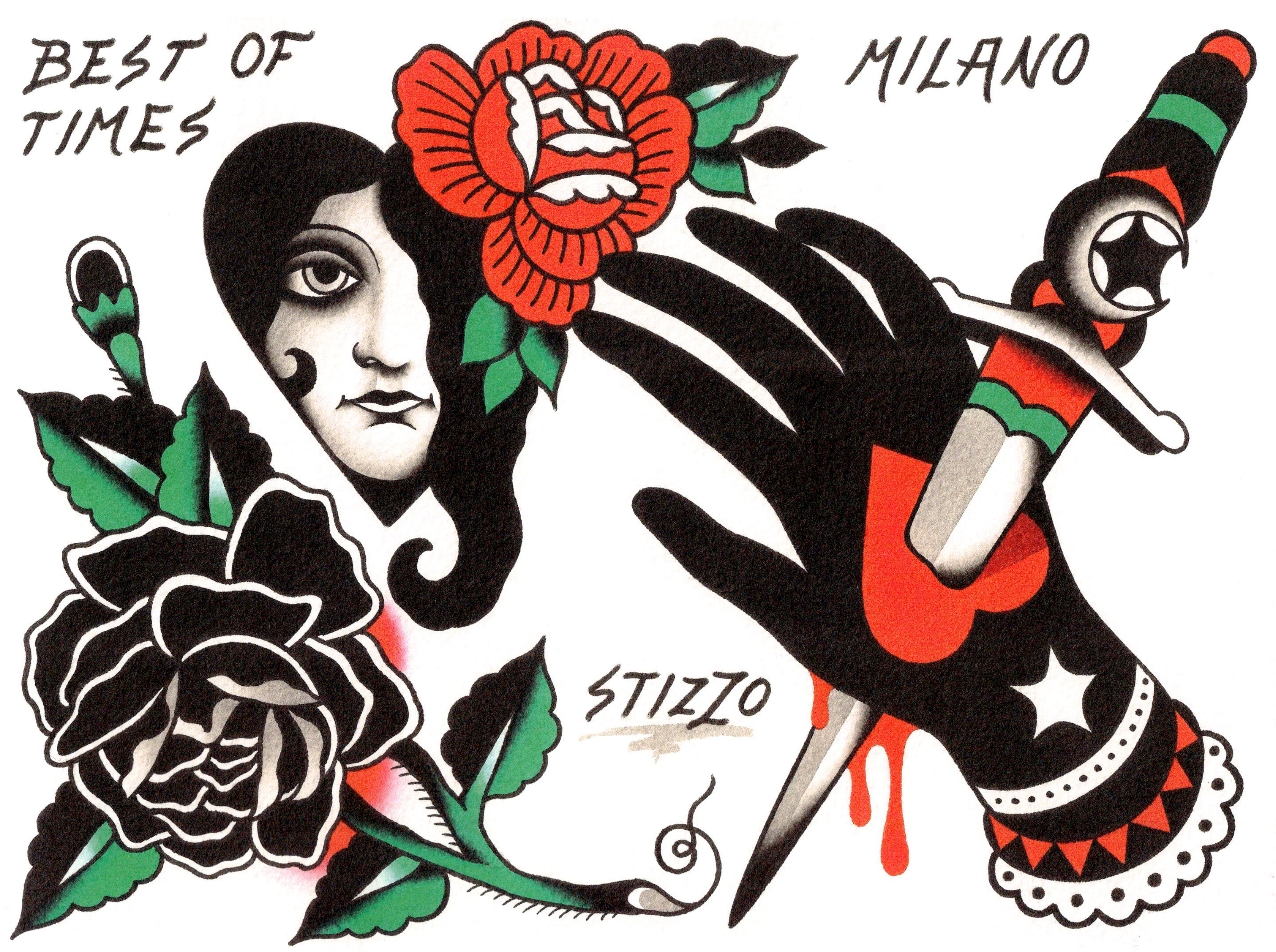
BEST OF
TIMES
MILANO
STIZZO

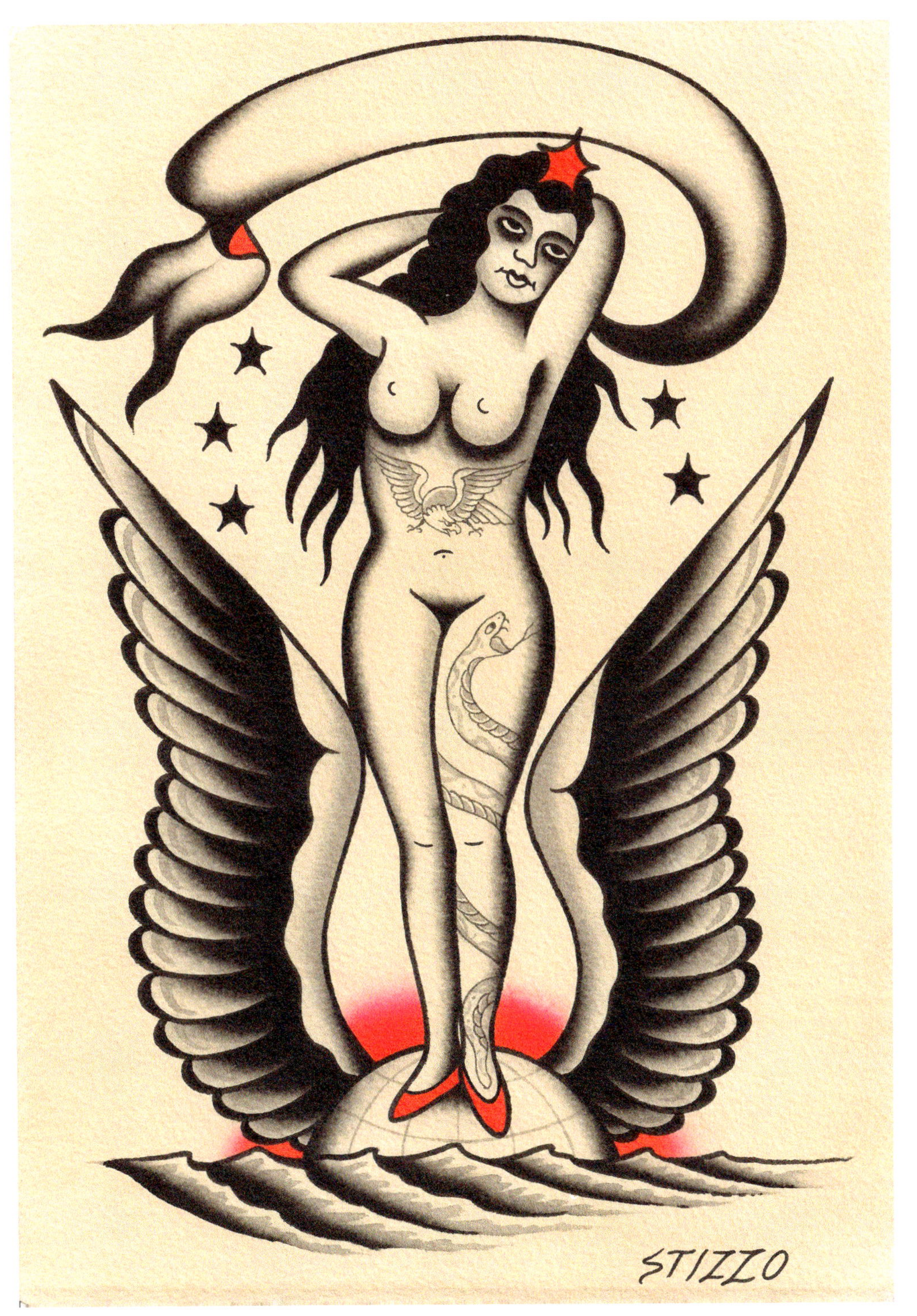
STIZZO

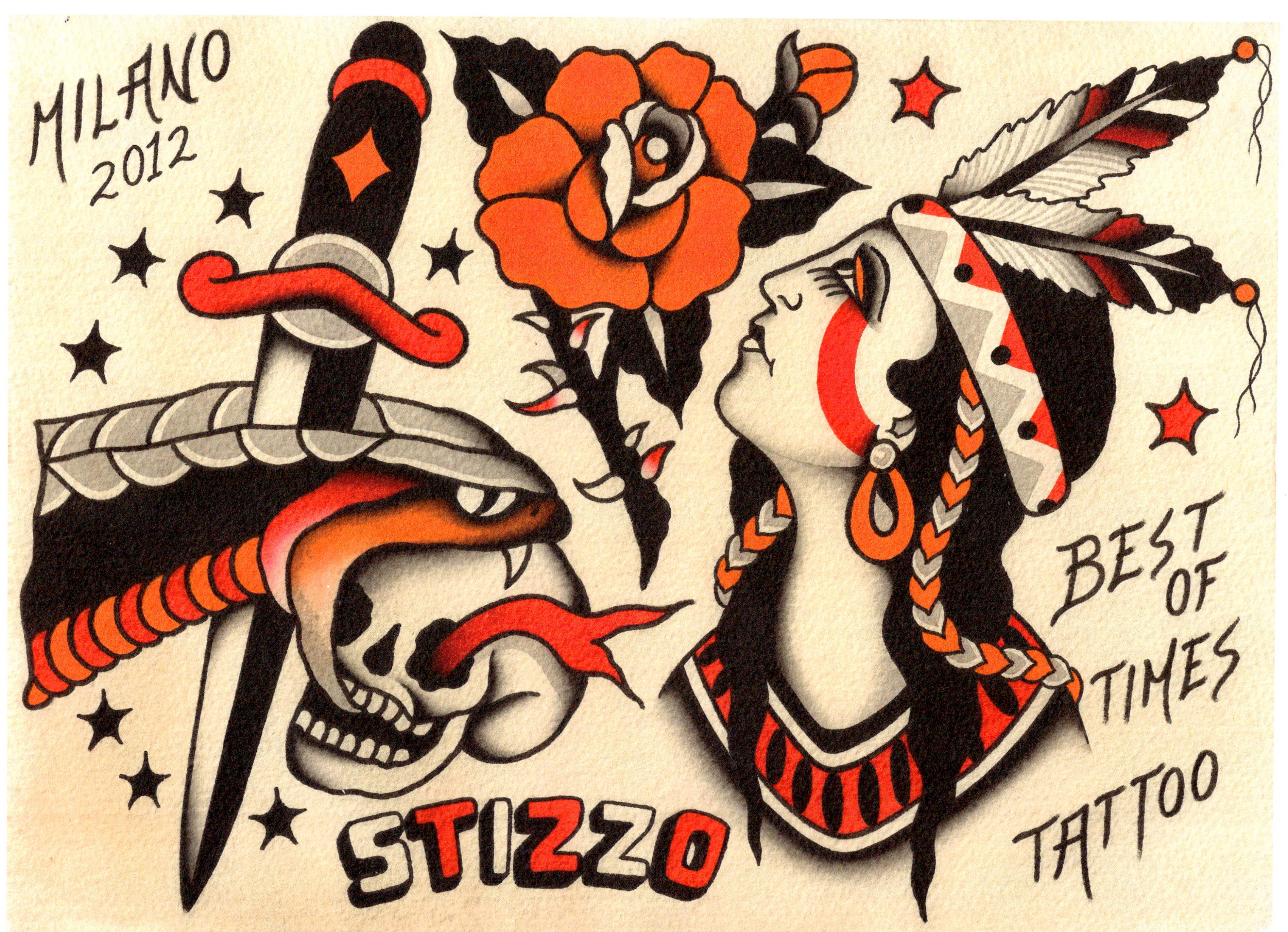
MILANO
2012
BEST
OF
TIMES
TATTOO
STIZZO

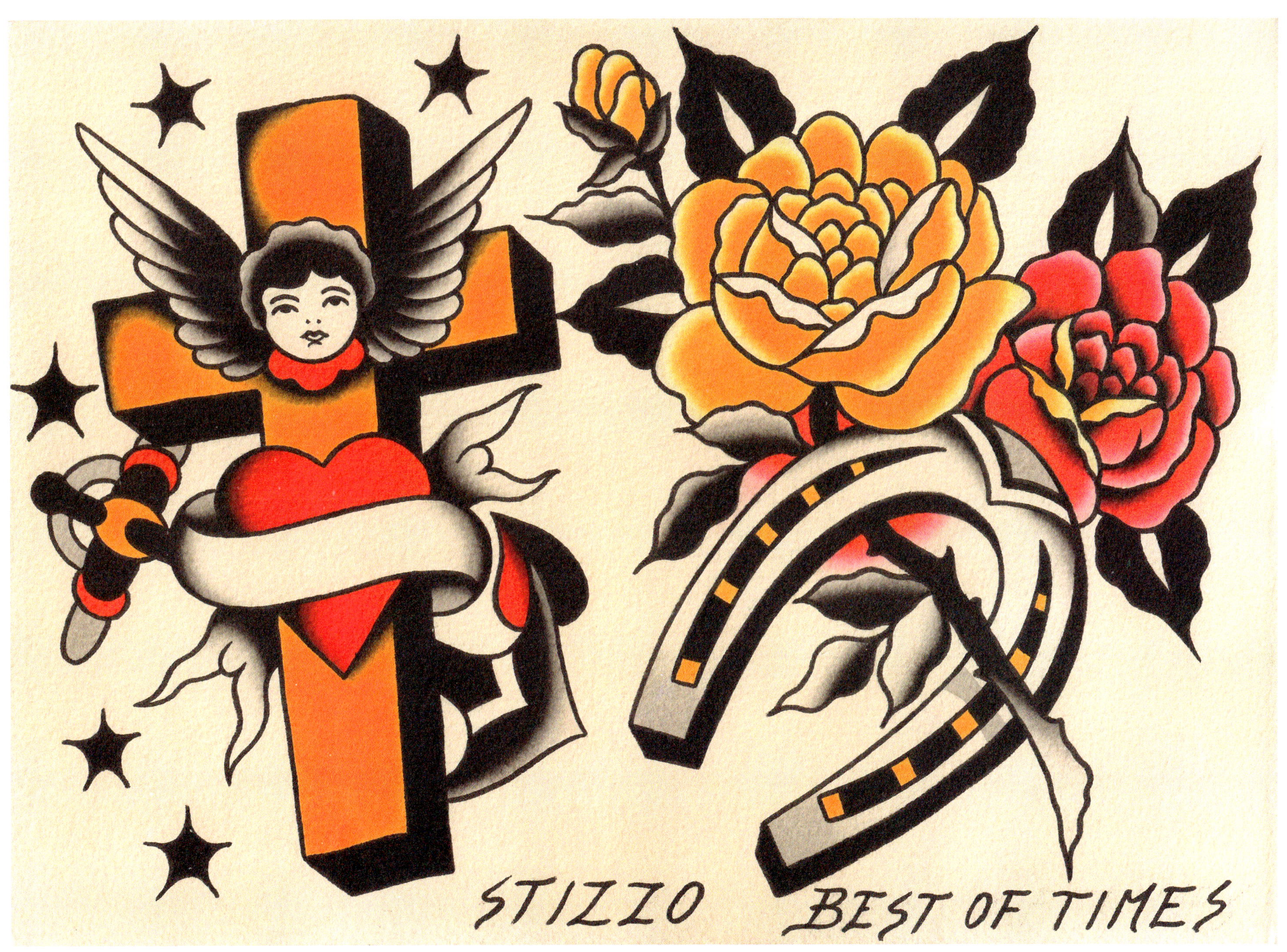
STIZZO
BEST OF TIMES

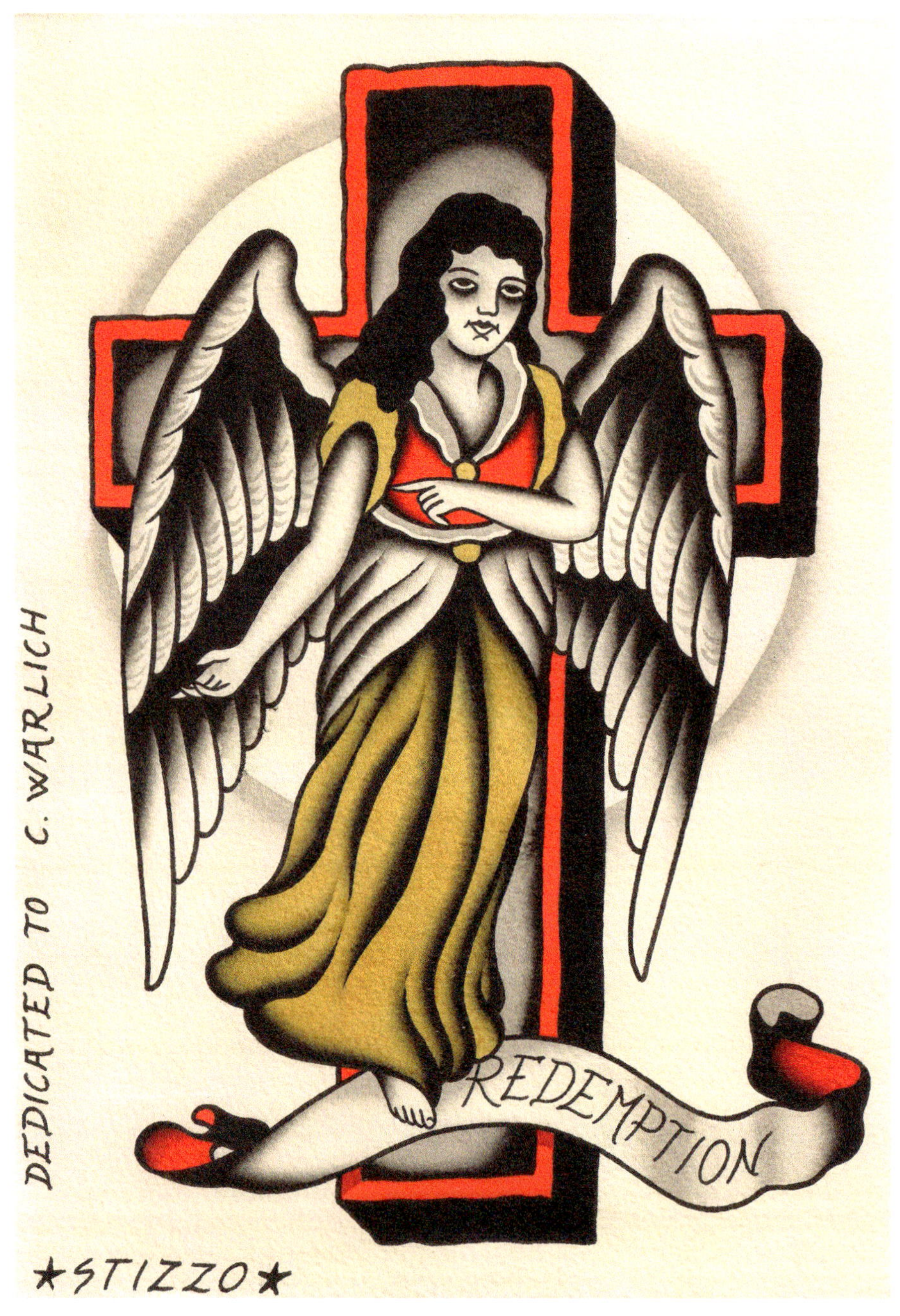
DEDICATED TO C. WARLICH
REDEMPTION
★STIZZO★

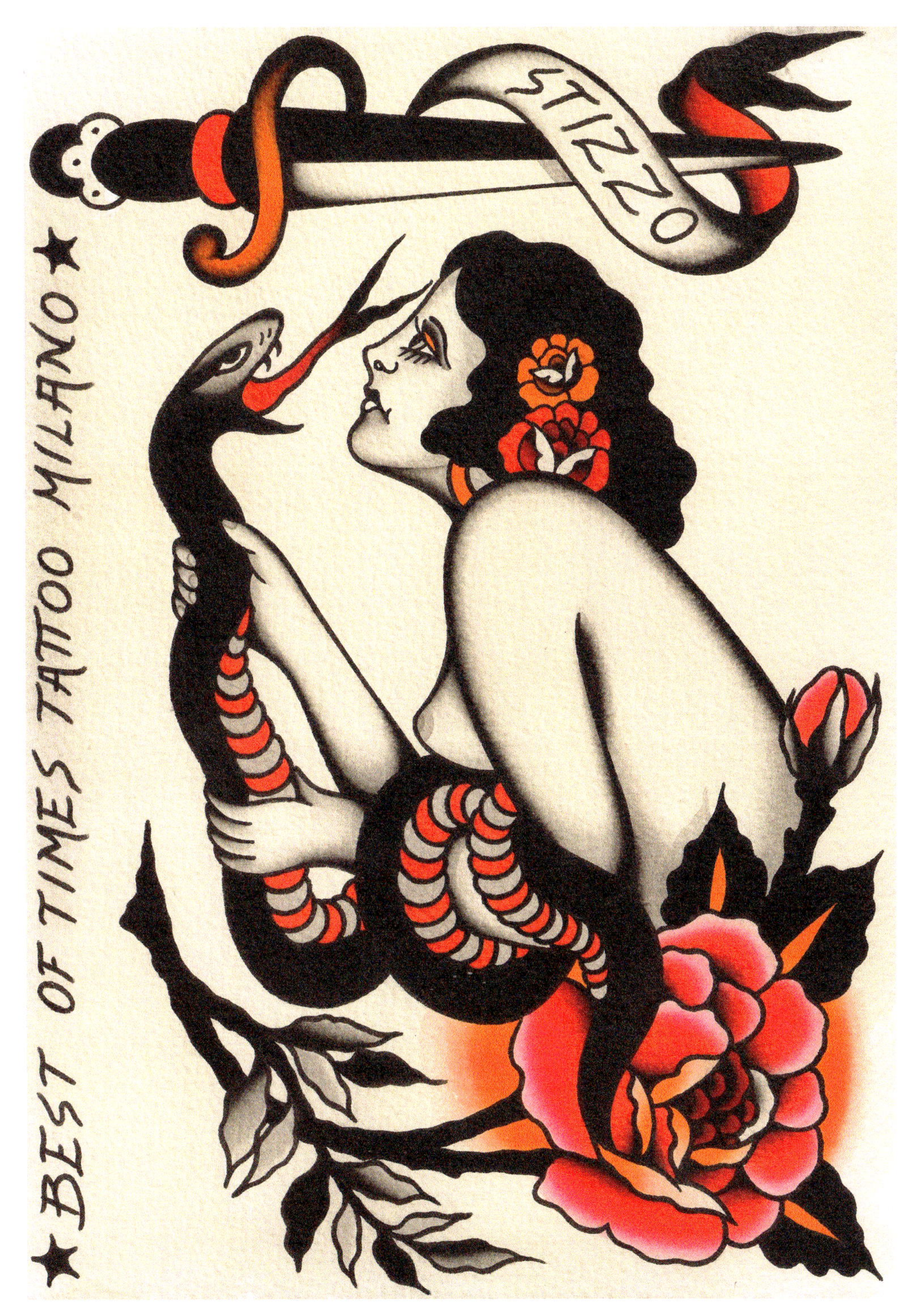
STIZZO
★ BEST OF TIMES TATTOO MILANO ★

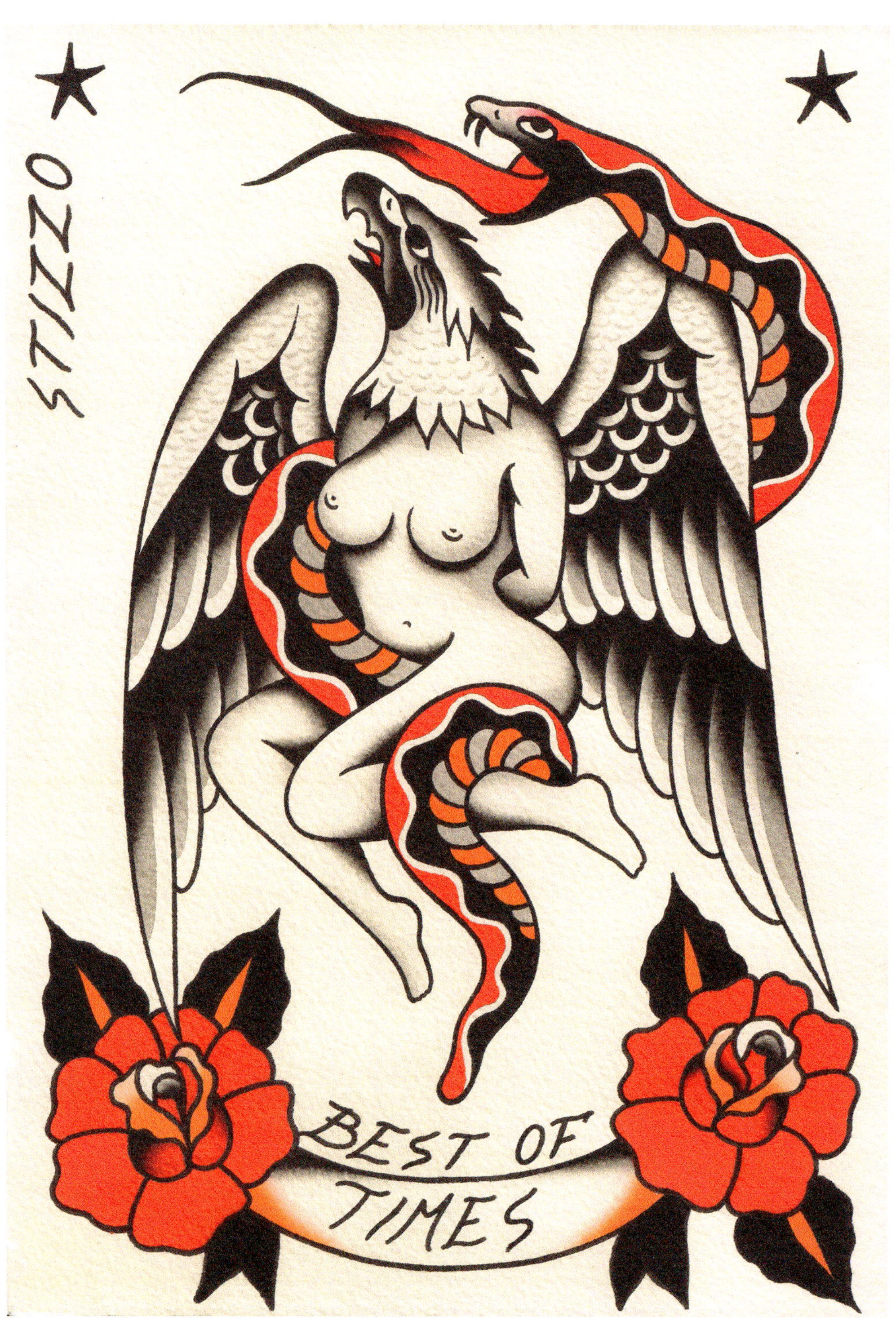
STIZZO
BEST OF
TIMES

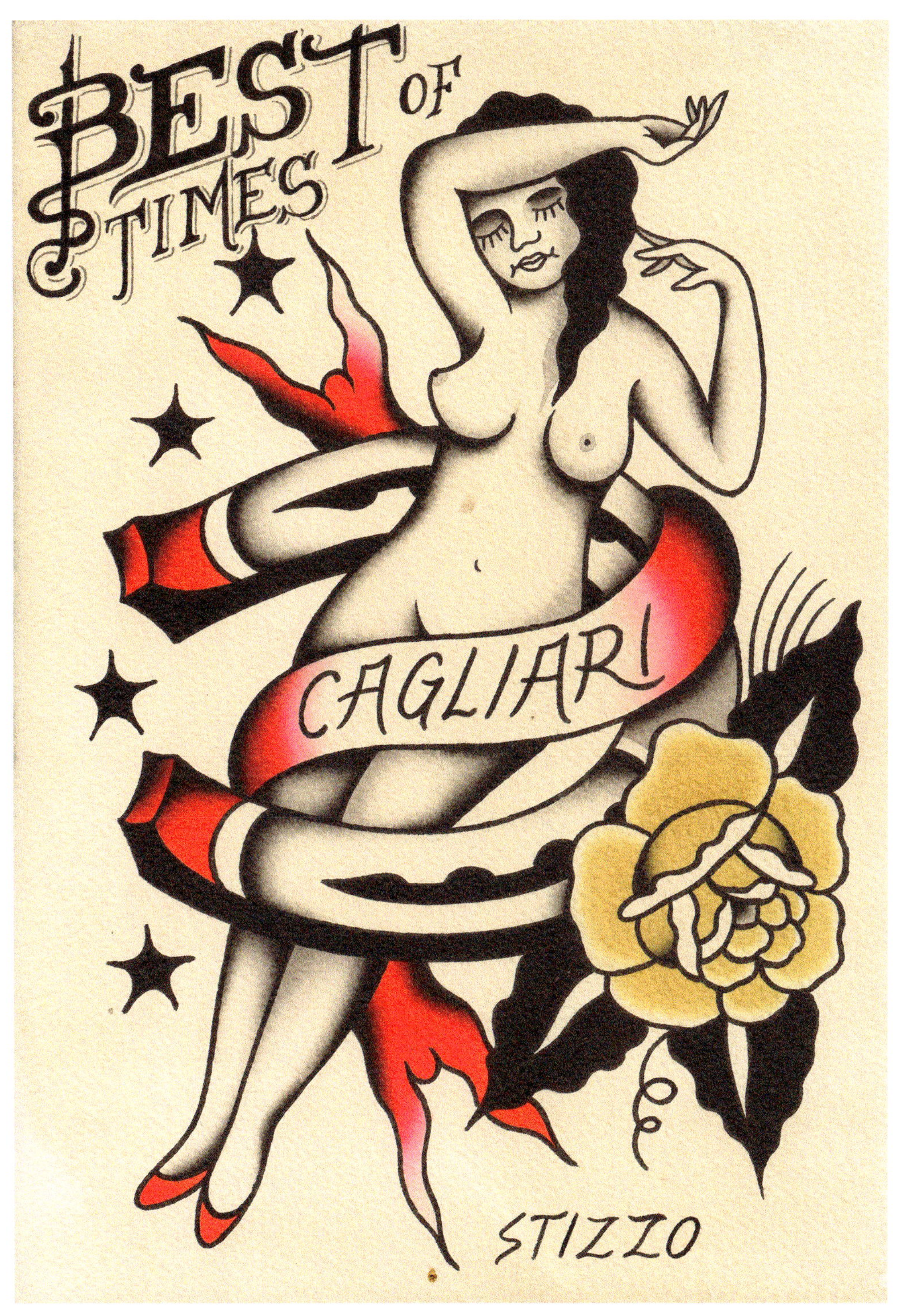
BEST OF TIMES
CAGLIARI
STIZZO

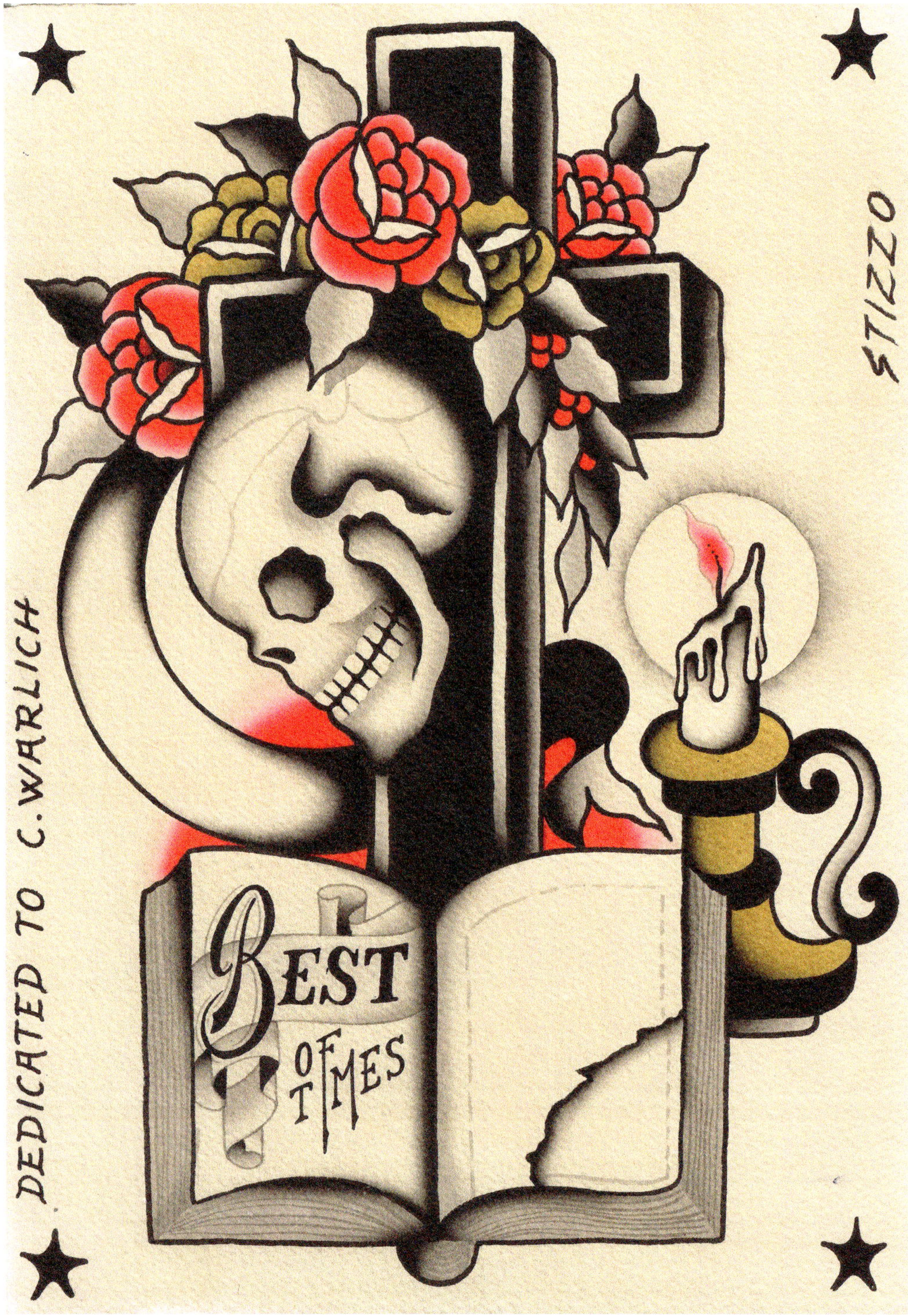

DEDICATED TO C.WARLICH

BEST OF TIMES

STIZZO

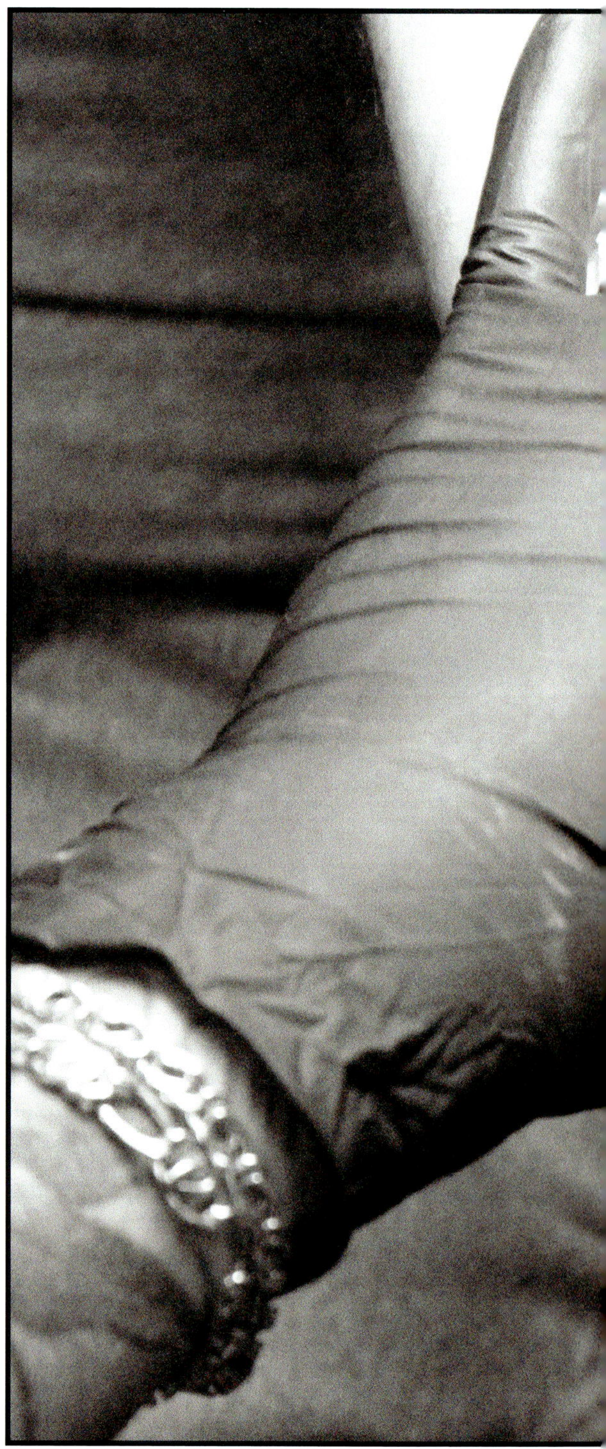

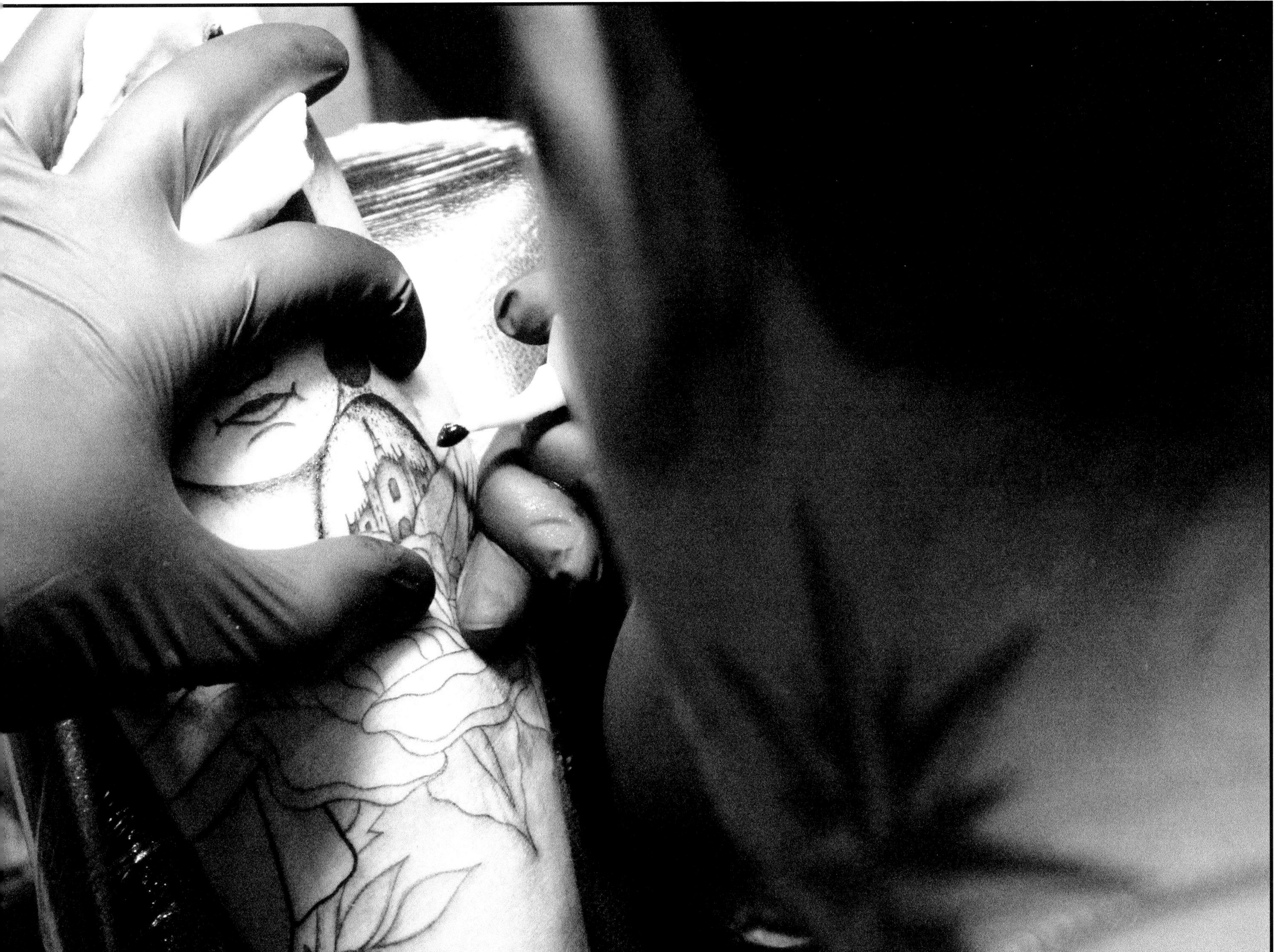

MAX BRAIN

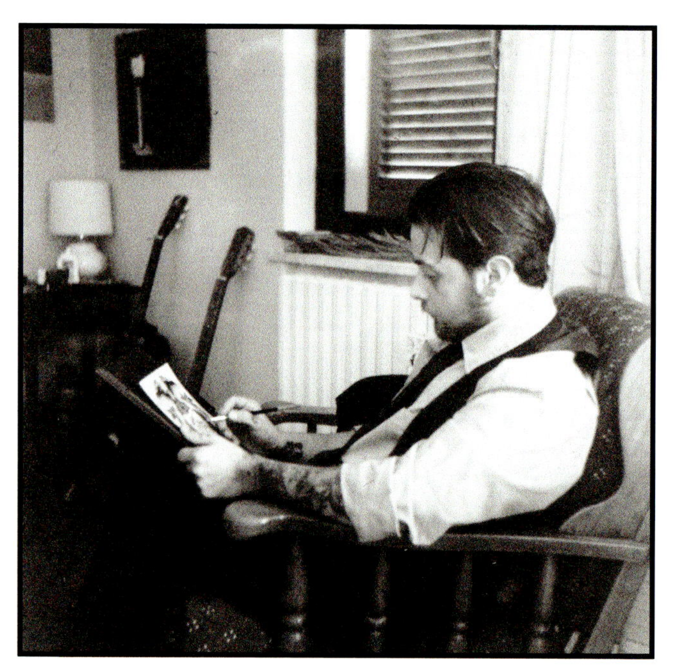

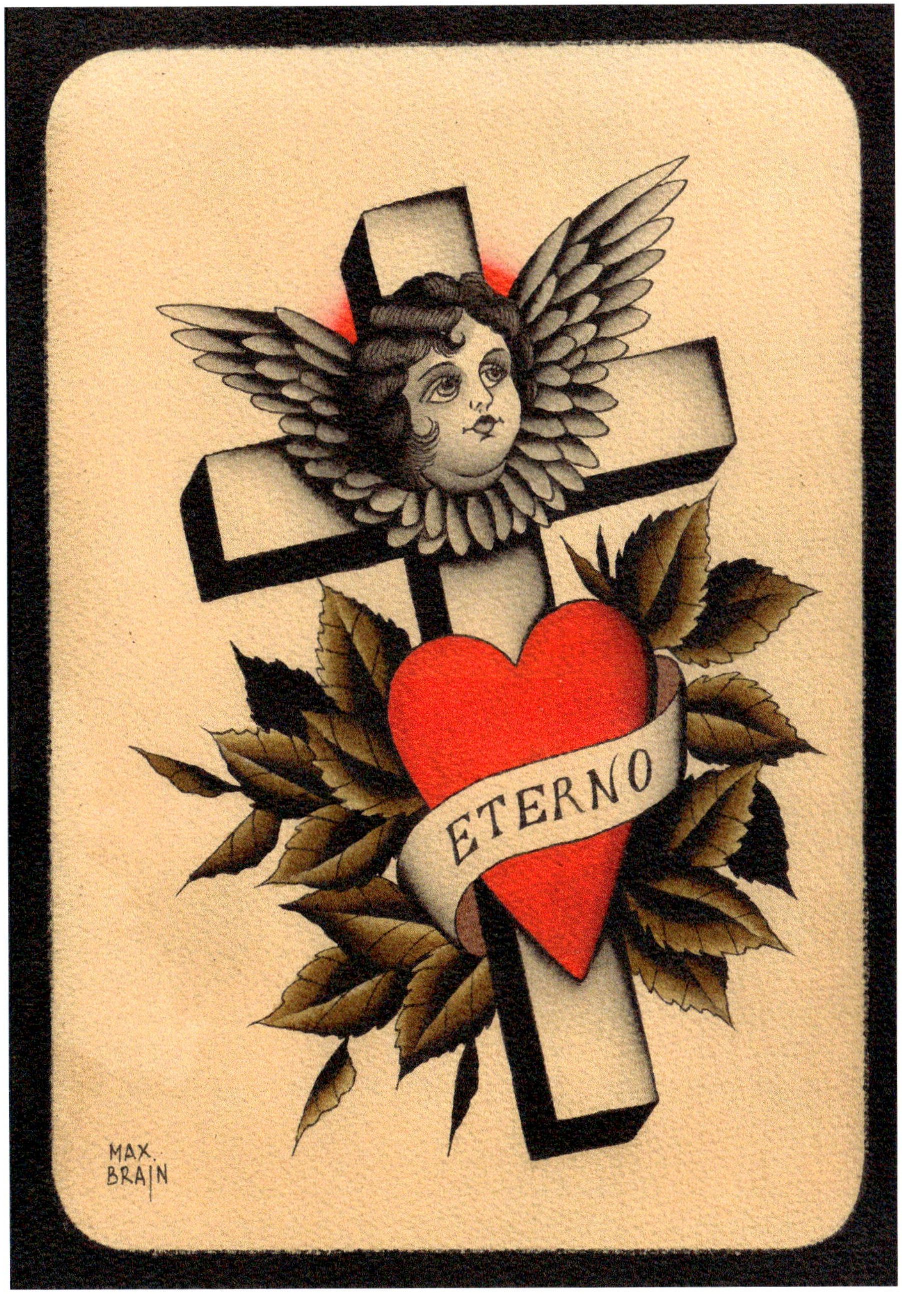

ETERNO
MAX BRAIN

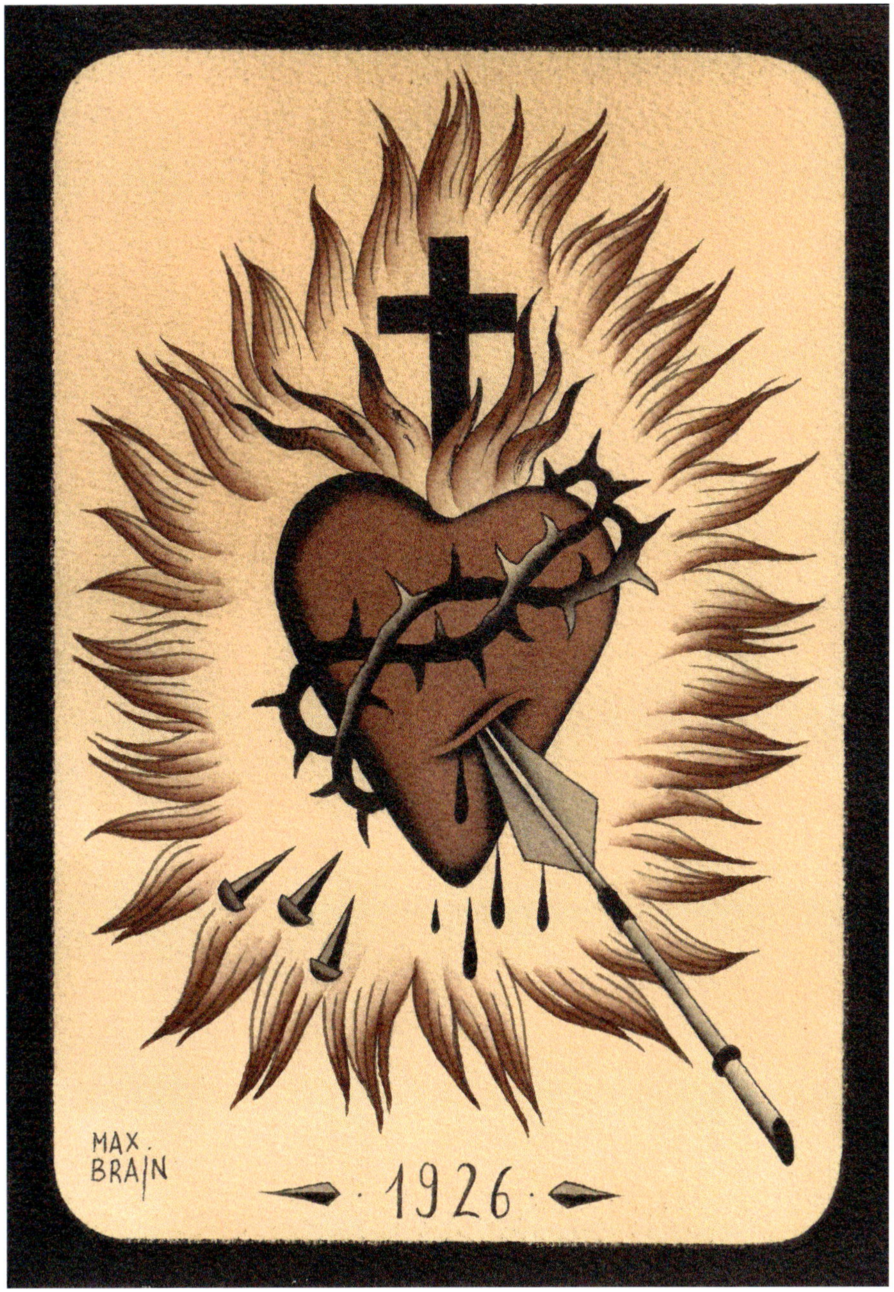

MAX BRAIN
1926

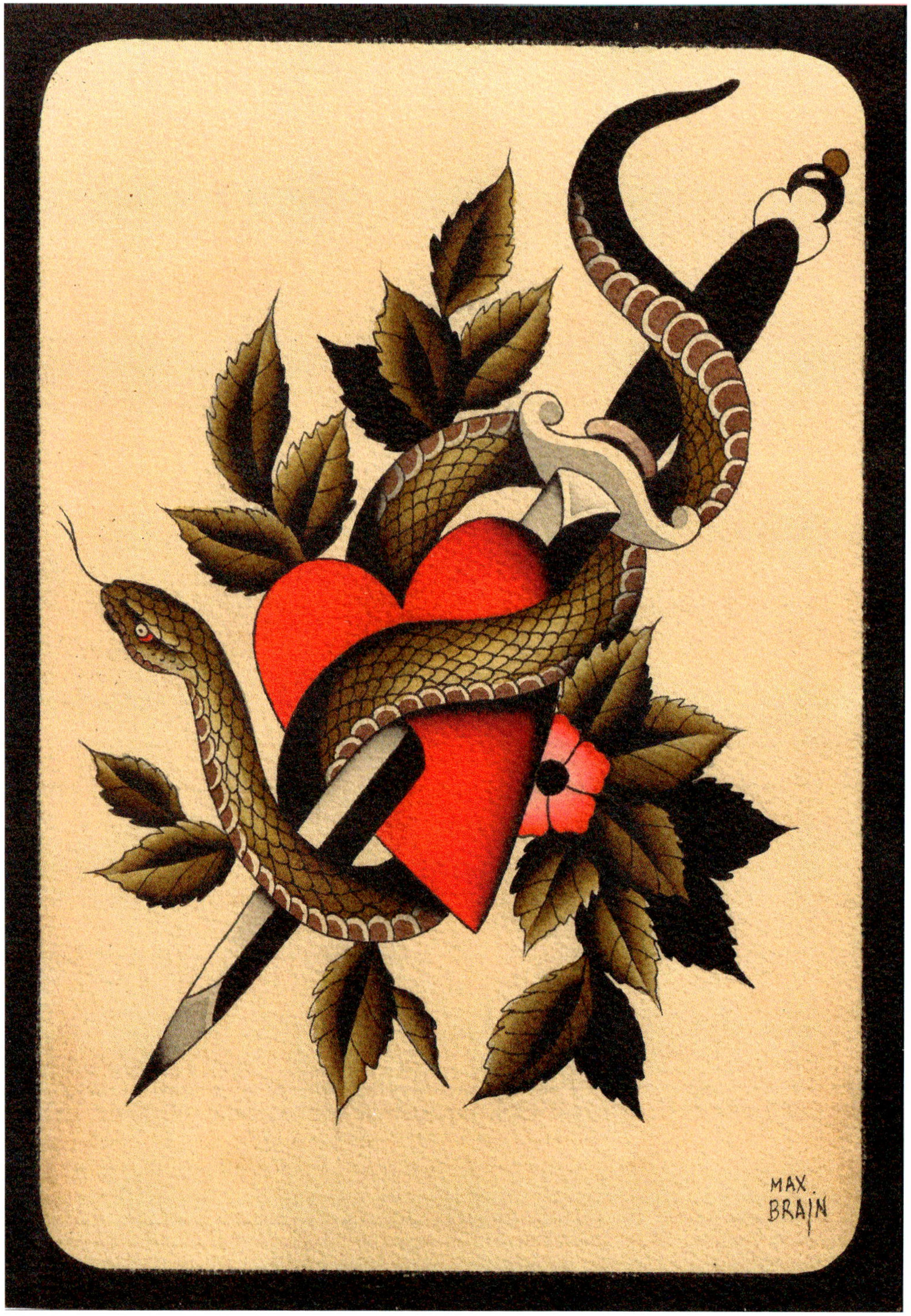

MAX
BRAIN

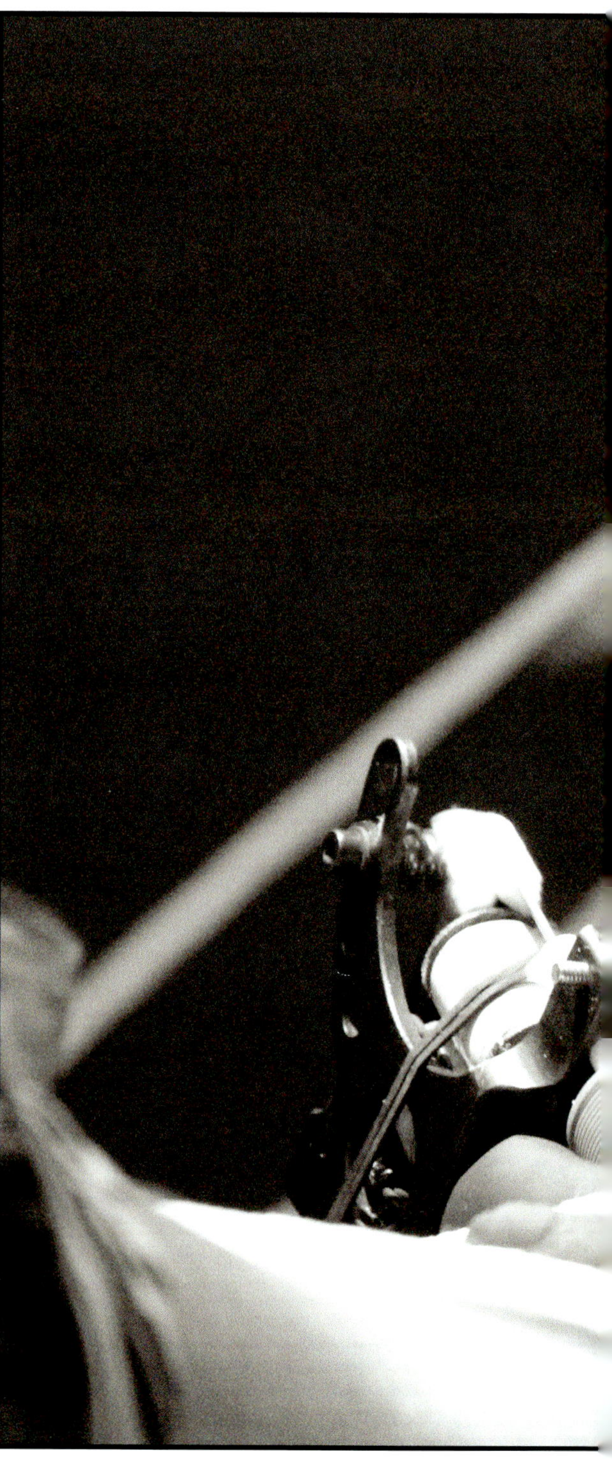

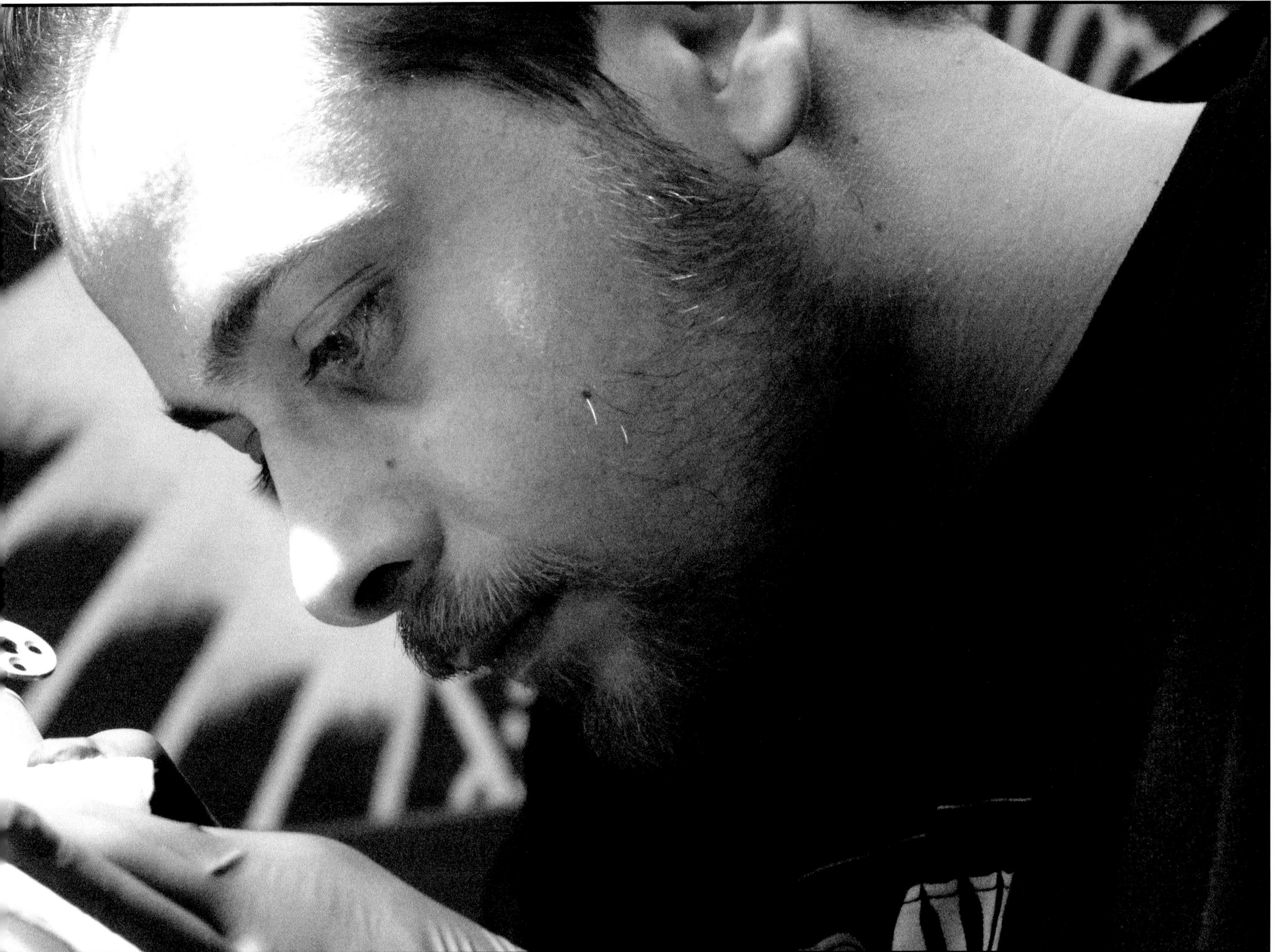

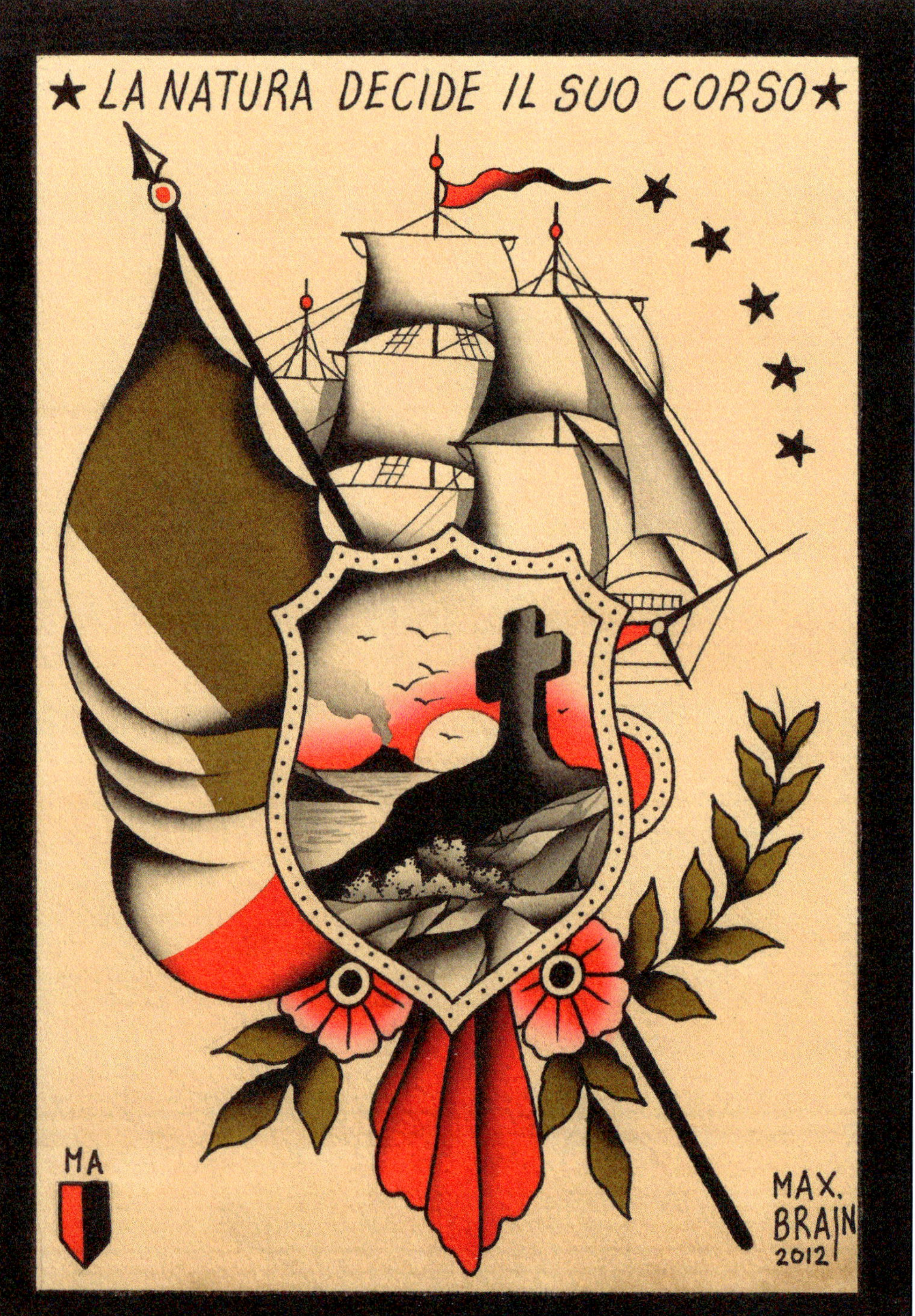
★ LA NATURA DECIDE IL SUO CORSO ★
MA
MAX.
BRAIN
2012

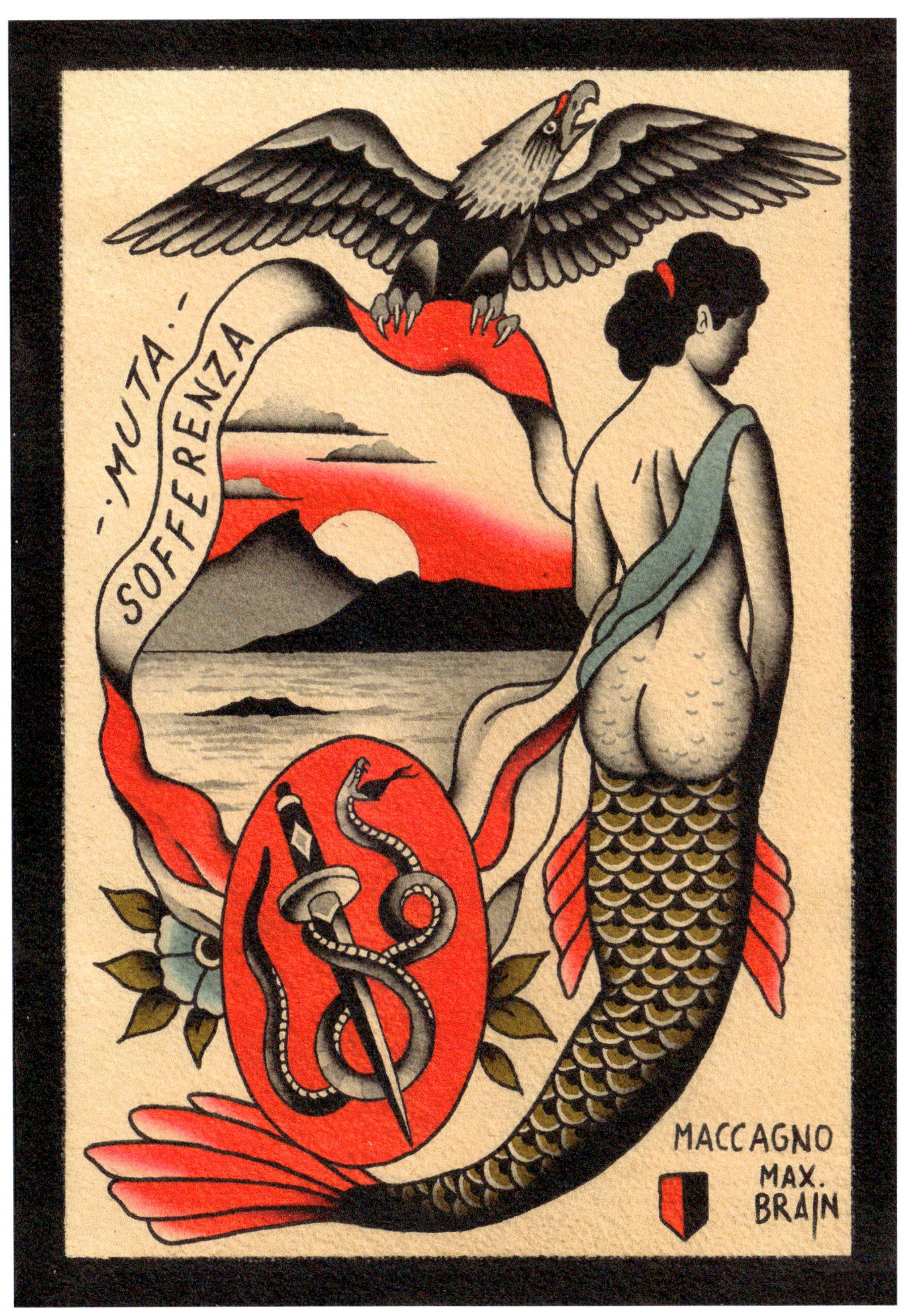
MUTA SOFFERENZA
MACCAGNO
MAX.
BRAIN

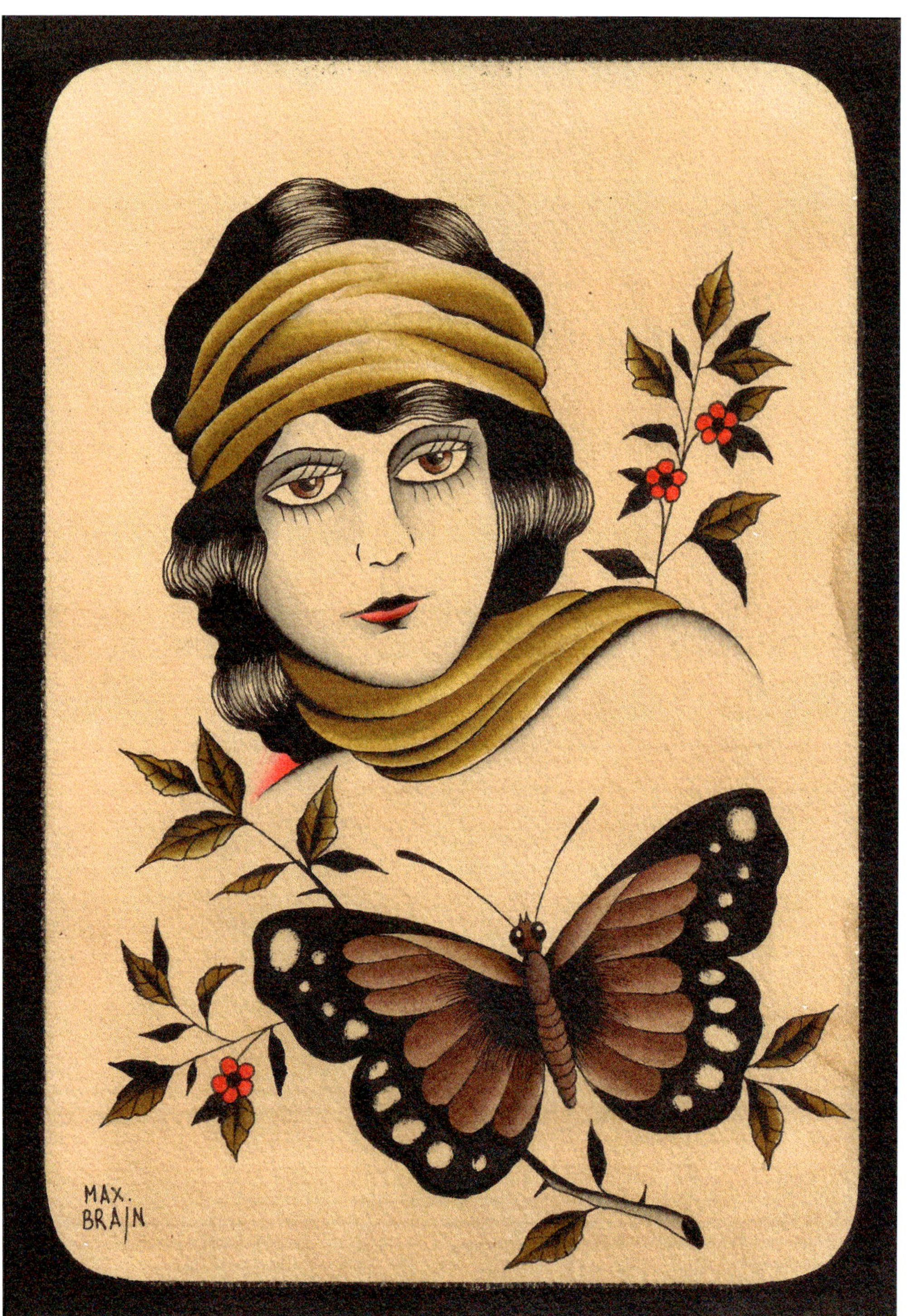
MAX.
BRAIN

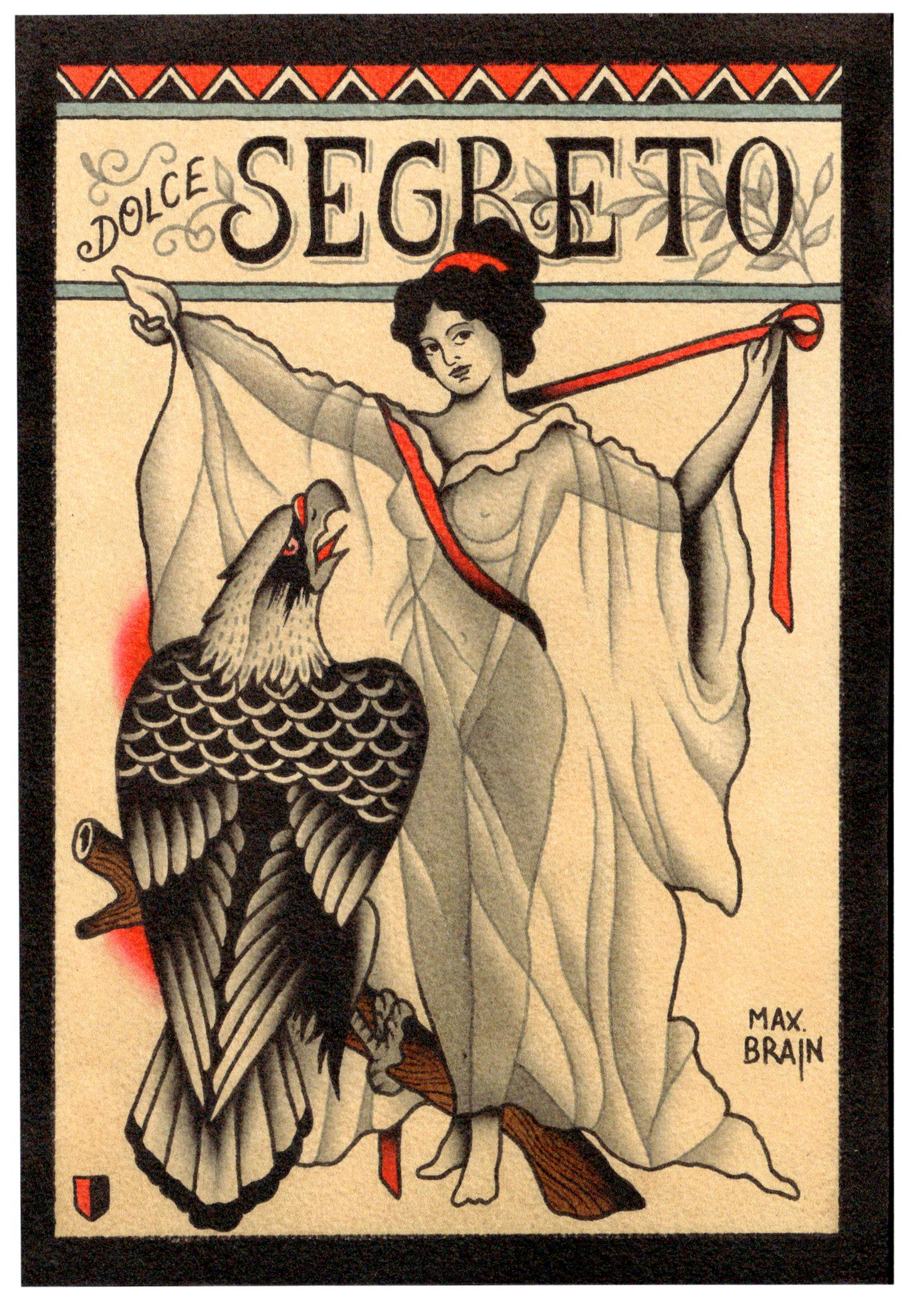
DOLCE SEGRETO
MAX.
BRAIN

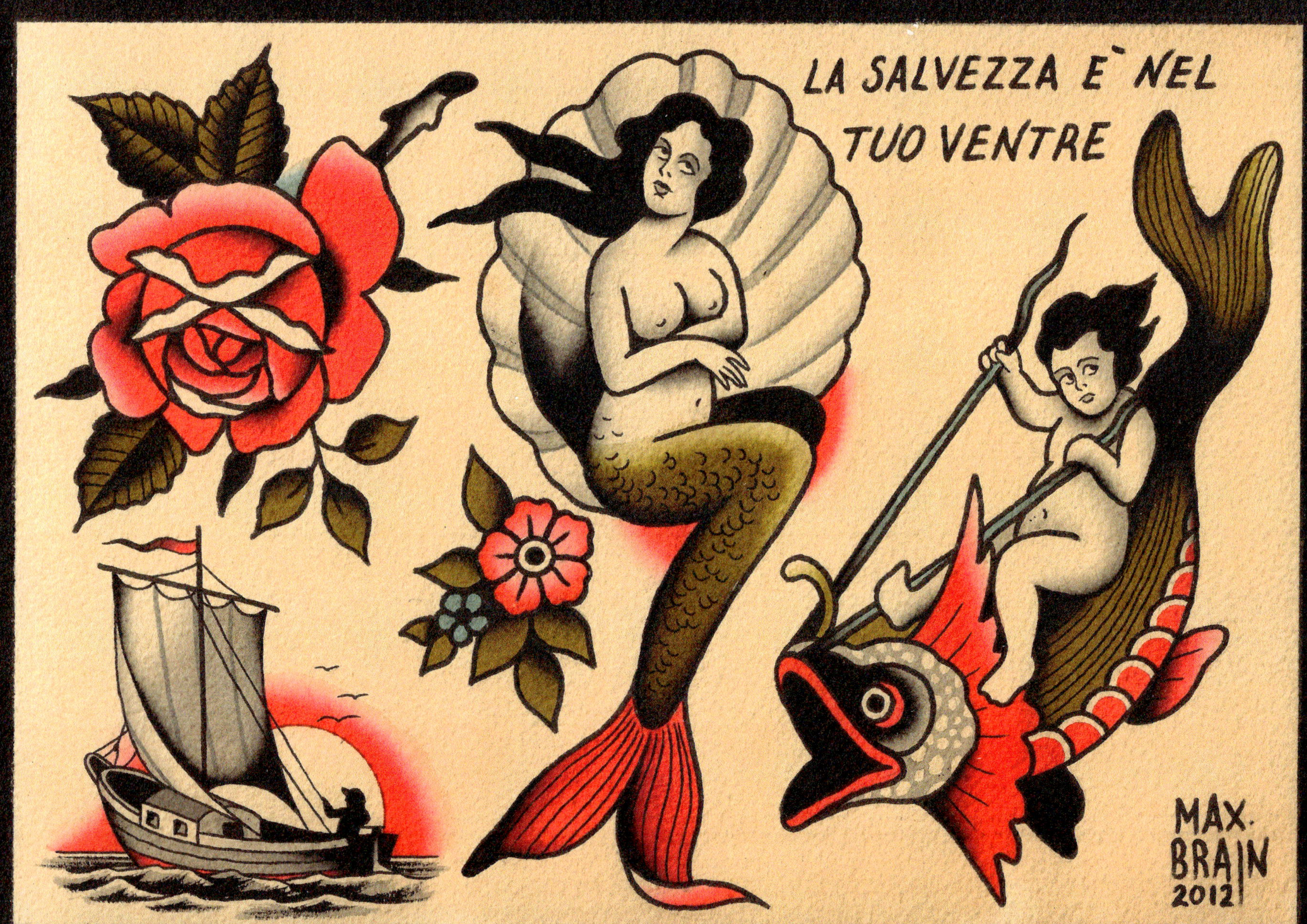
LA SALVEZZA E` NEL
TUO VENTRE
MAX.
BRAIN
2012

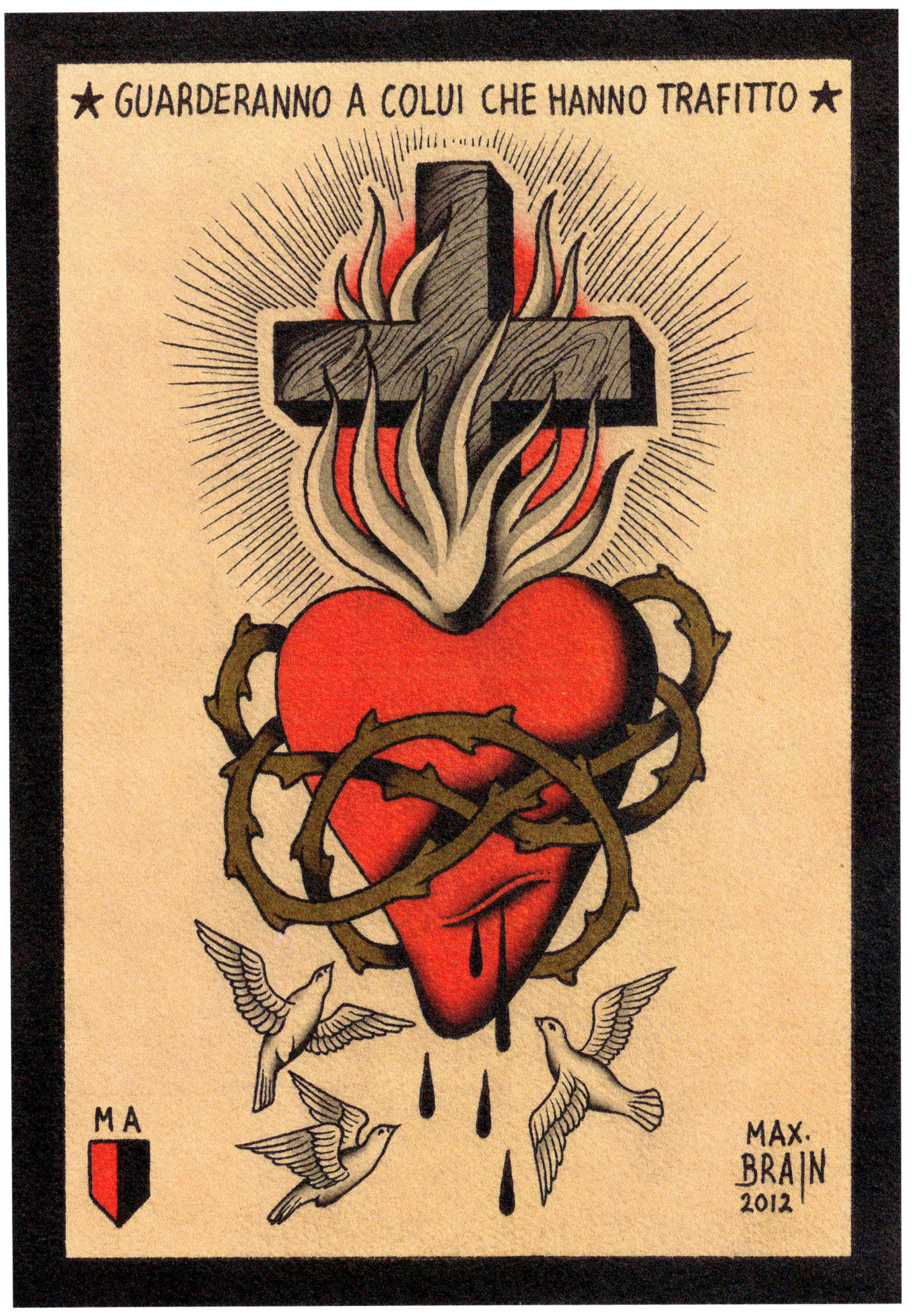
★ GUARDERANNO A COLUI CHE HANNO TRAFITTO ★
MA
MAX.
BRAIN
2012

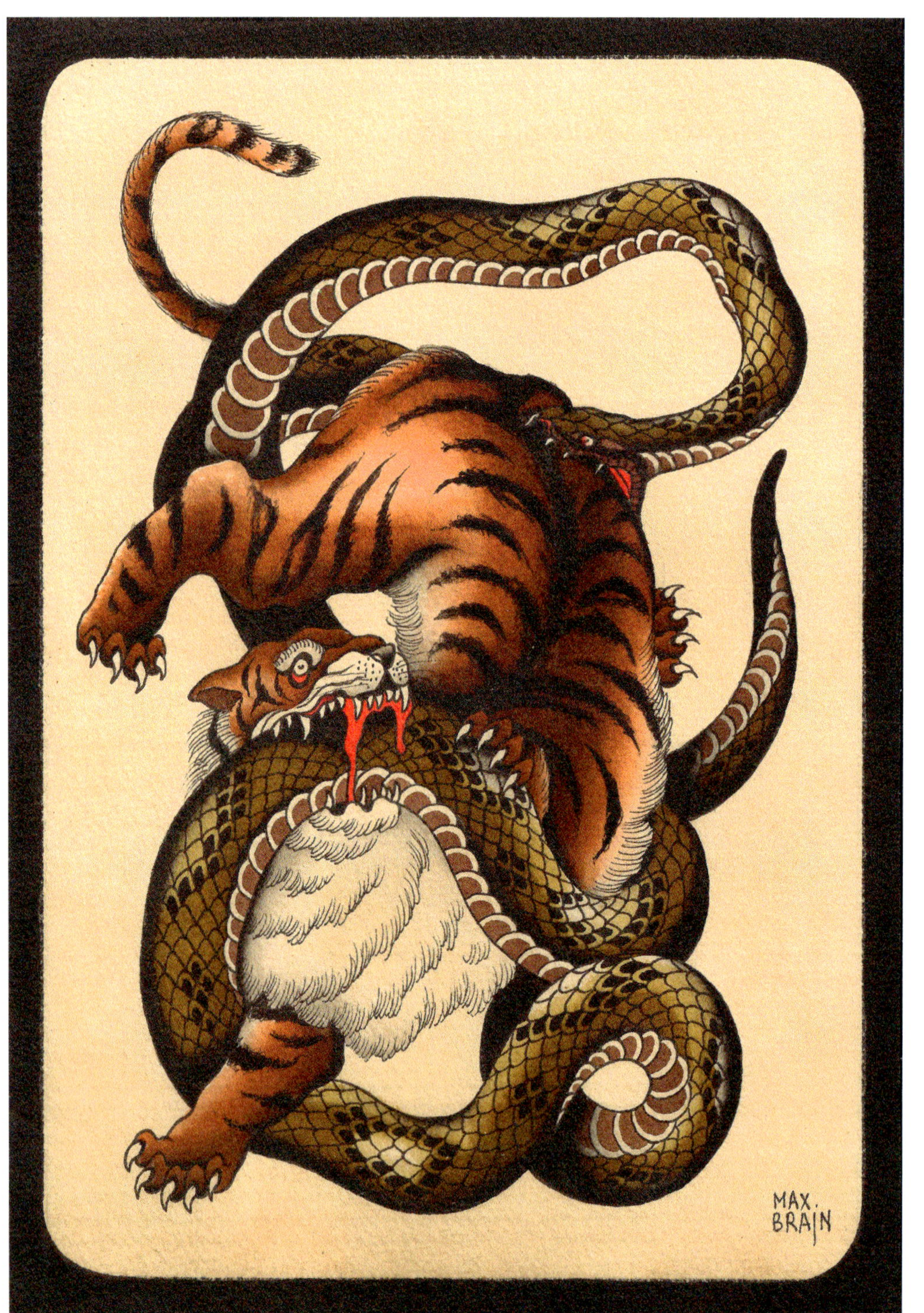
MAX.
BRAIN

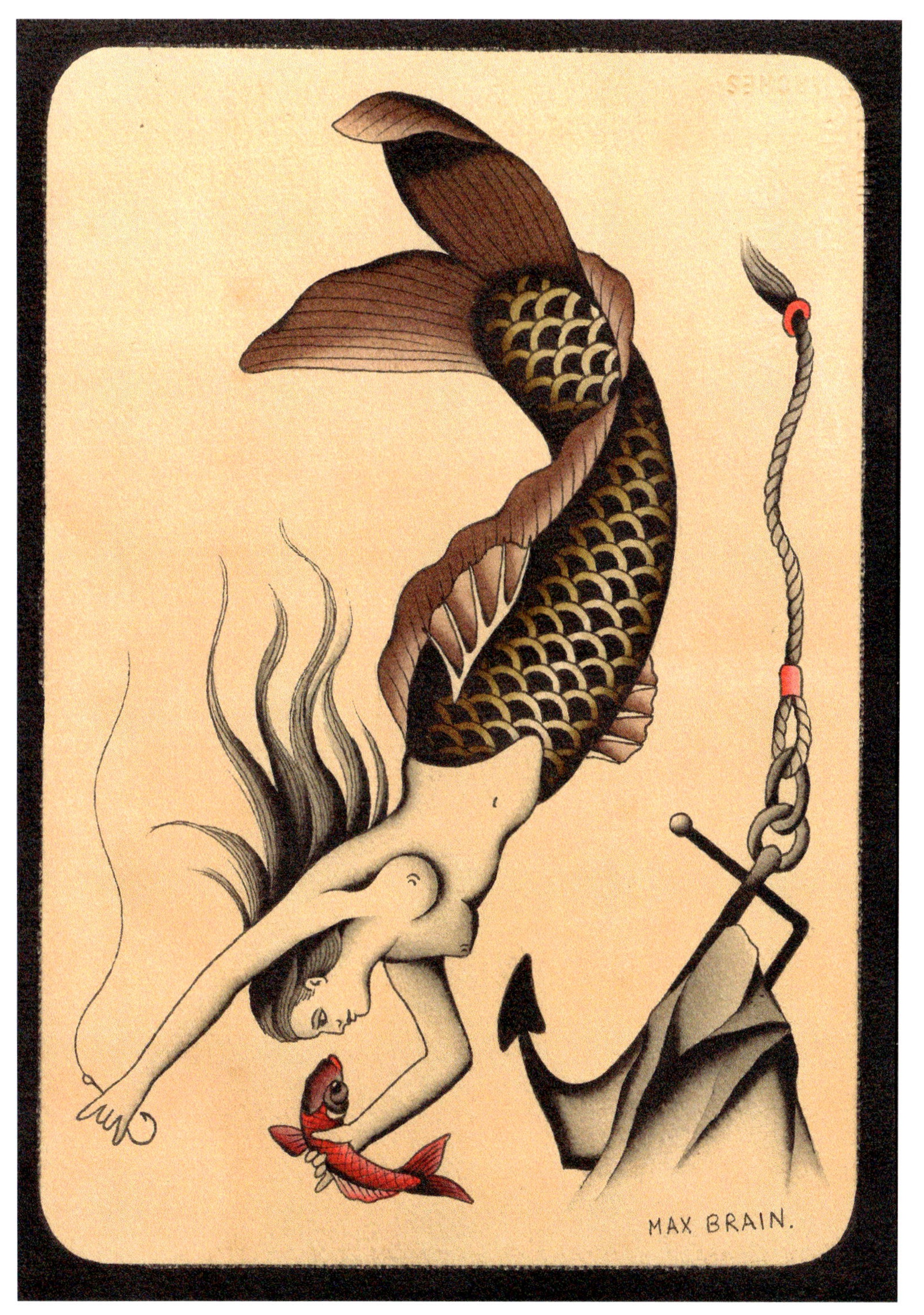
MAX BRAIN.

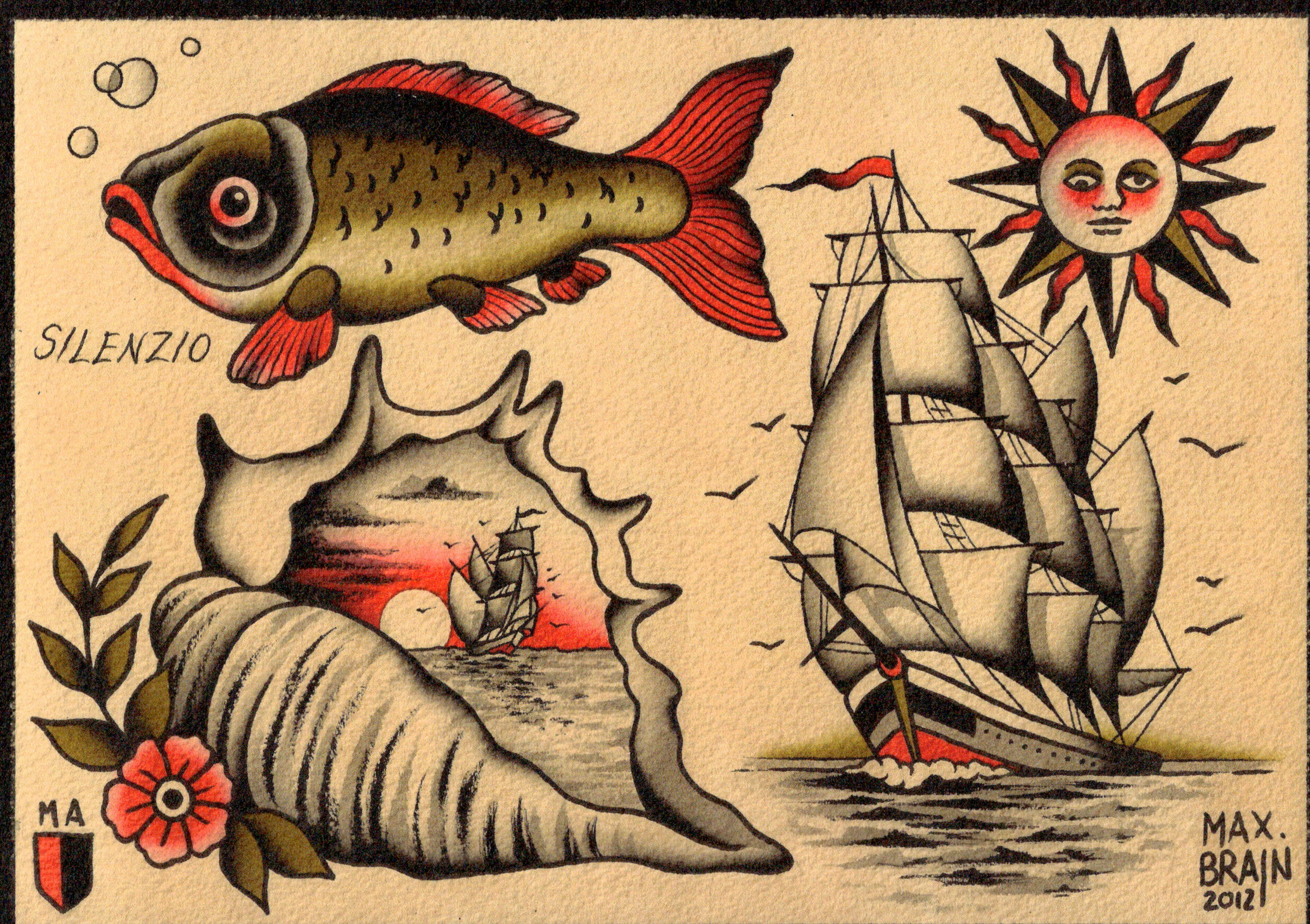
SILENZIO
MA
MAX.
BRAIN
2012

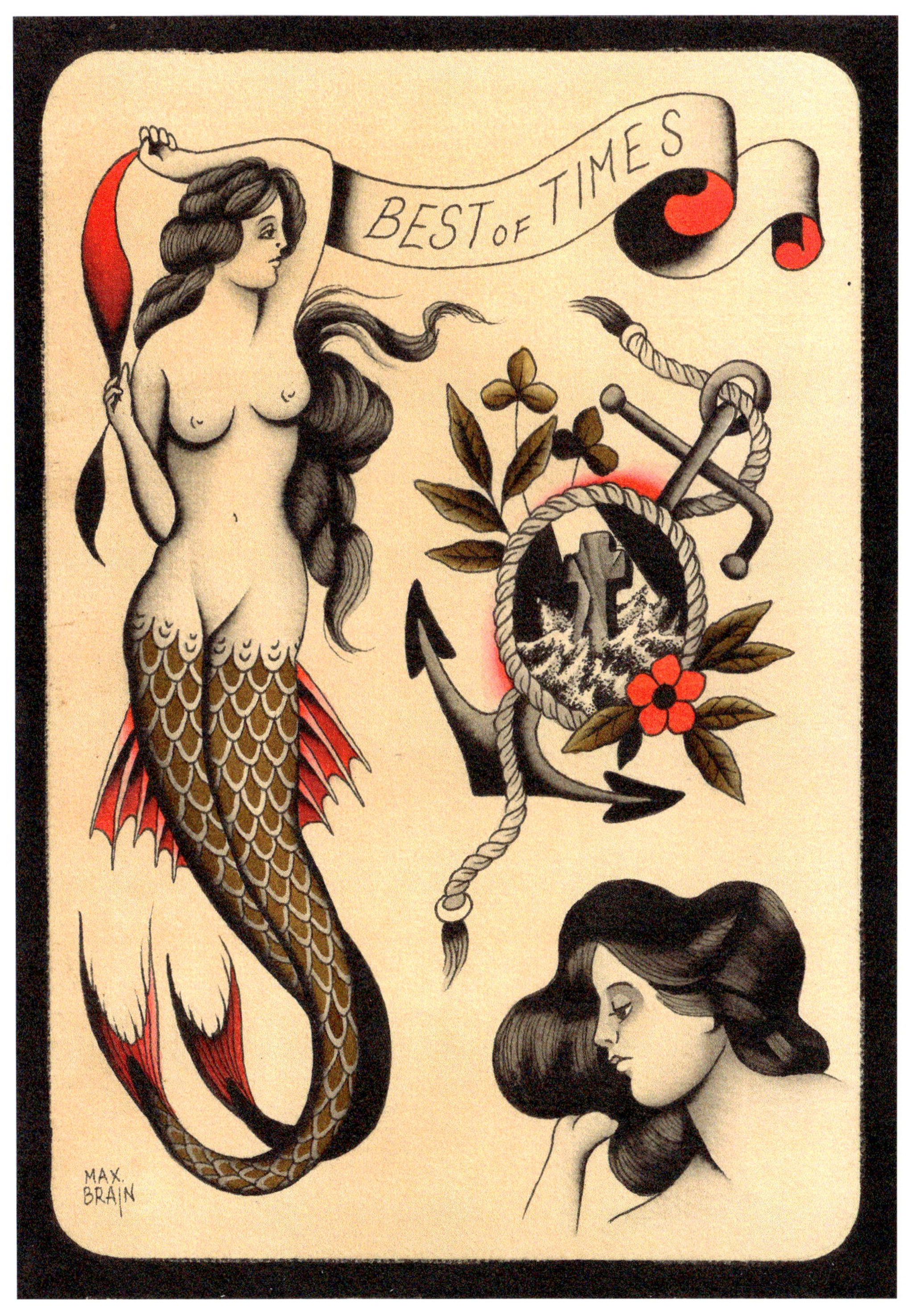
BEST OF TIMES
MAX.
BRAIN

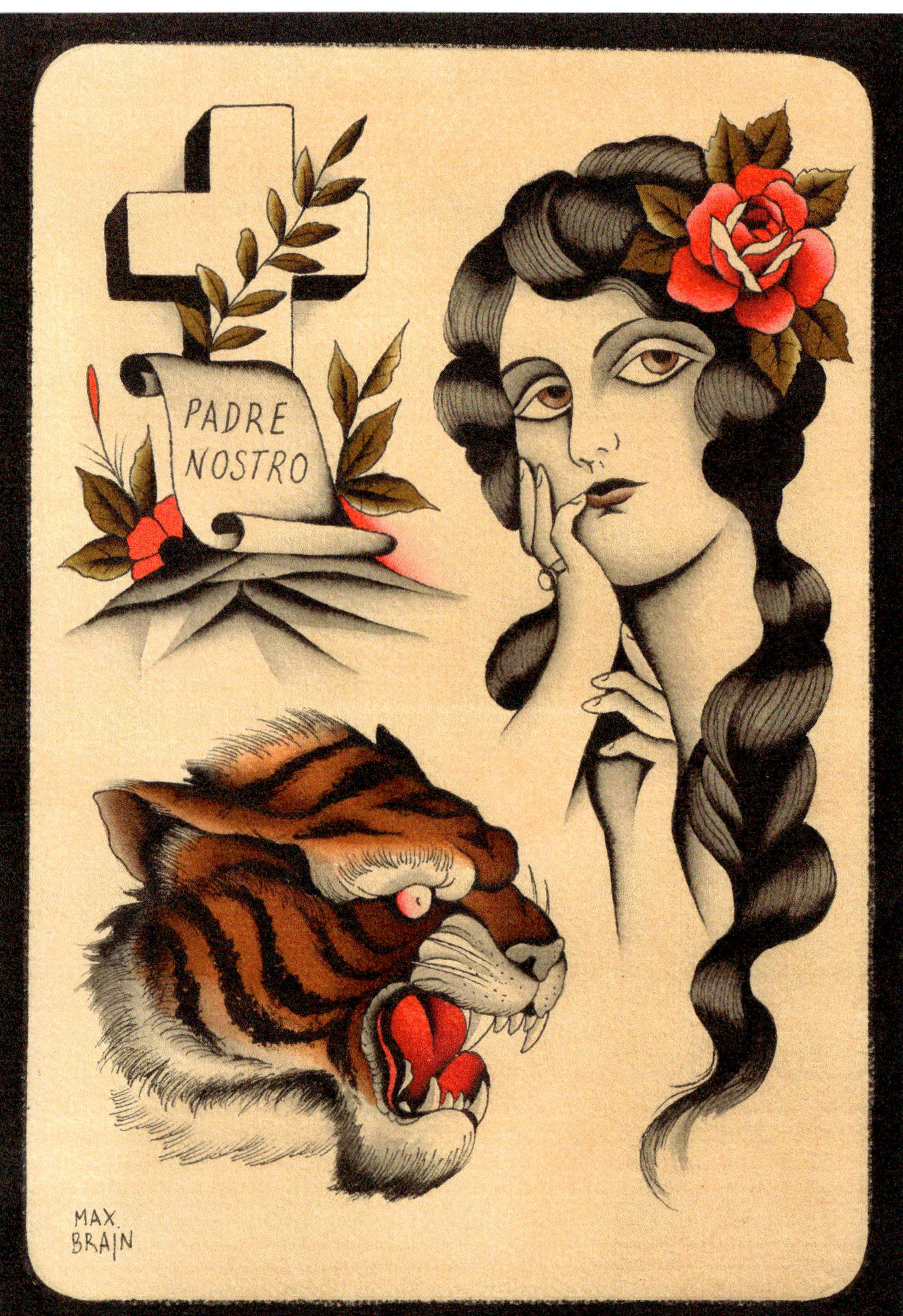
PADRE NOSTRO
MAX. BRAIN

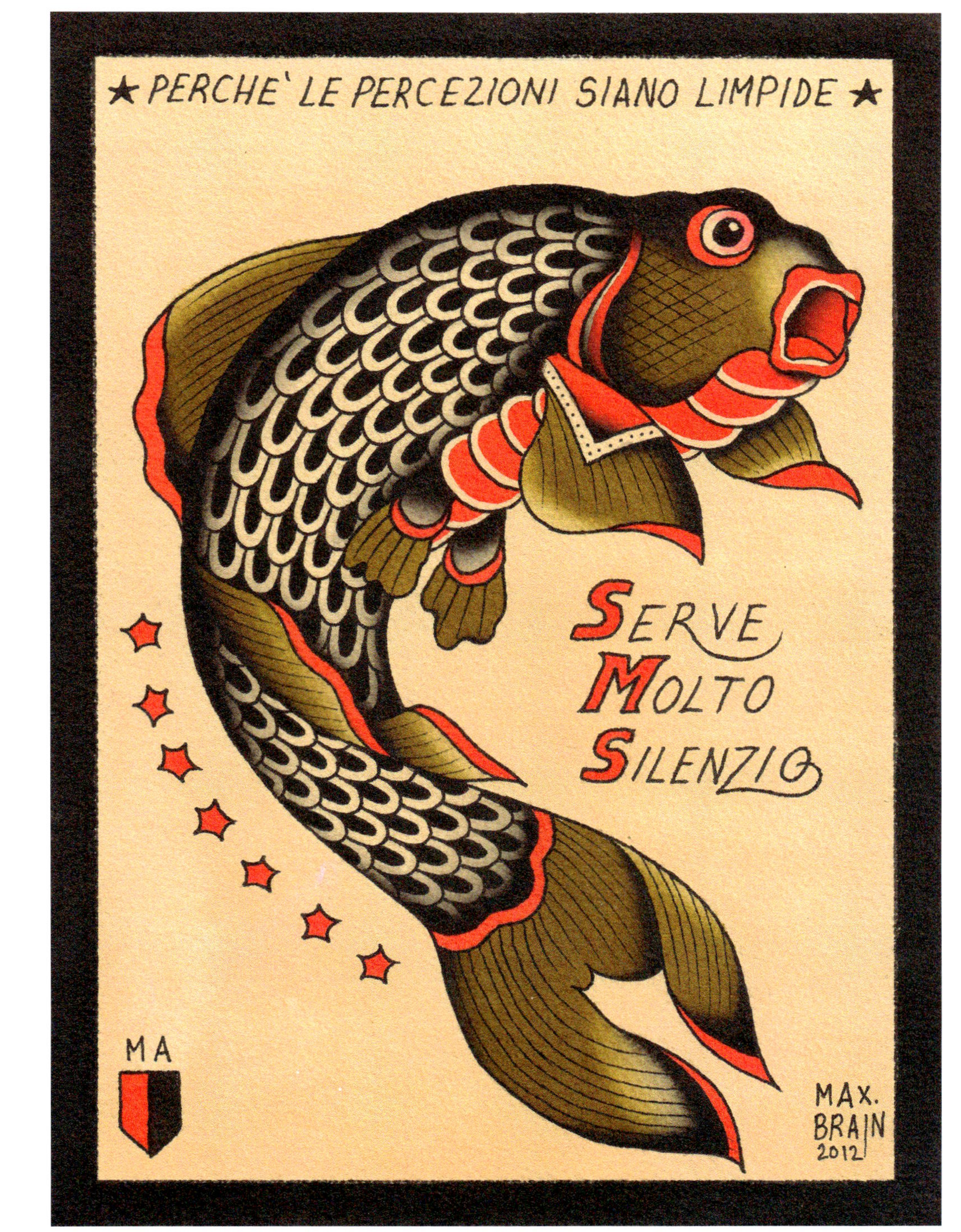
★ PERCHE' LE PERCEZIONI SIANO LIMPIDE ★
SERVE
MOLTO
SILENZIO
MA
MAX.
BRAIN
2012

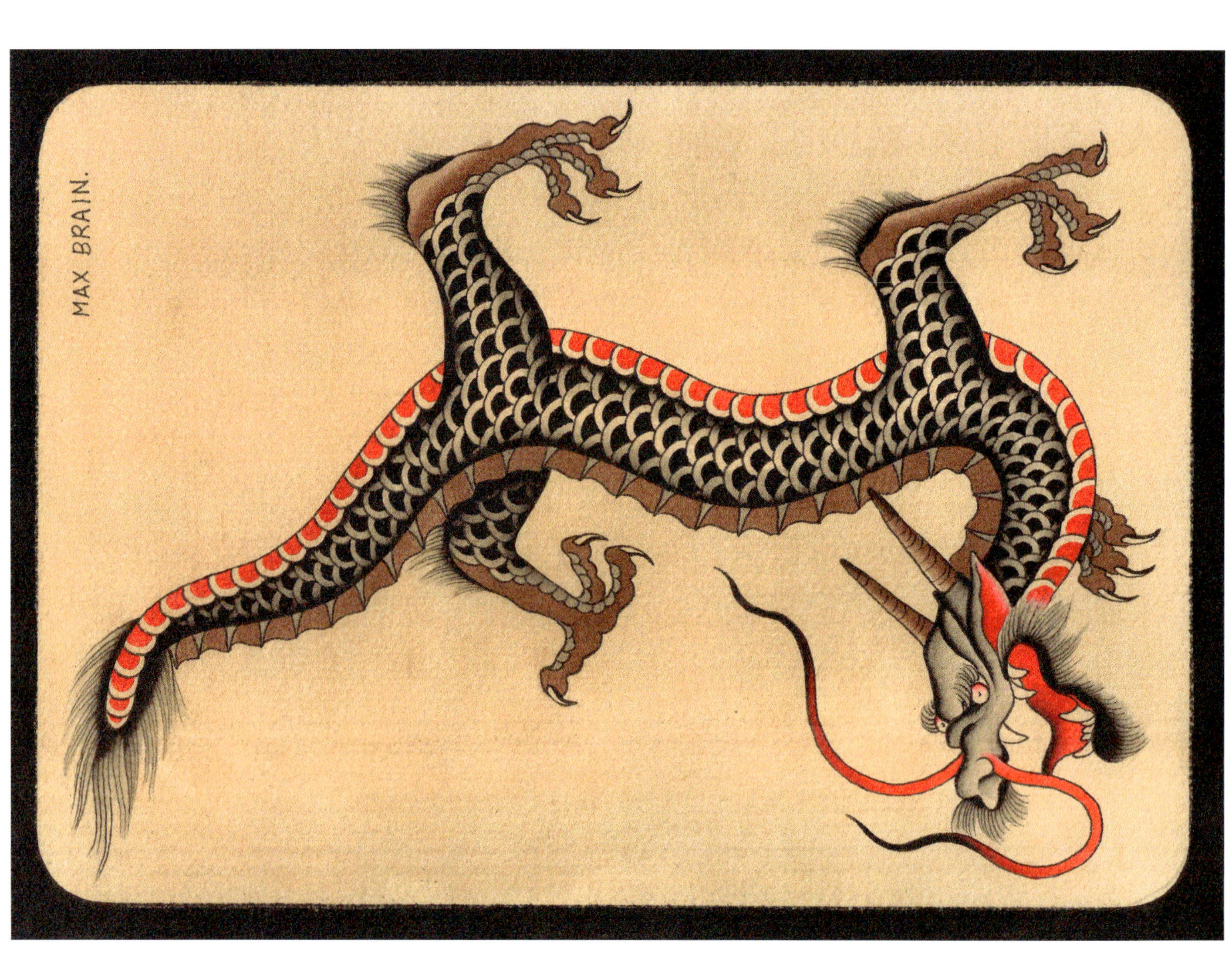
MAX BRAIN.

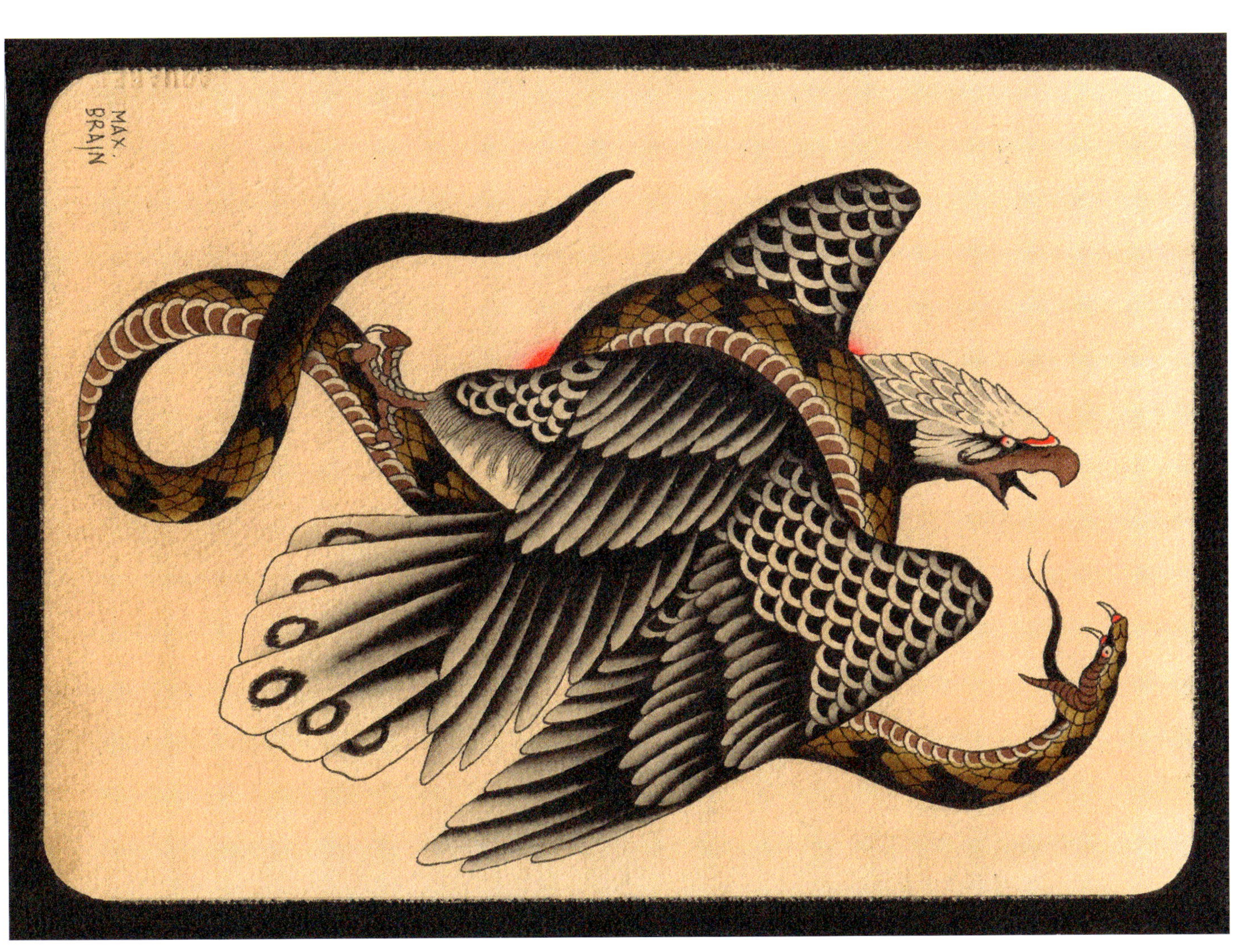
MAX.
BRAIN

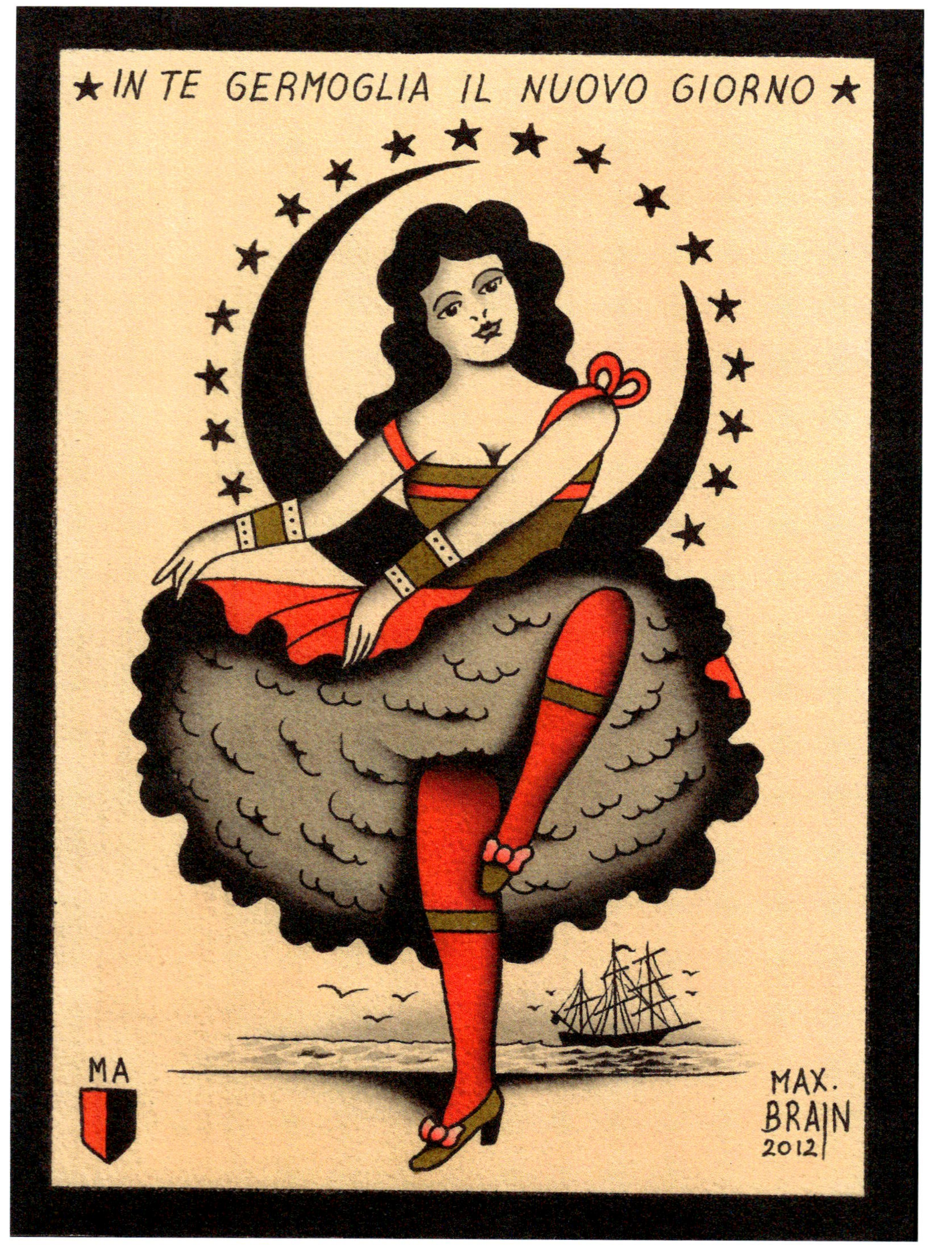
★ IN TE GERMOGLIA IL NUOVO GIORNO ★
MA
MAX. BRAIN 2012

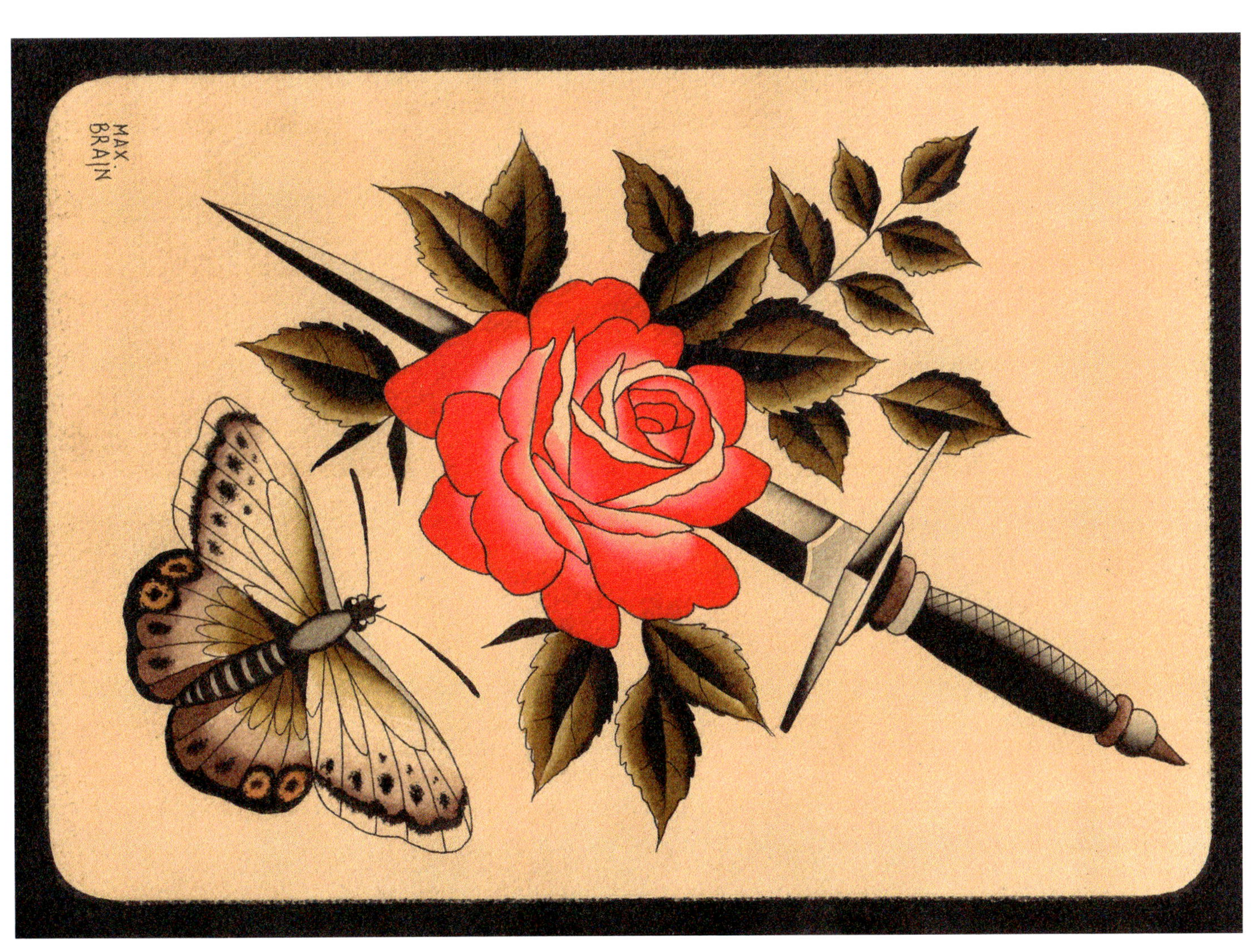
MAX
BRAJN

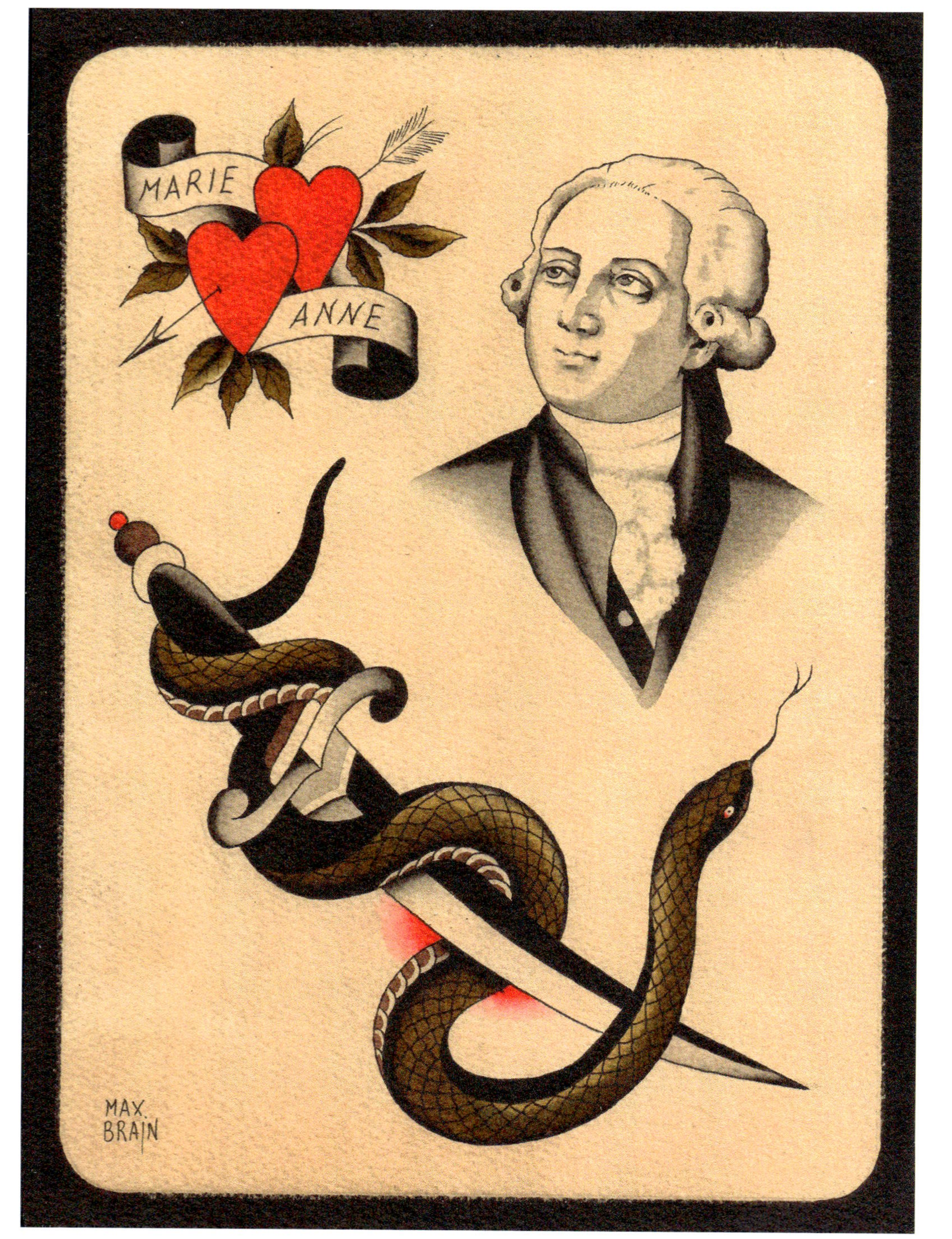
MARIE
ANNE
MAX.
BRAIN

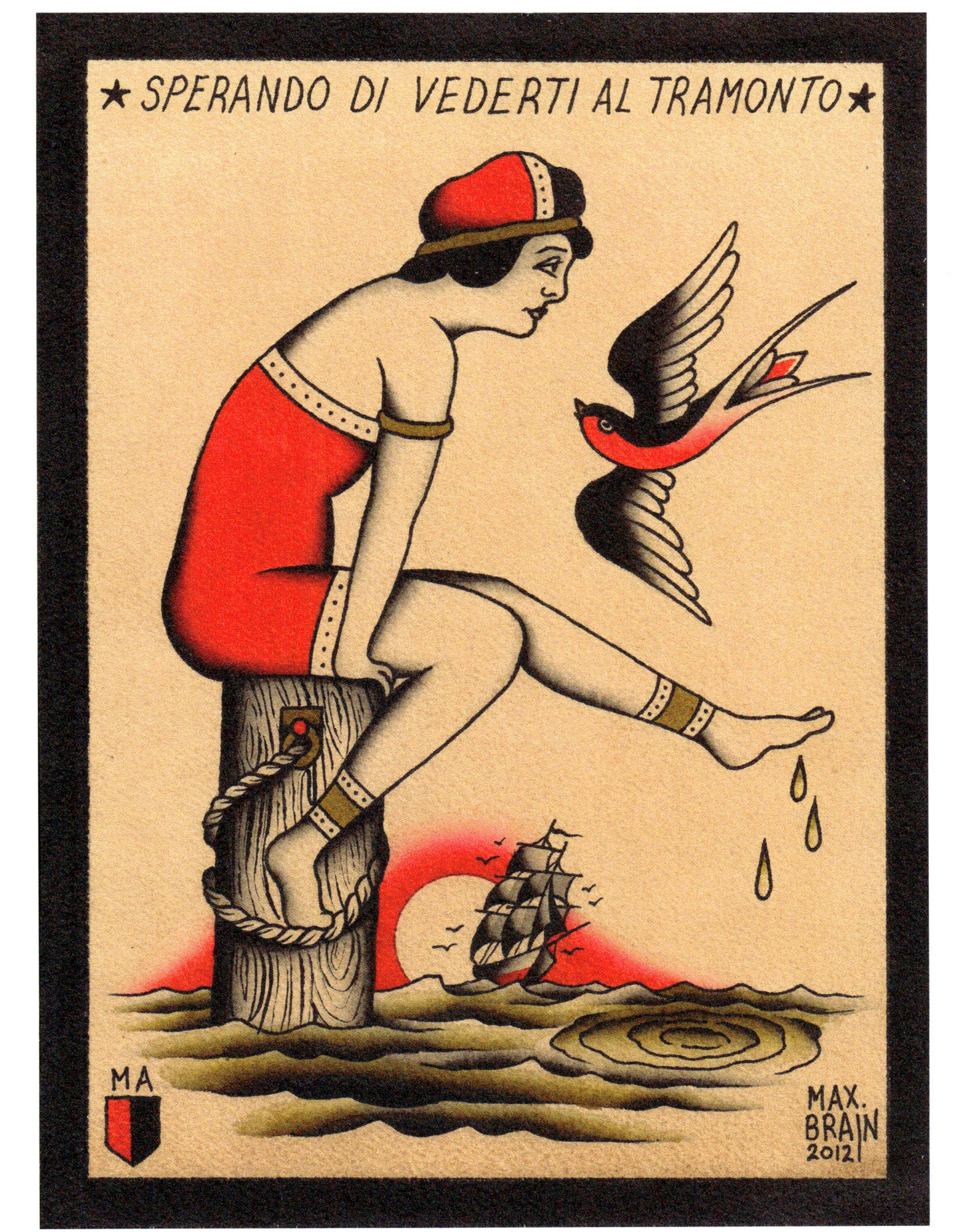
★ SPERANDO DI VEDERTI AL TRAMONTO ★
MA
MAX.
BRAIN
2012

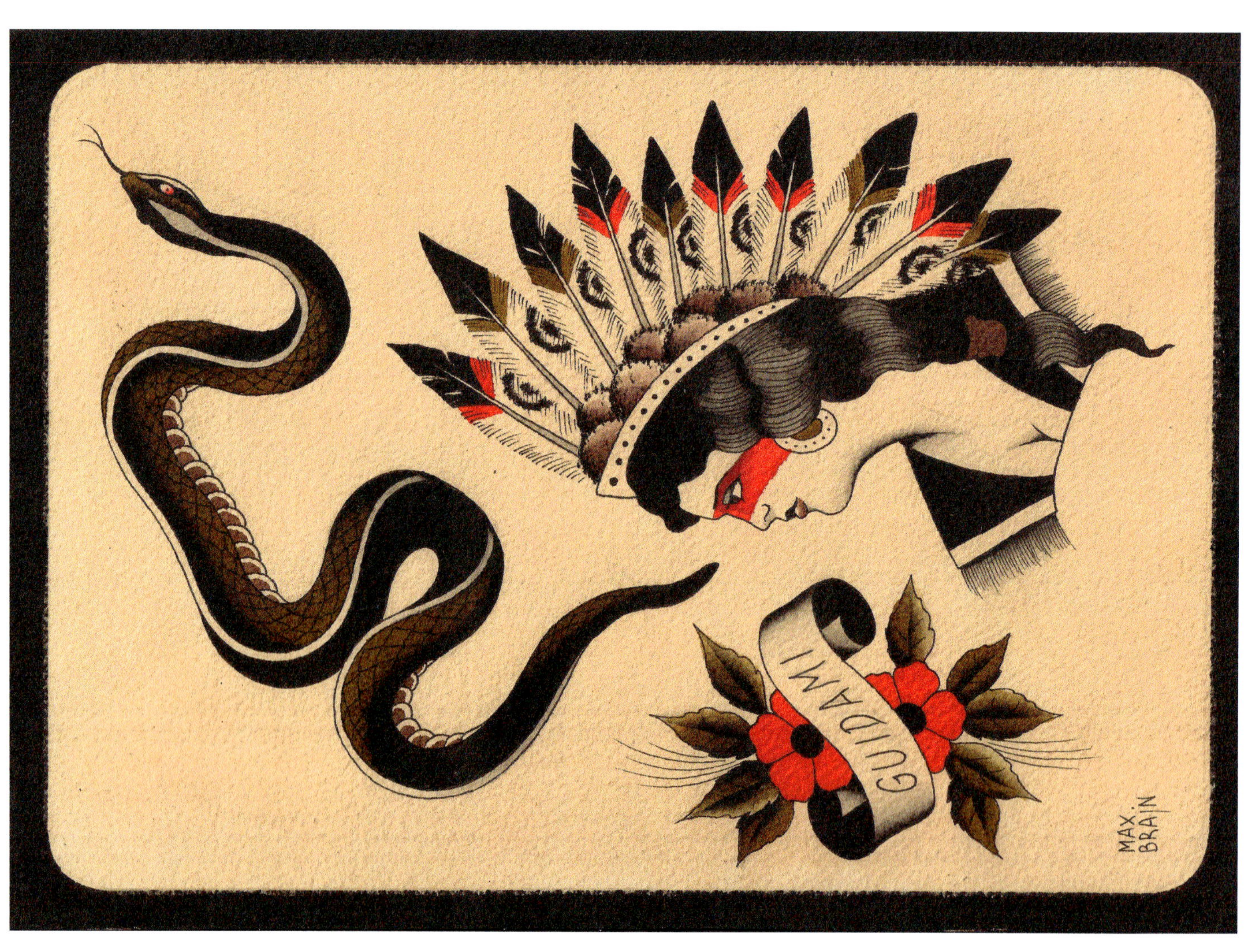
GUIDAMI
MAX.
BRAIN

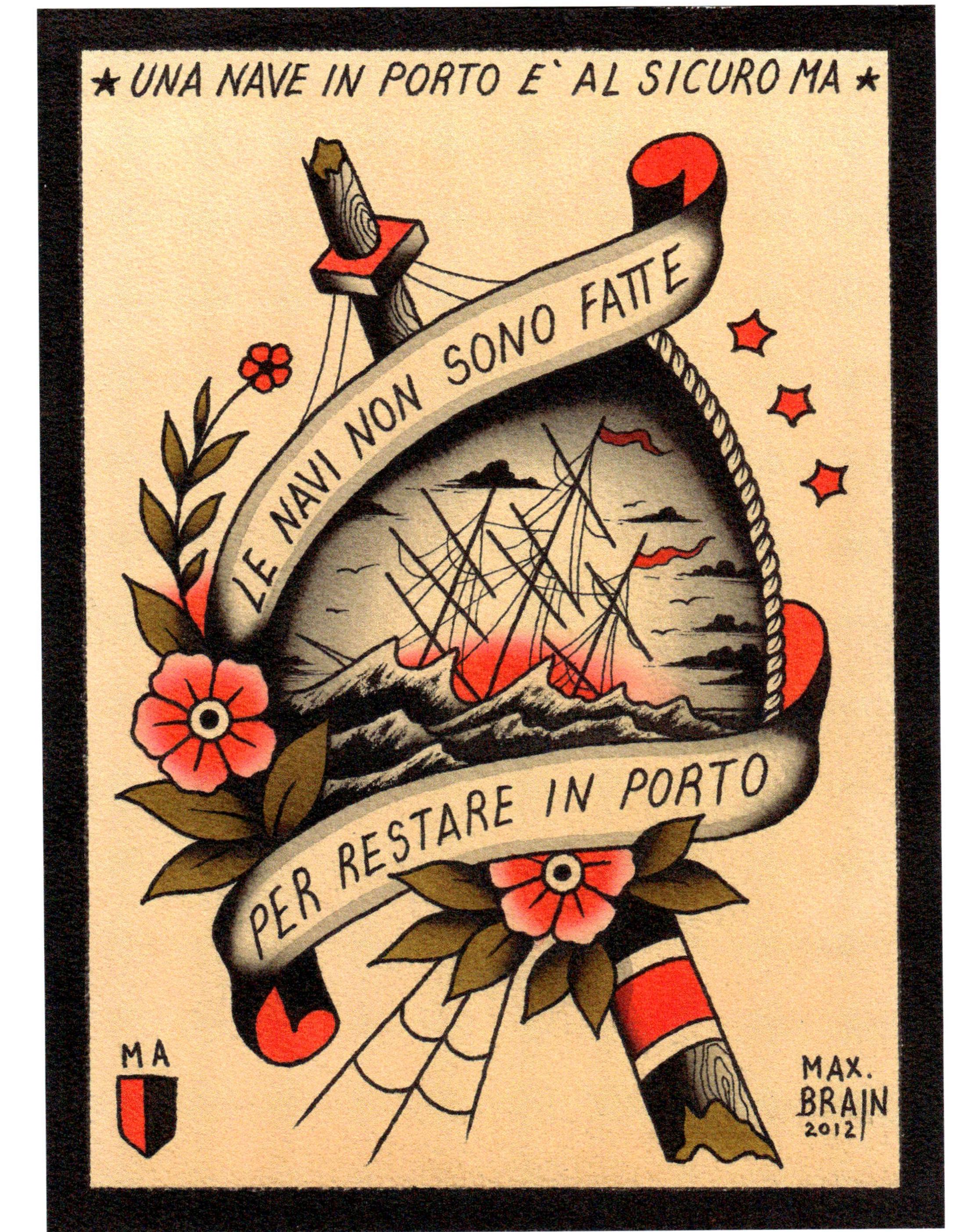
★ UNA NAVE IN PORTO E` AL SICURO MA ★
LE NAVI NON SONO FATTE
PER RESTARE IN PORTO
MA
MAX. BRAIN 2012

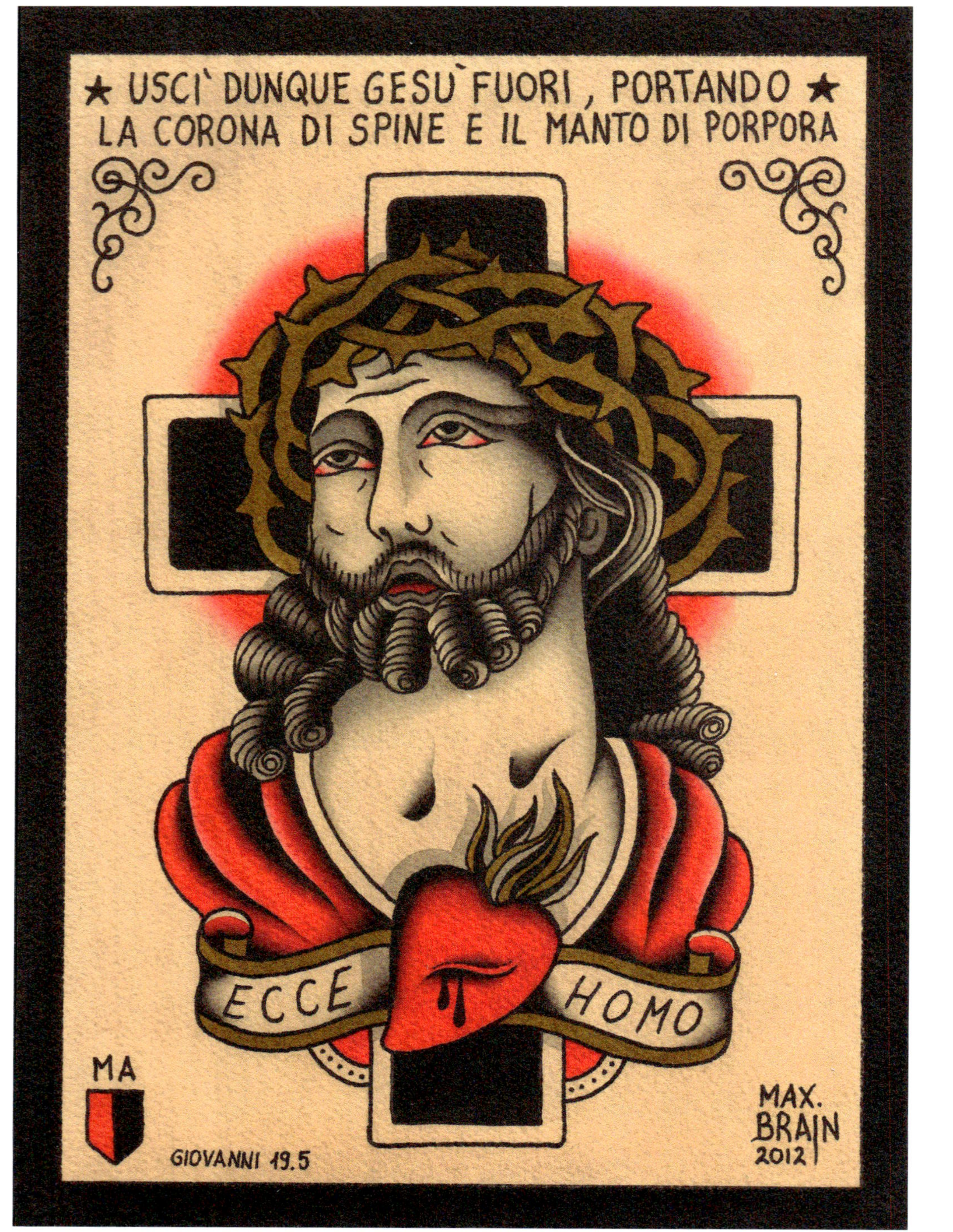
★ USCI' DUNQUE GESU' FUORI, PORTANDO ★
LA CORONA DI SPINE E IL MANTO DI PORPORA
ECCE HOMO
MA
GIOVANNI 19.5
MAX. BRAIN 2012

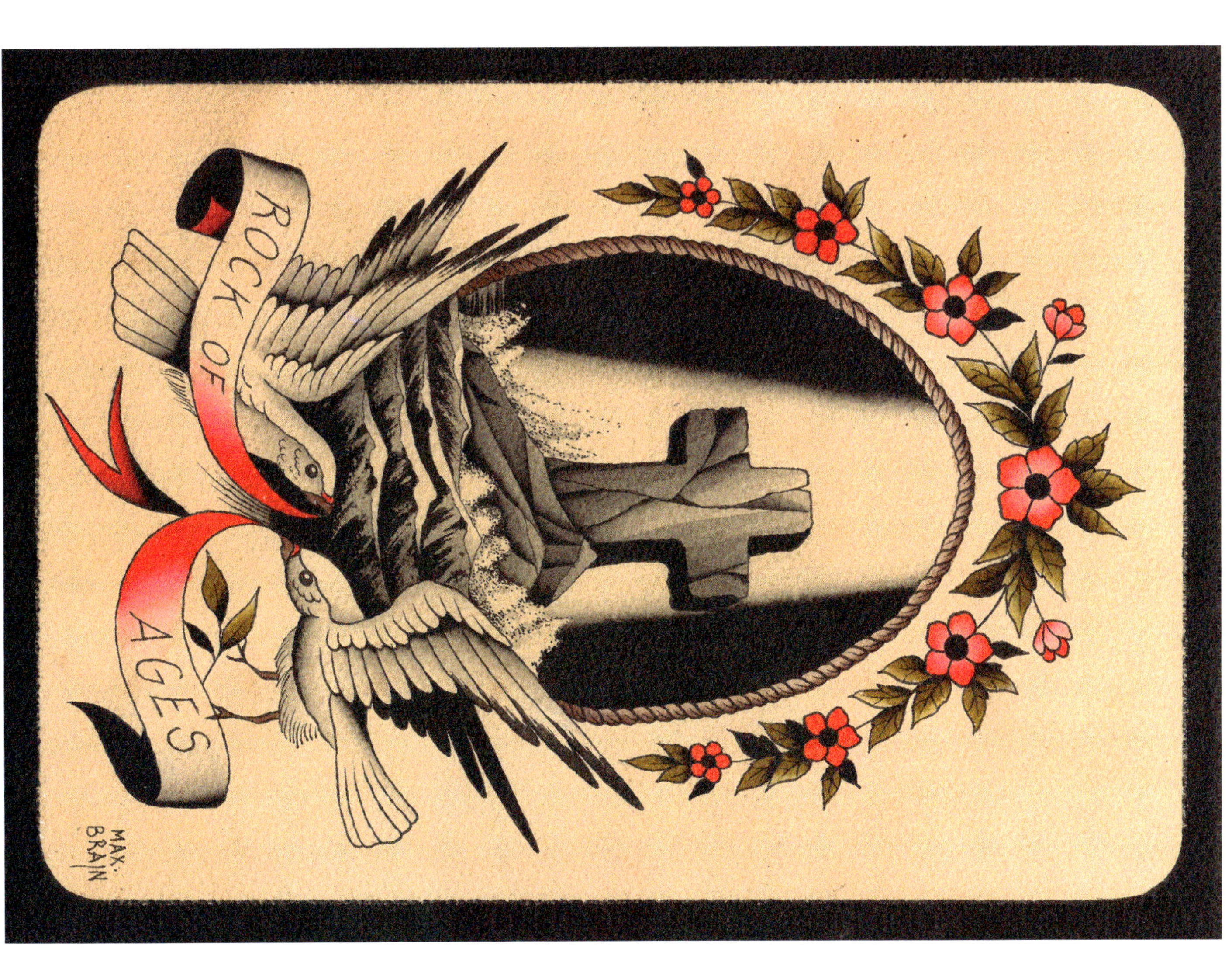
ROCK OF
AGES
MAX. BRAIN

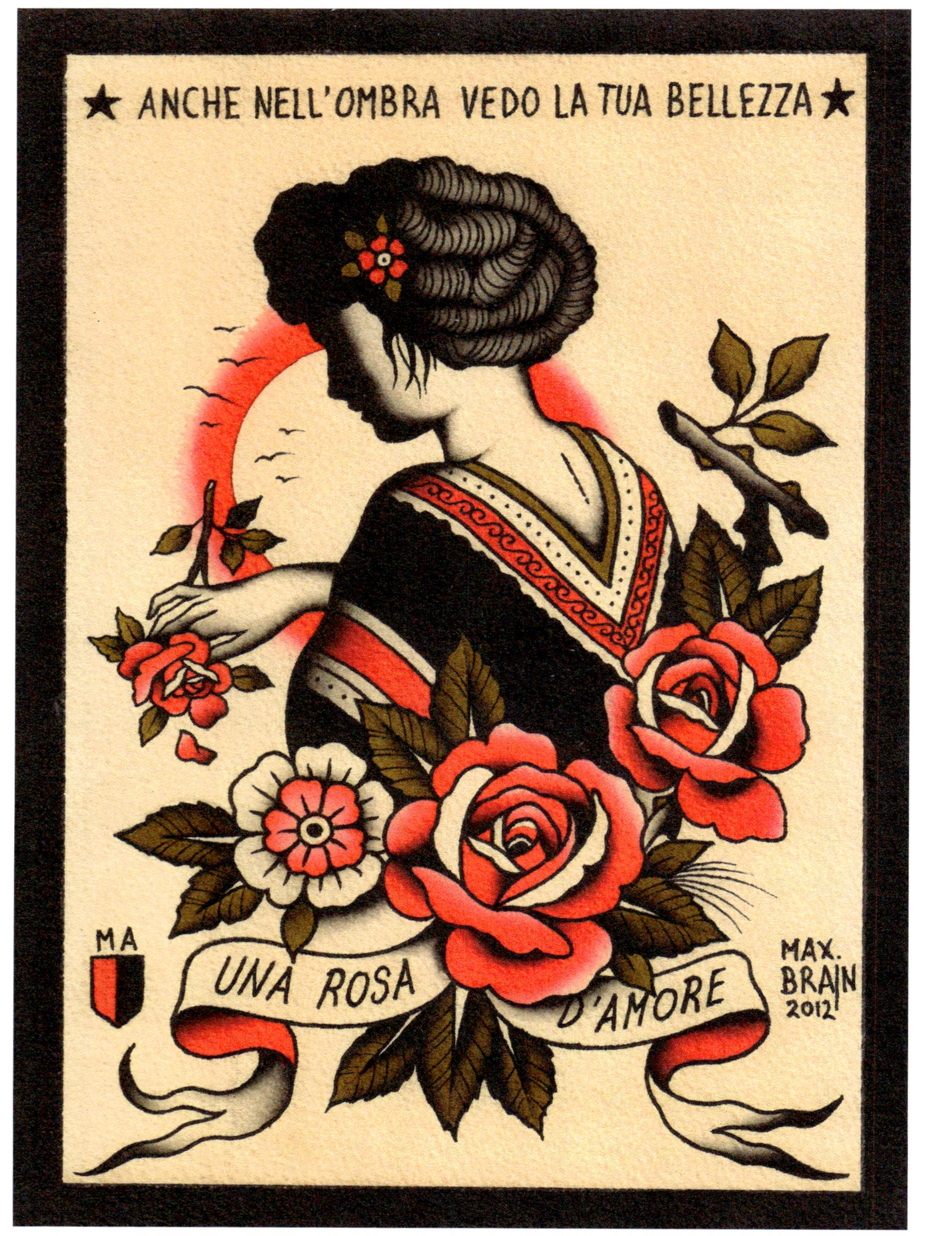
★ ANCHE NELL'OMBRA VEDO LA TUA BELLEZZA ★
MA
UNA ROSA D'AMORE
MAX. BRAIN 2012

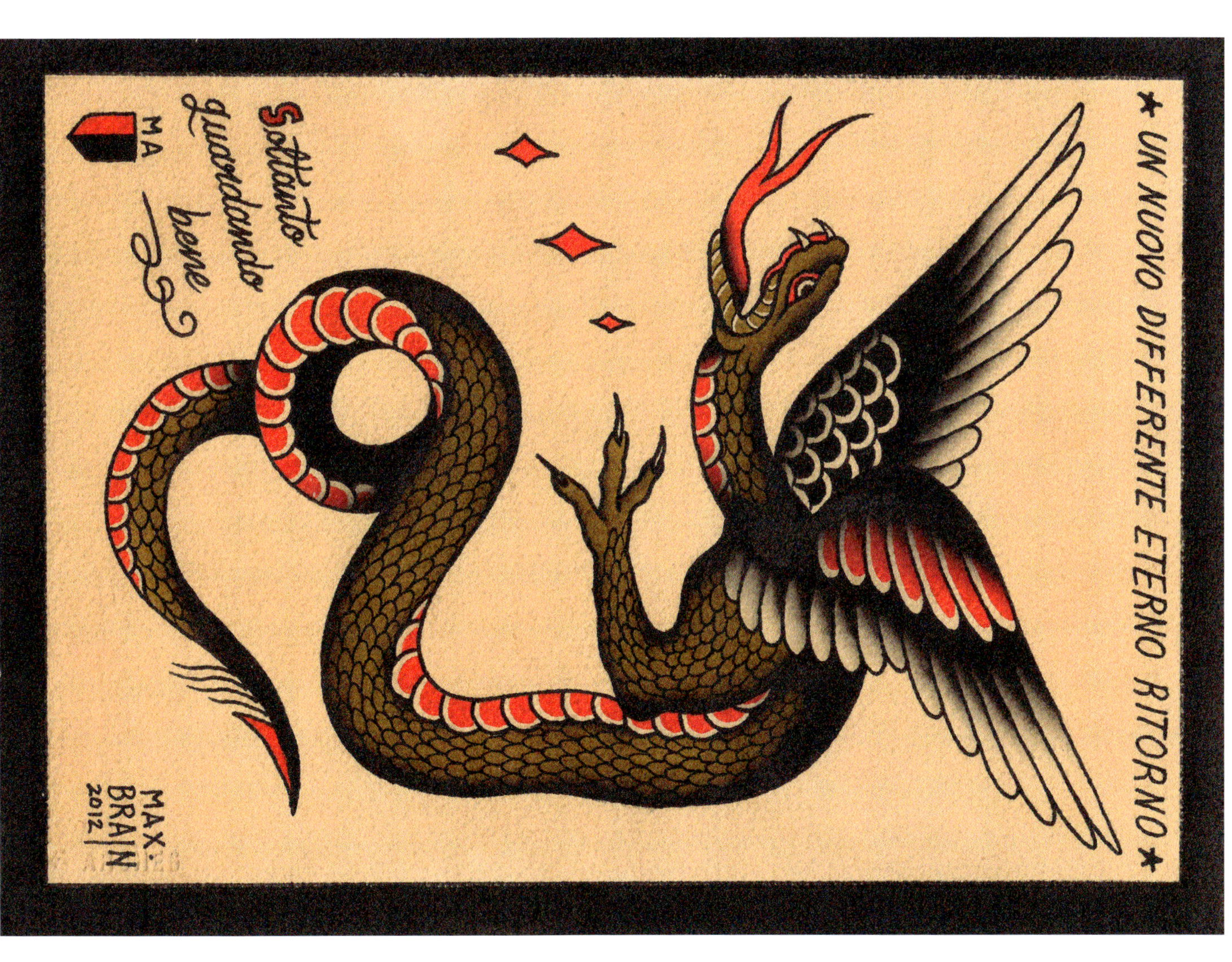
★ UN NUOVO DIFFERENTE ETERNO RITORNO ★
Soltanto
guardando
bene
MA
MAX.
BRAIN
2012

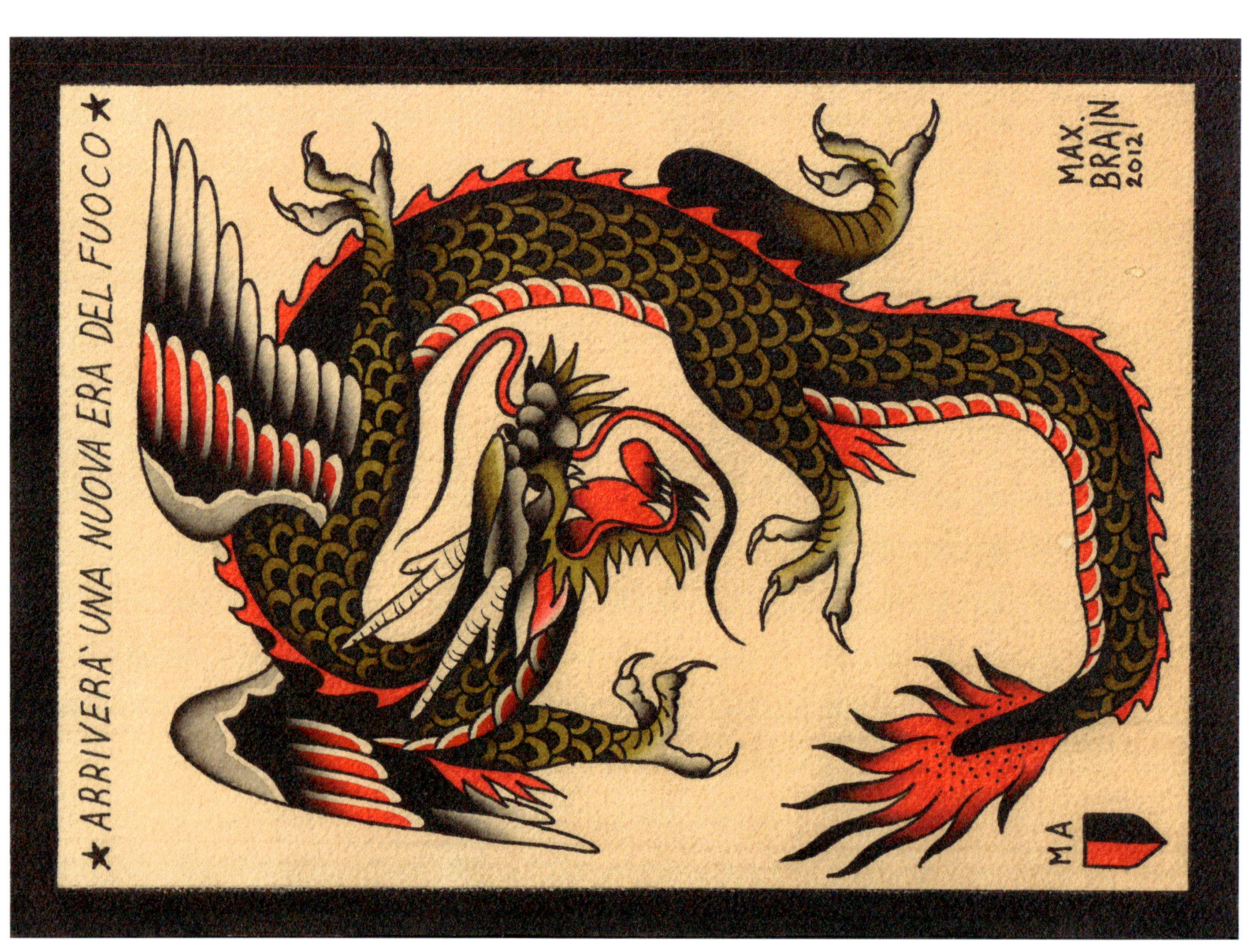
★ ARRIVERA' UNA NUOVA ERA DEL FUOCO ★
MAX. BRAIN 2012
MA

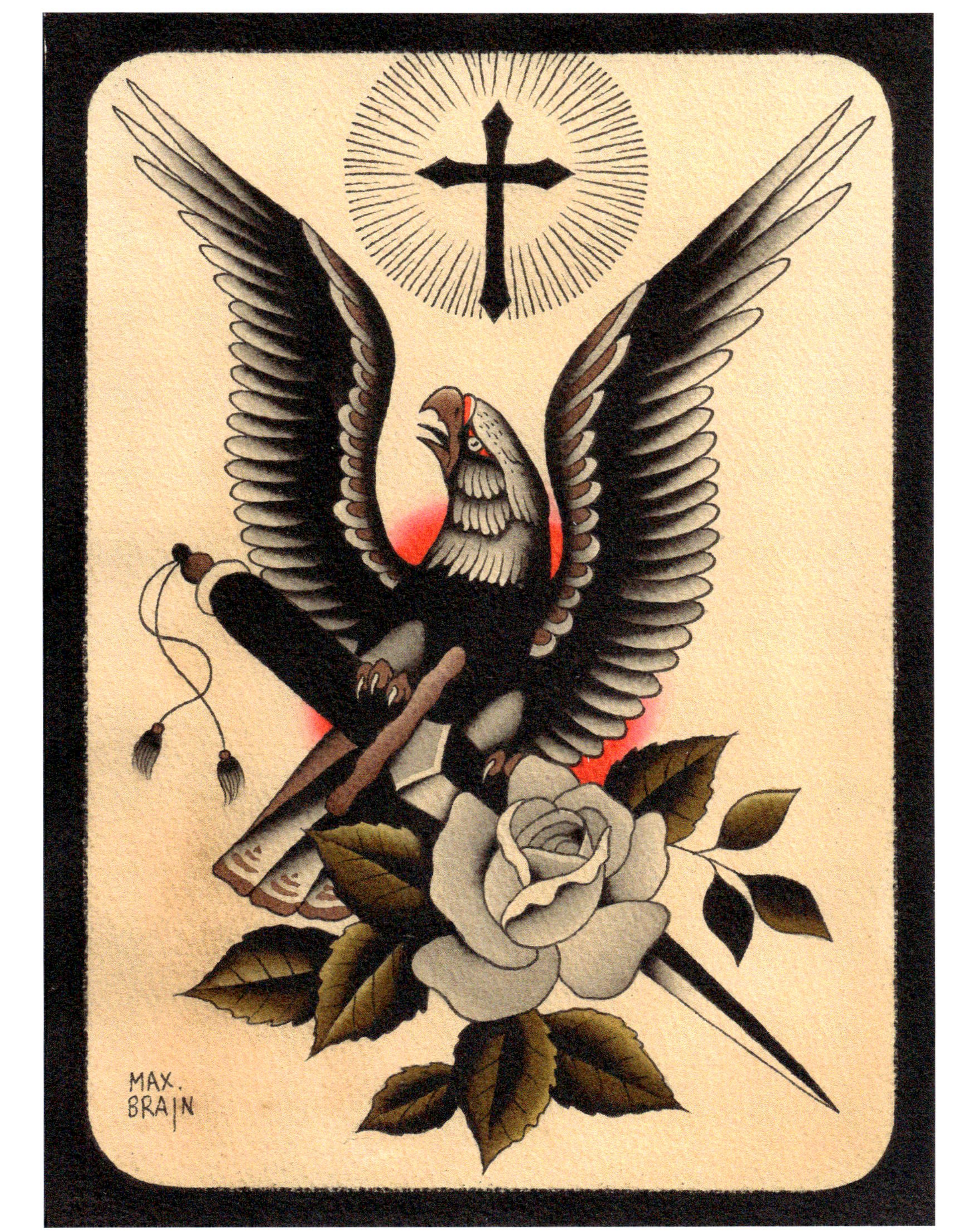
MAX.
BRAIN

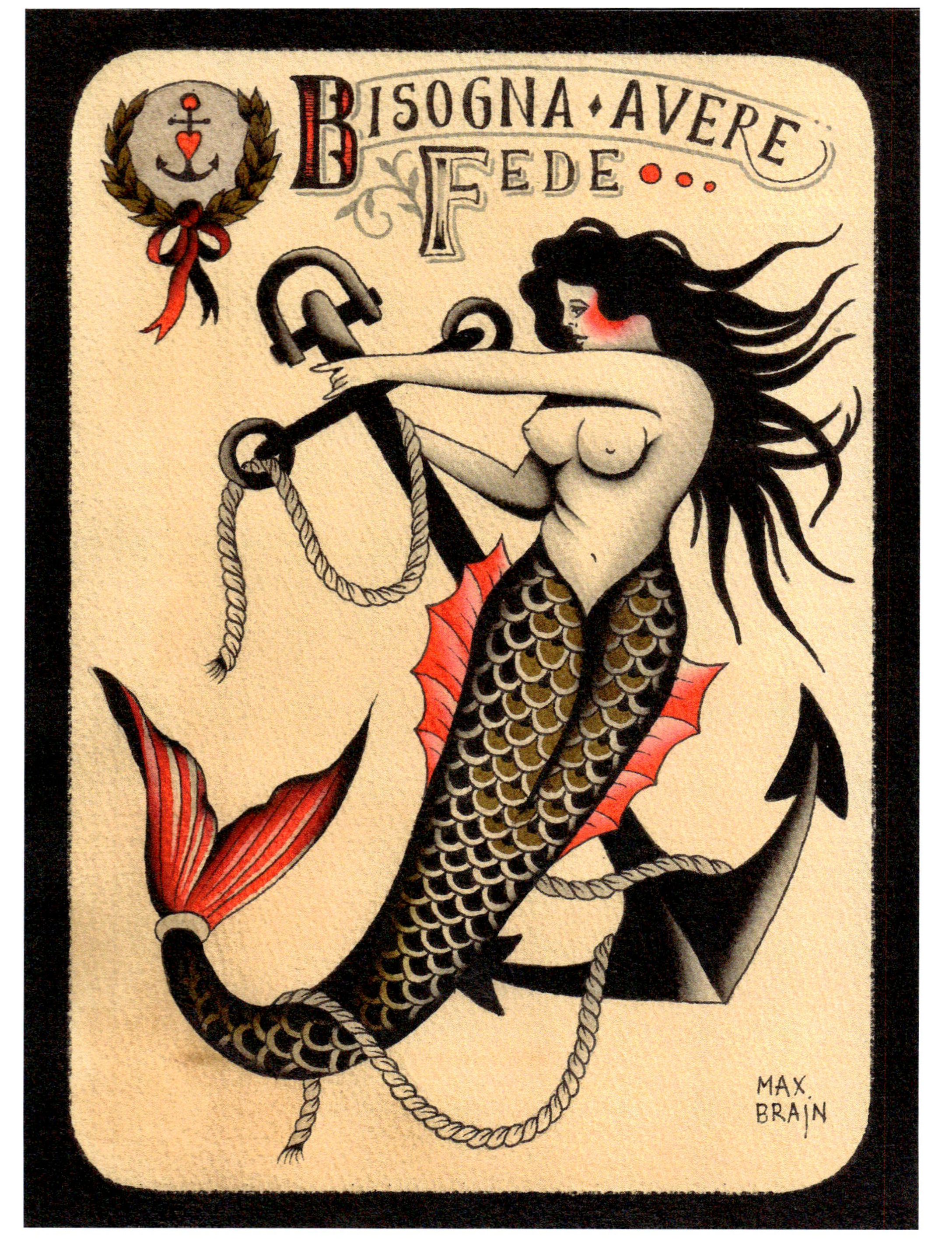
BISOGNA AVERE FEDE...
MAX BRAJN

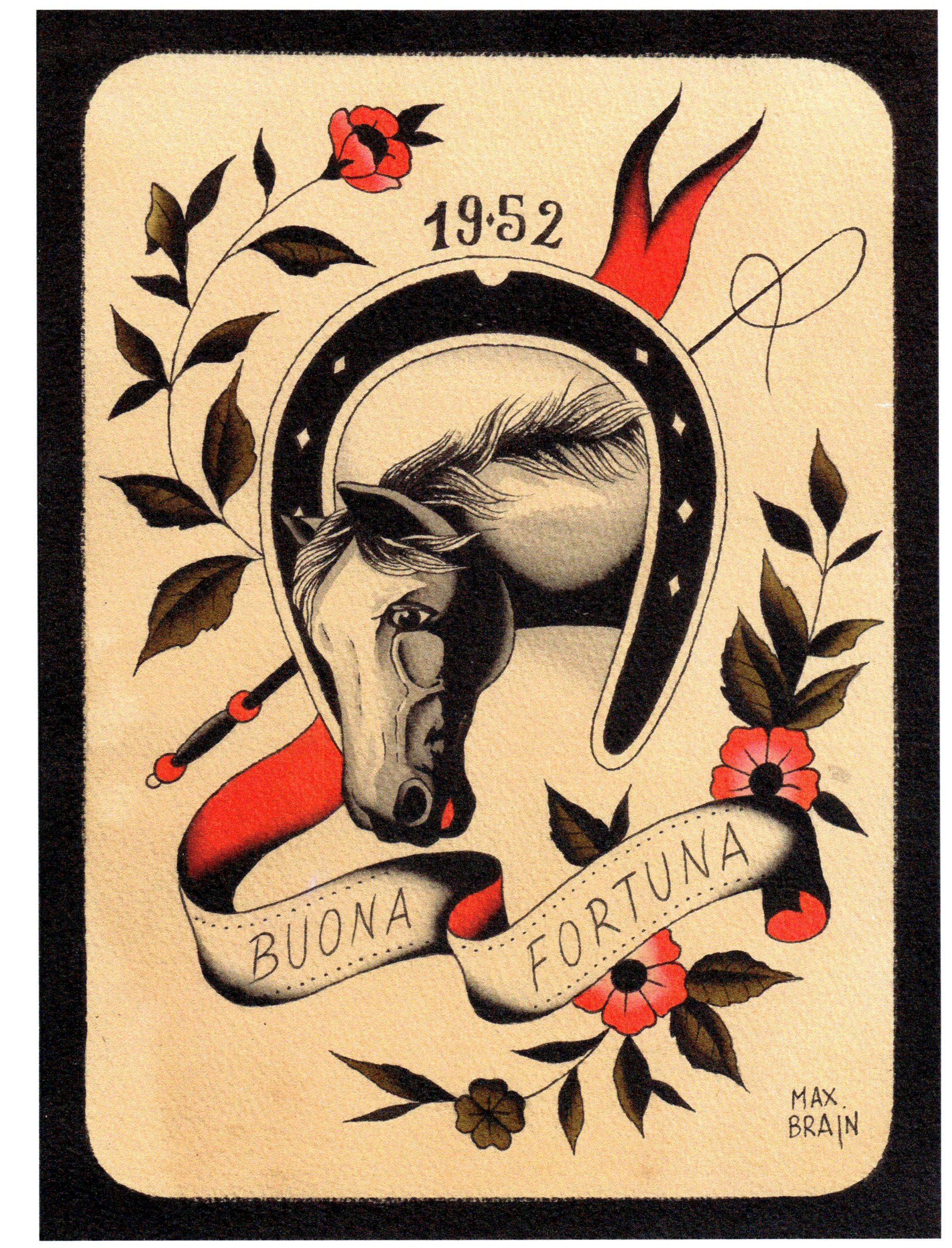
19·52
BUONA FORTUNA
MAX.
BRAIN

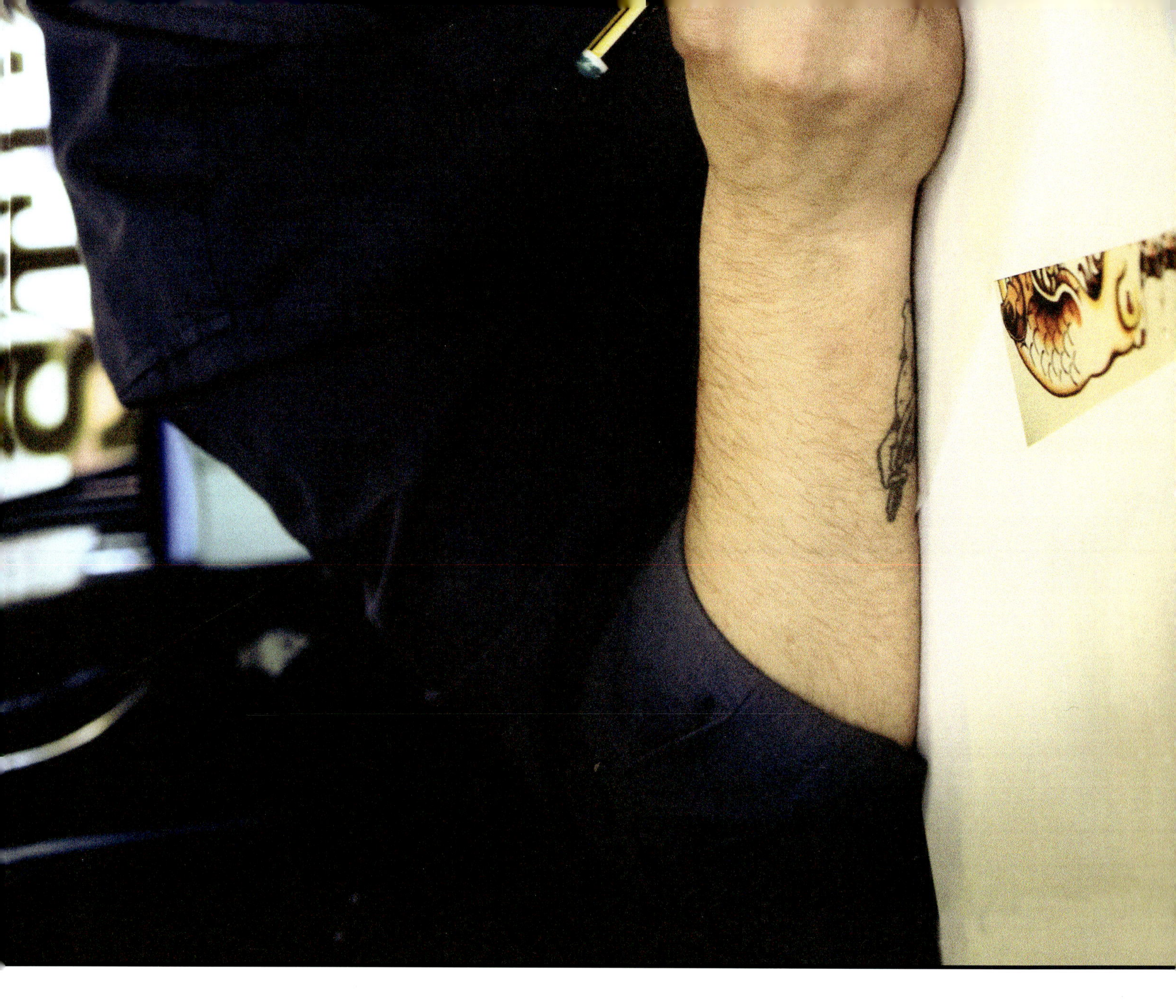

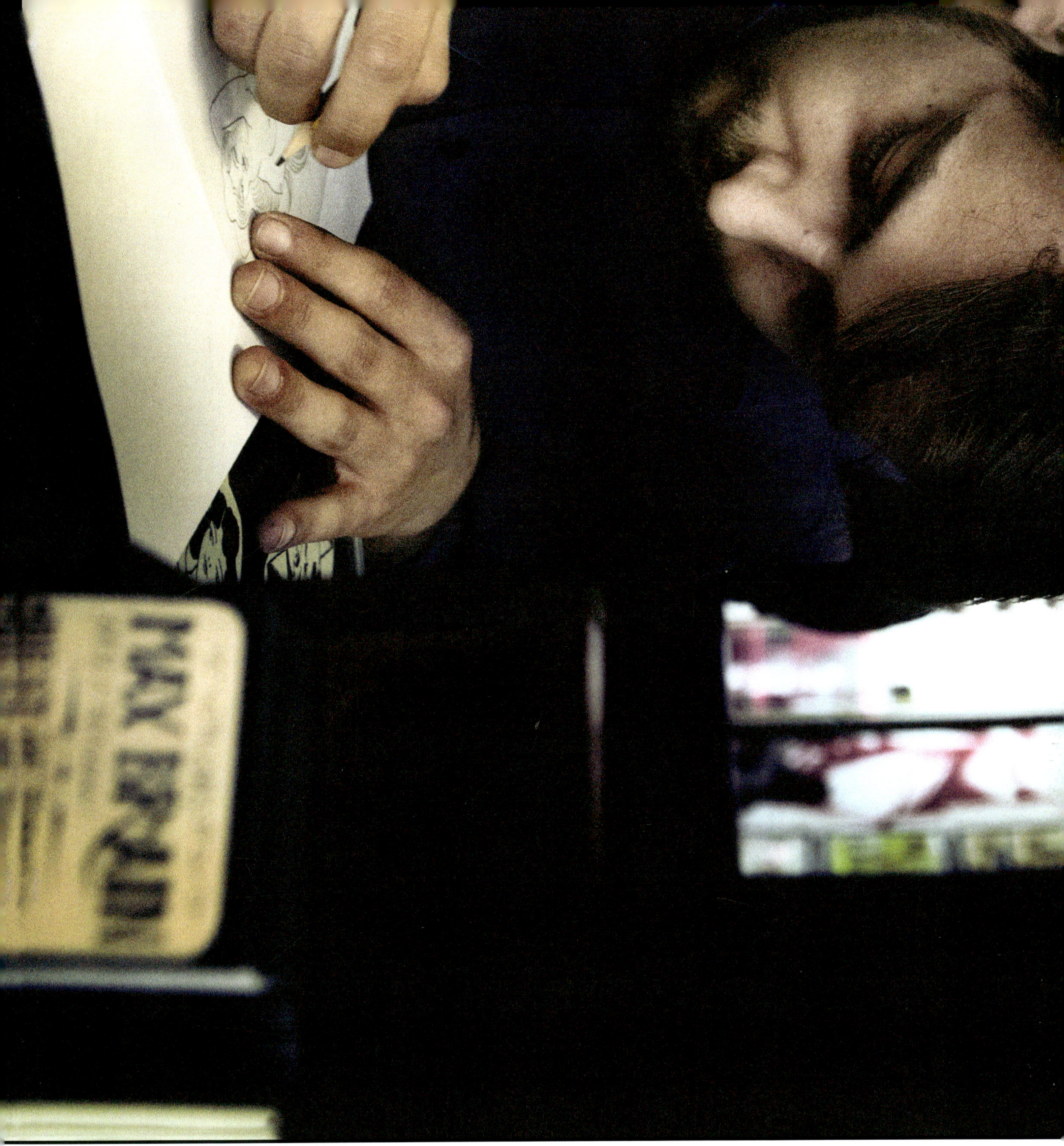

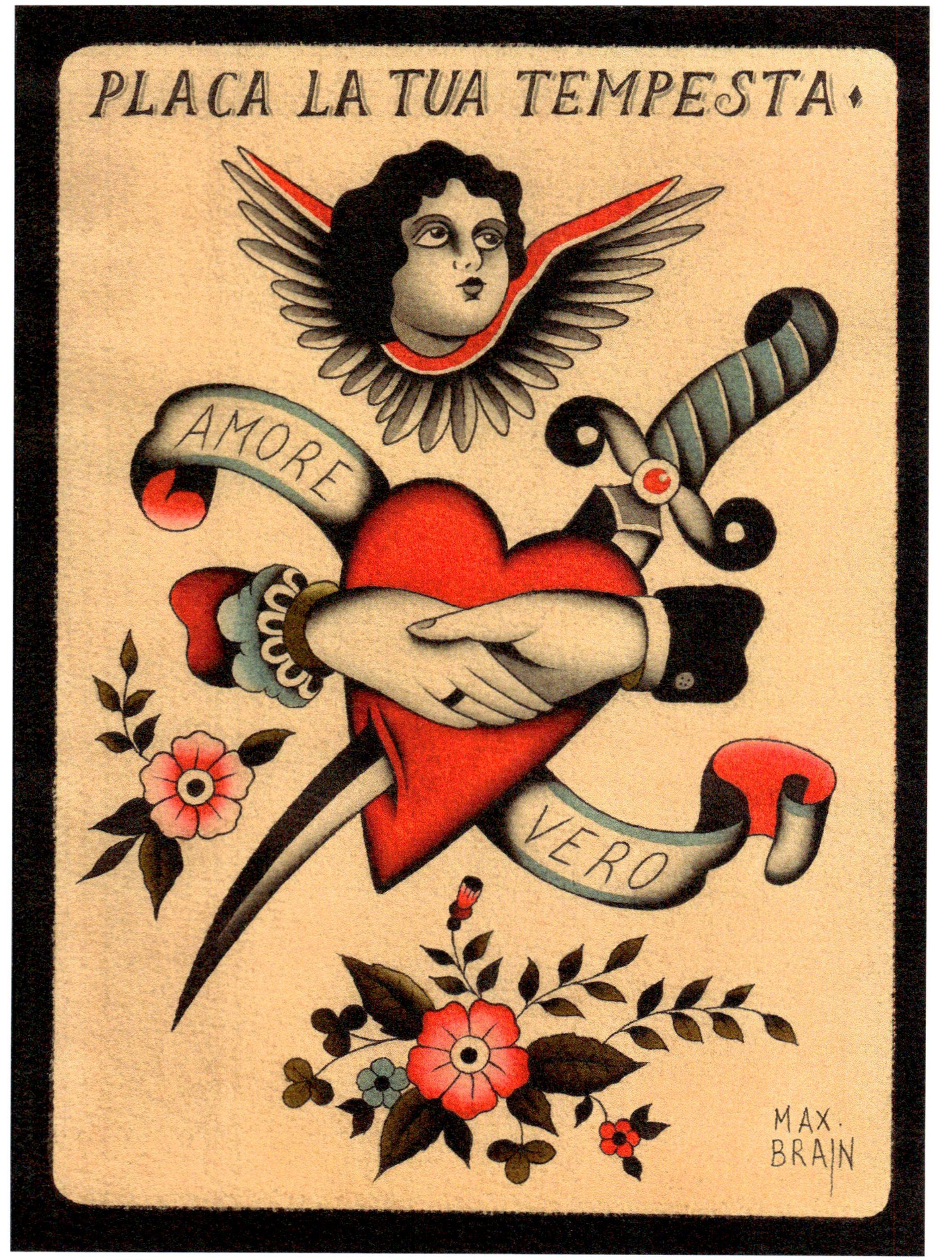
PLACA LA TUA TEMPESTA
AMORE
VERO
MAX.
BRAIN

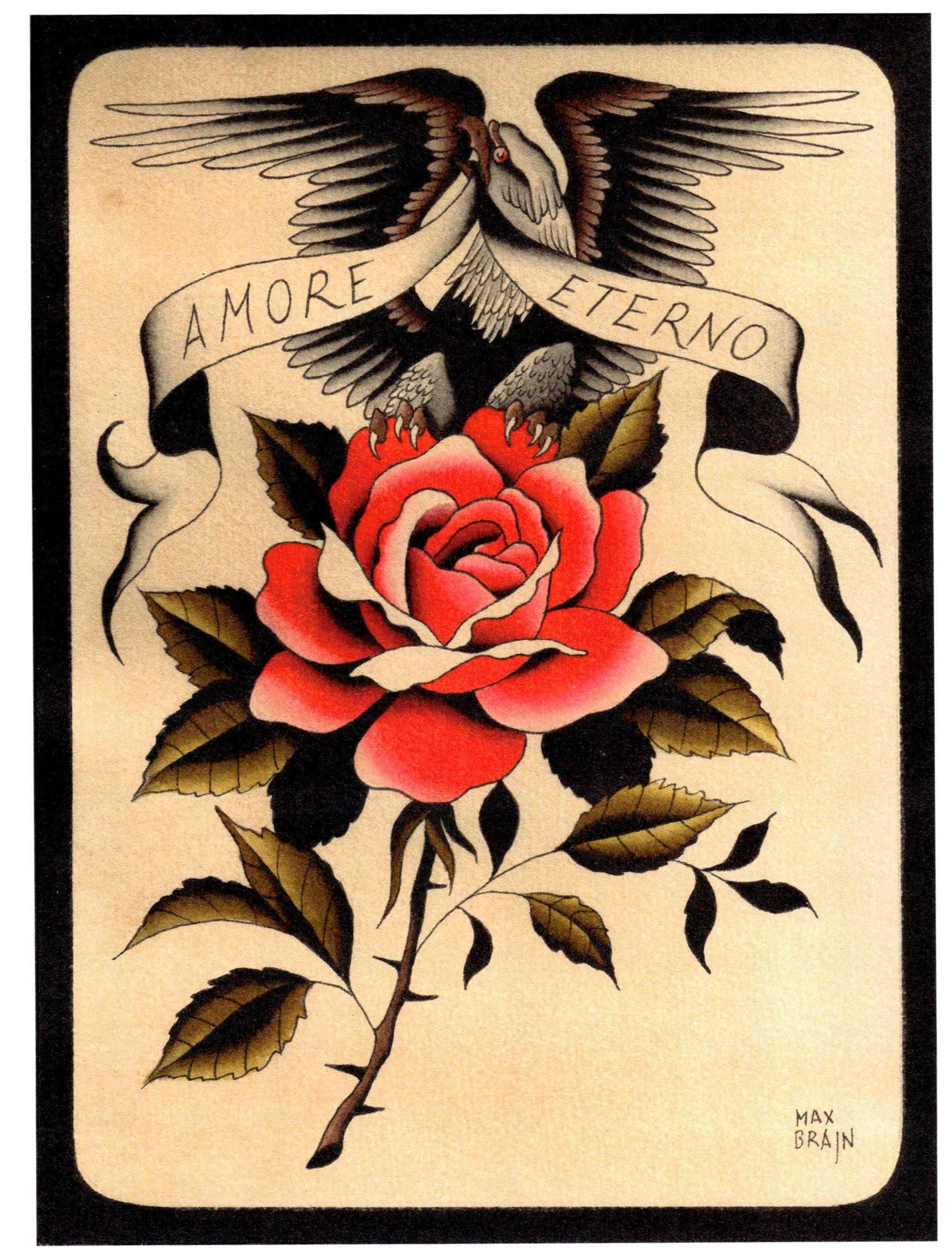
AMORE
ETERNO
MAX
BRAJN

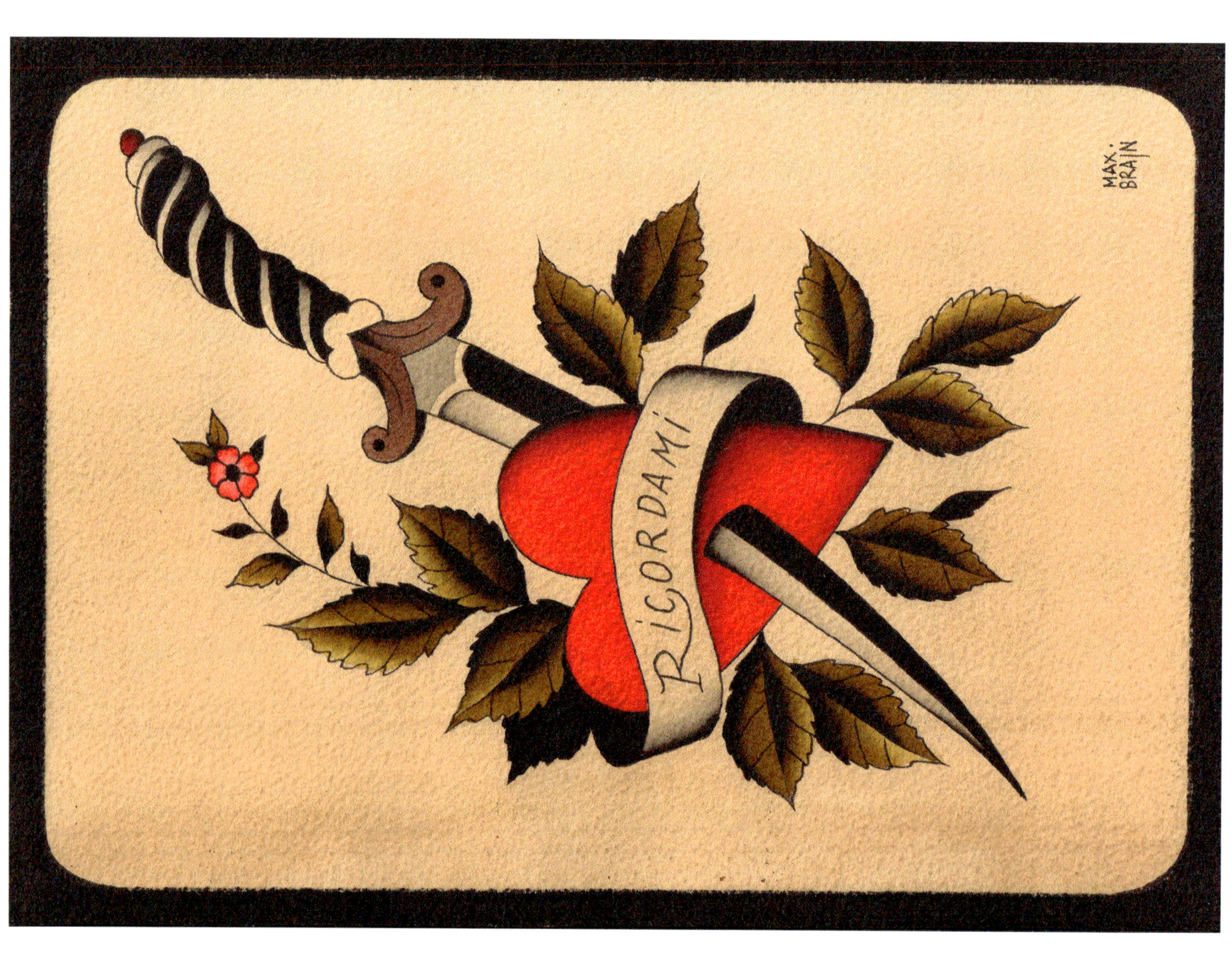
RICORDAMI
MAX. BRAIN

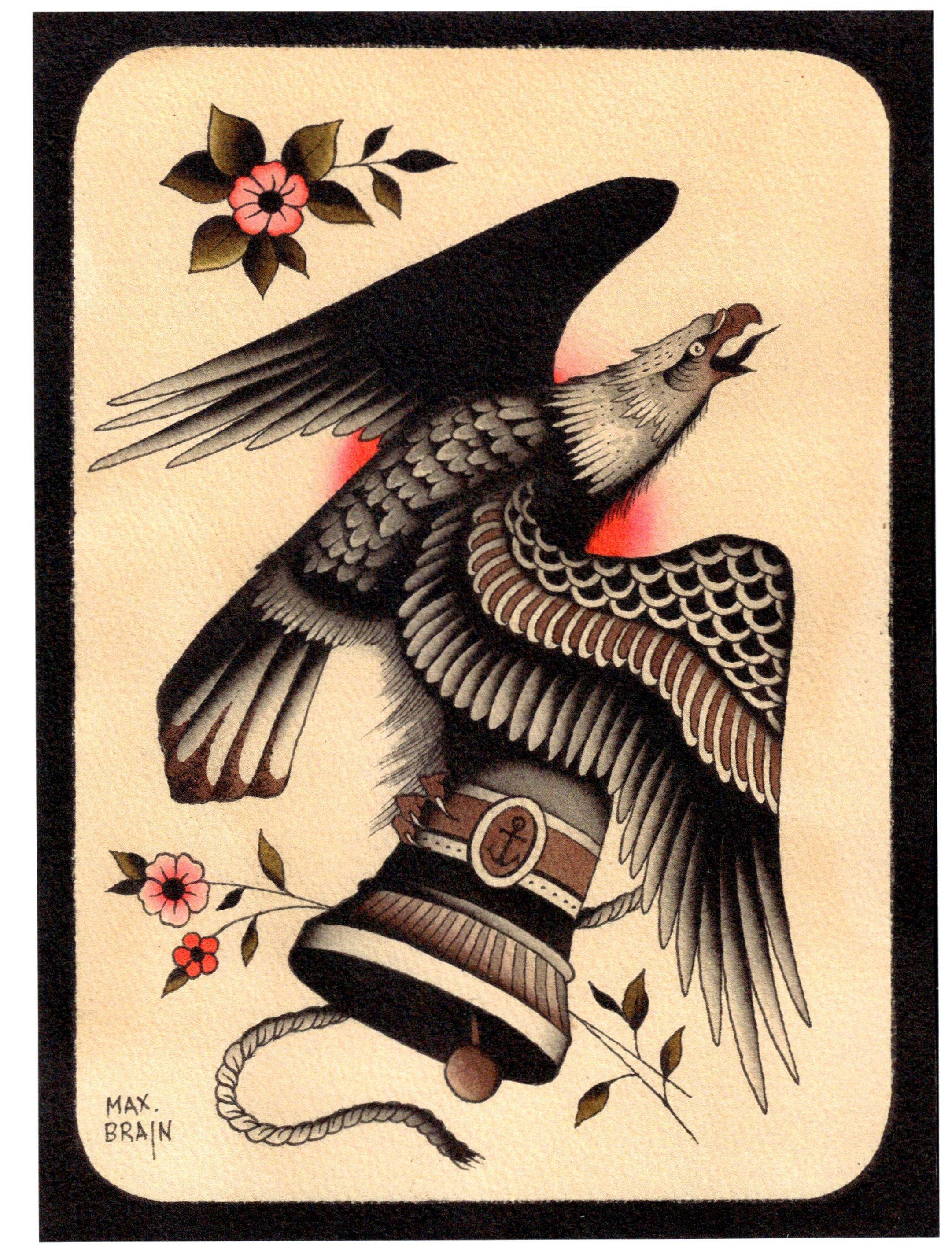
MAX.
BRAIN

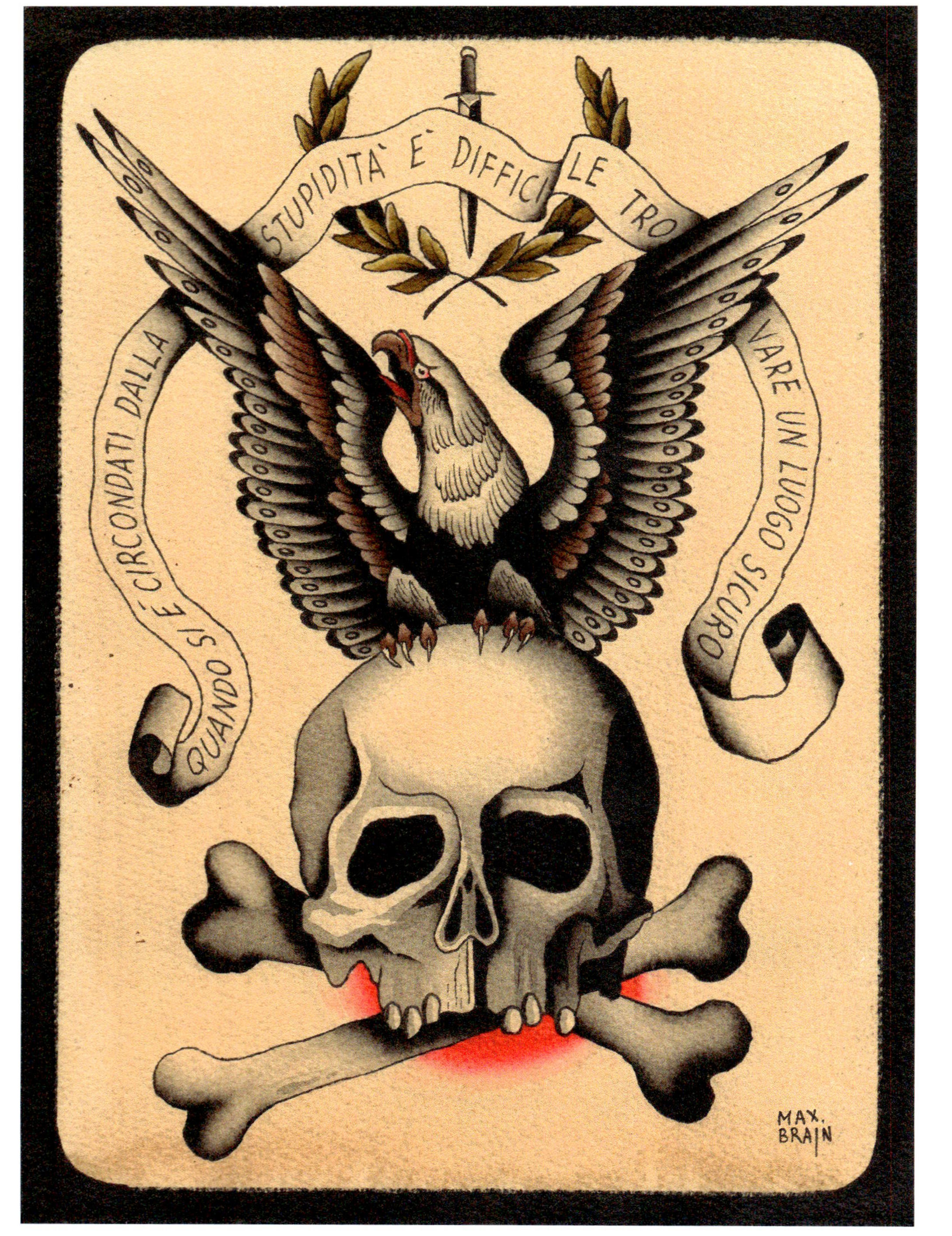
QUANDO SI È CIRCONDATI DALLA
STUPIDITÀ È DIFFICILE TROVARE UN LUOGO SICURO
MAX. BRAIN

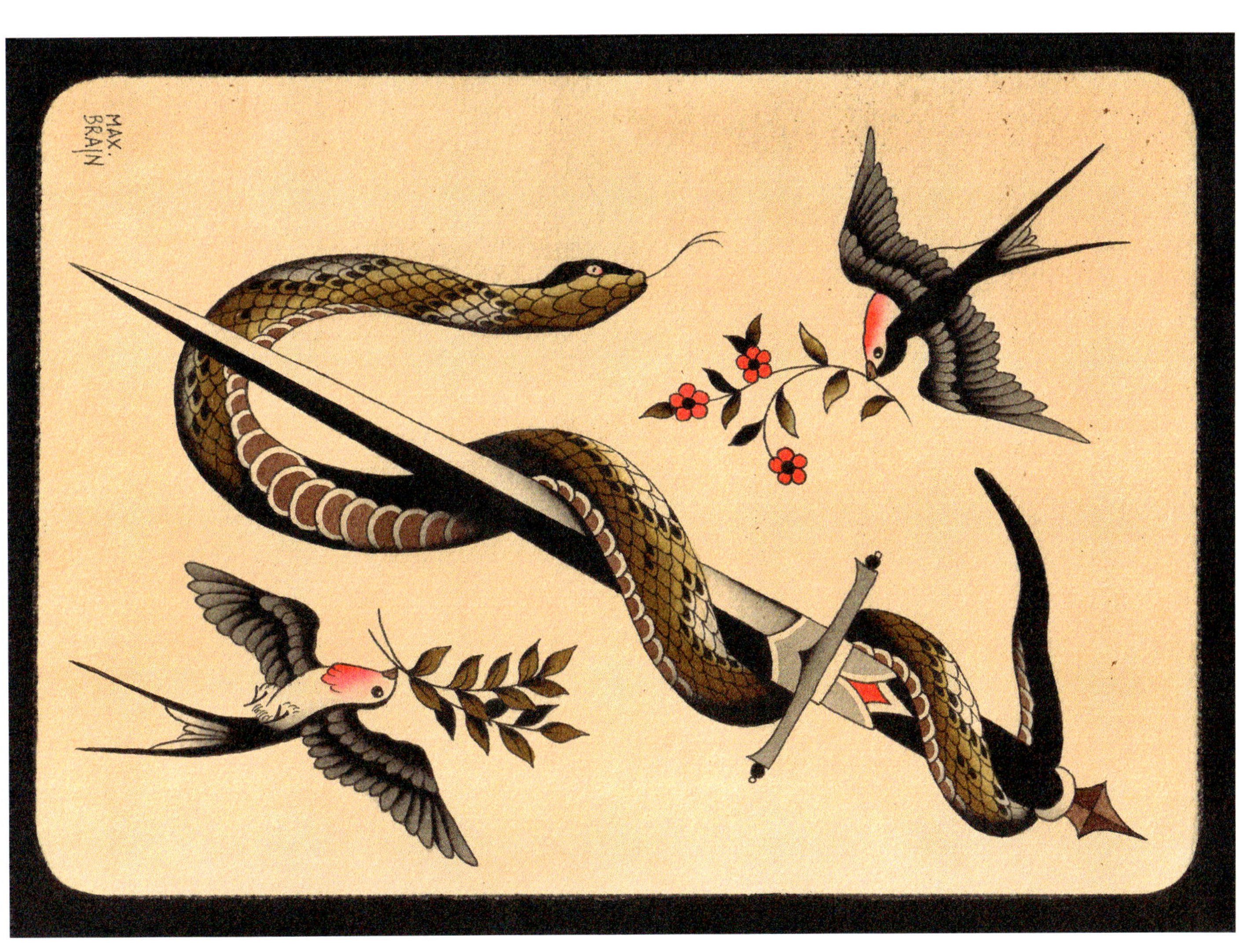
MAX
BRAIN

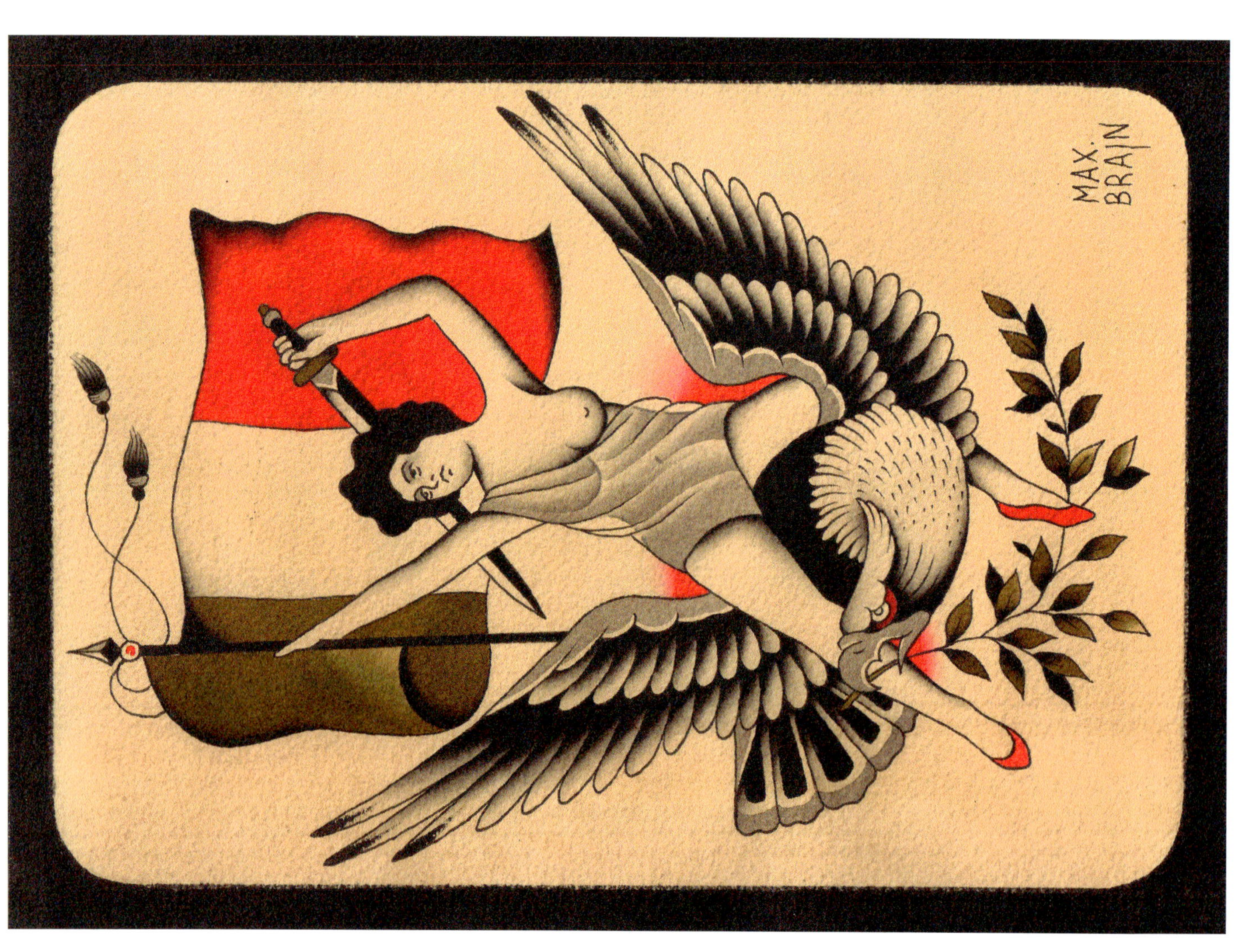
MAX.
BRAIN

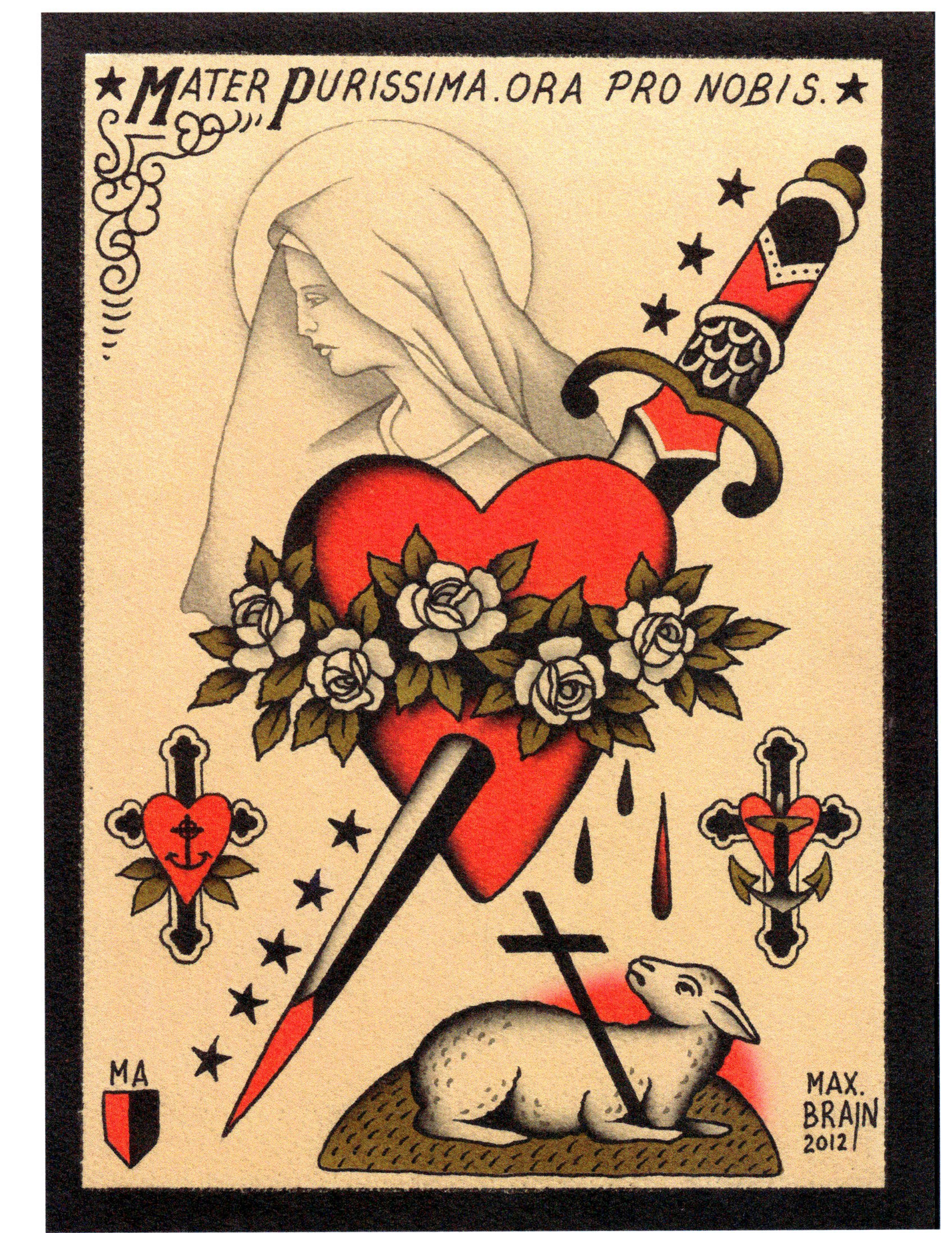
MATER PURISSIMA. ORA PRO NOBIS.
MA
MAX. BRAIN 2012

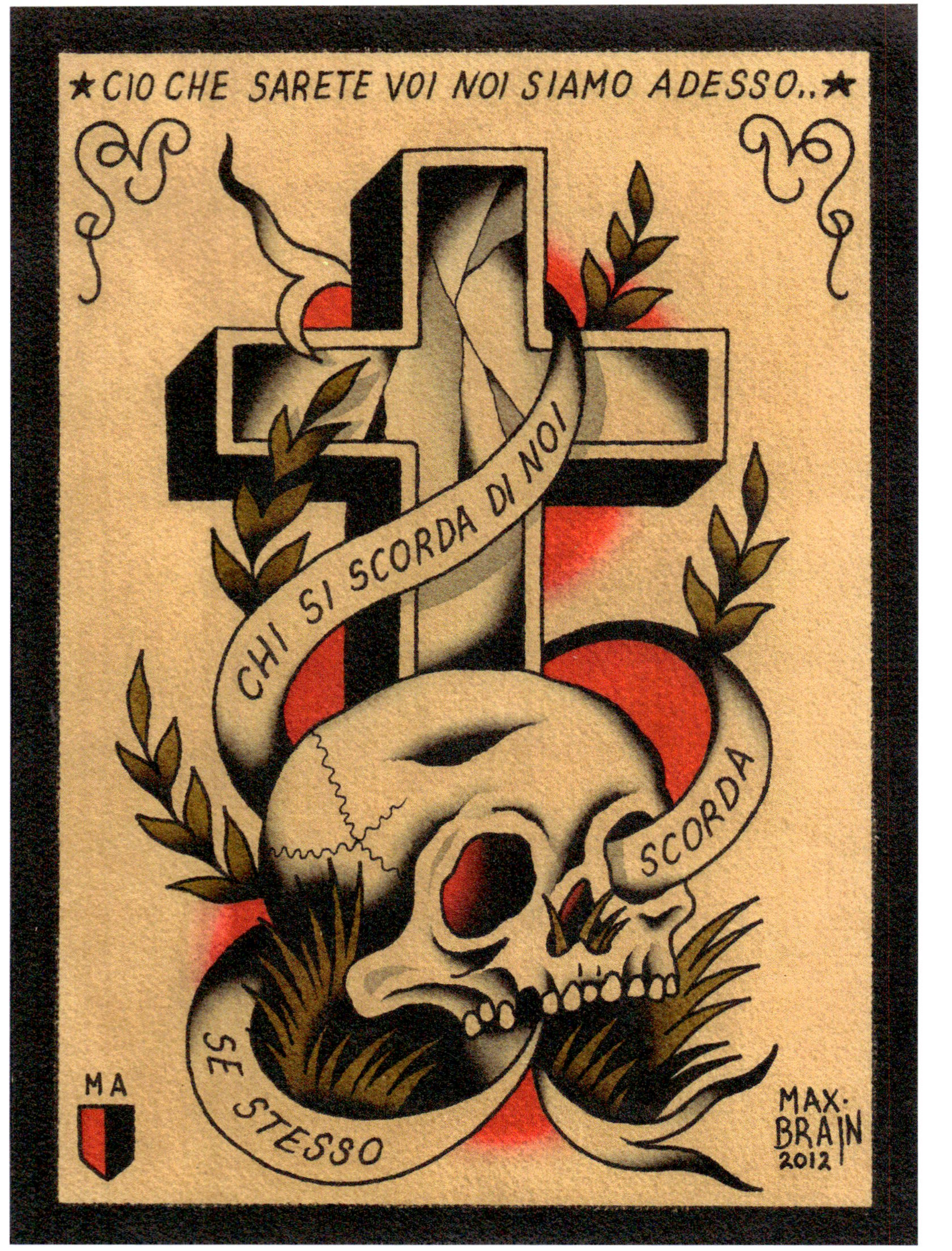
★ CIO CHE SARETE VOI NOI SIAMO ADESSO.. ★
CHI SI SCORDA DI NOI
SCORDA
SE STESSO
MA
MAX·
BRAIN
2012

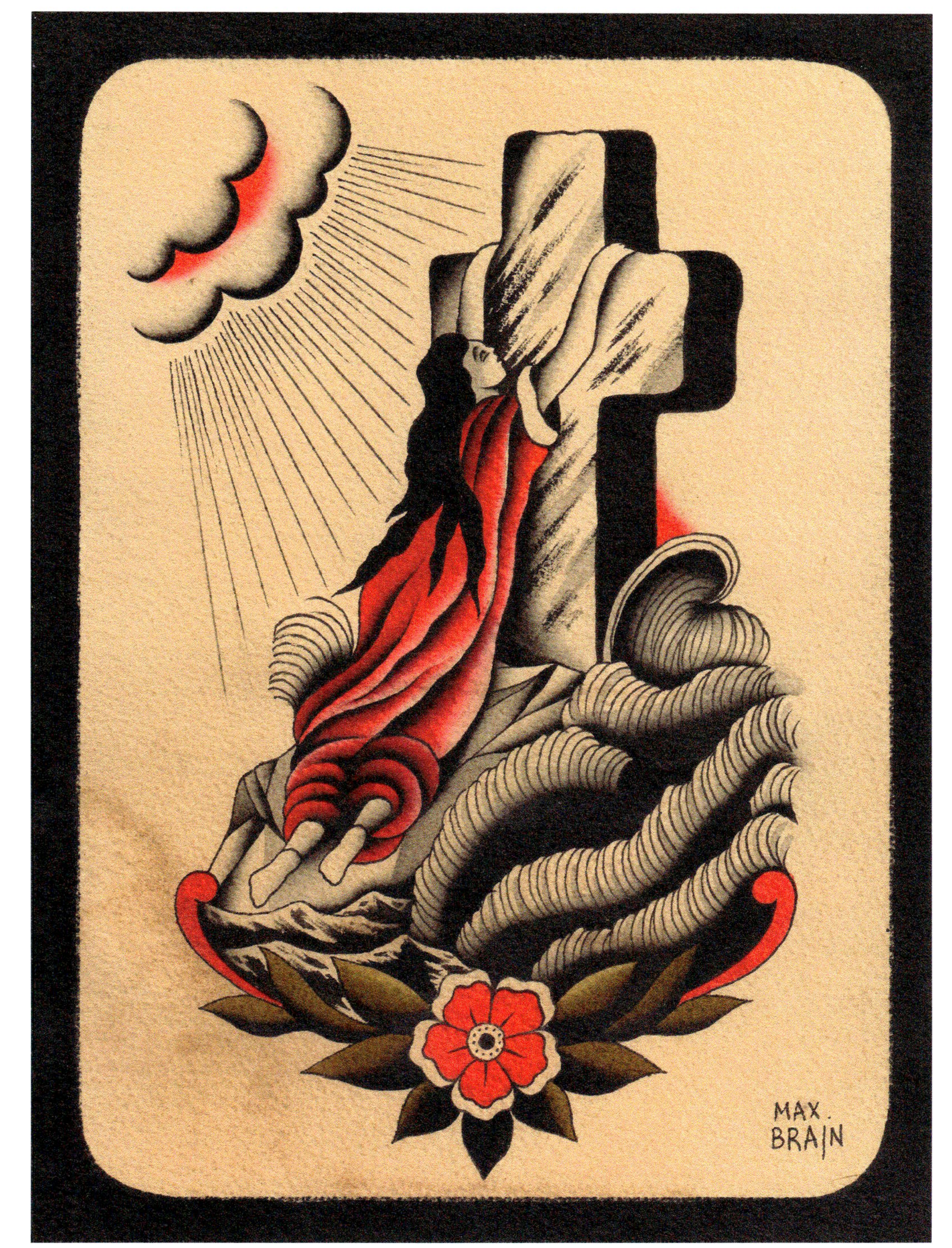
MAX.
BRAJN

SYLVIO PELLICO

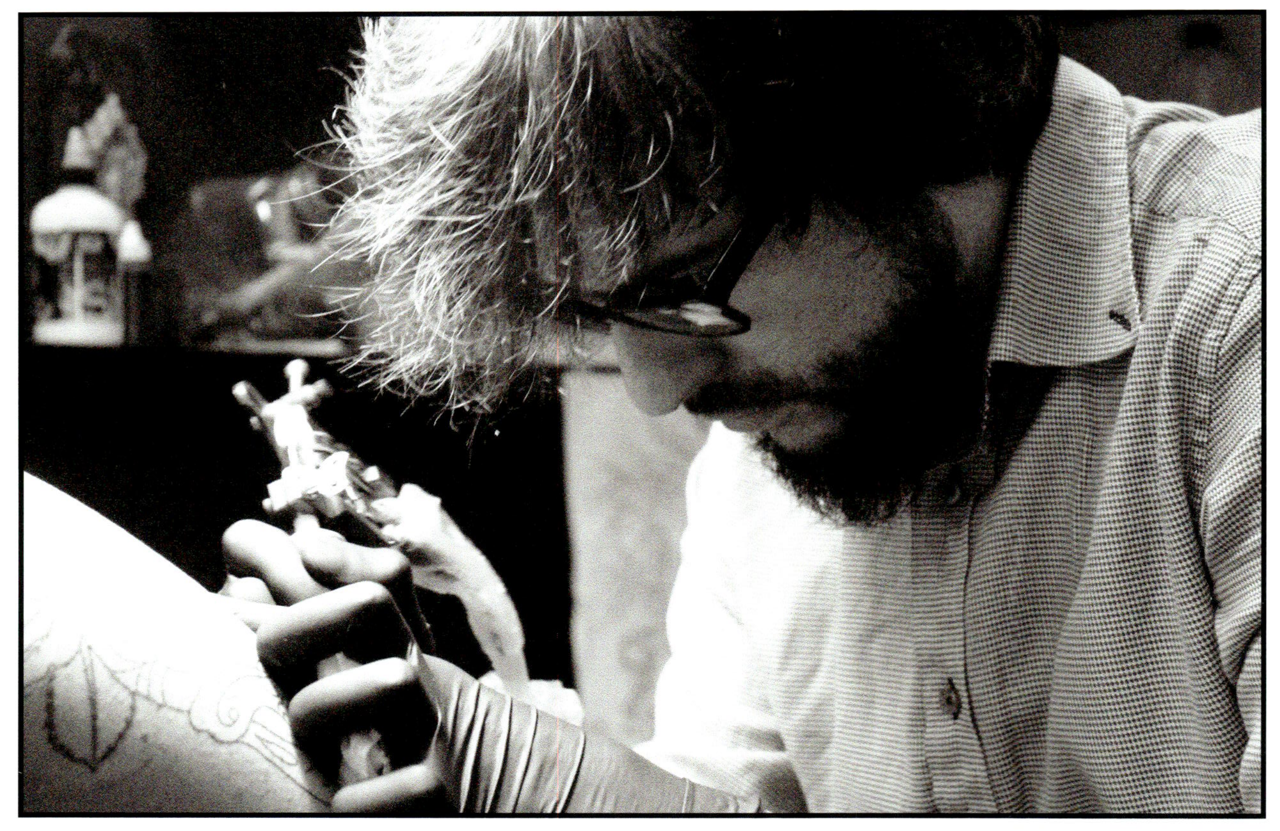

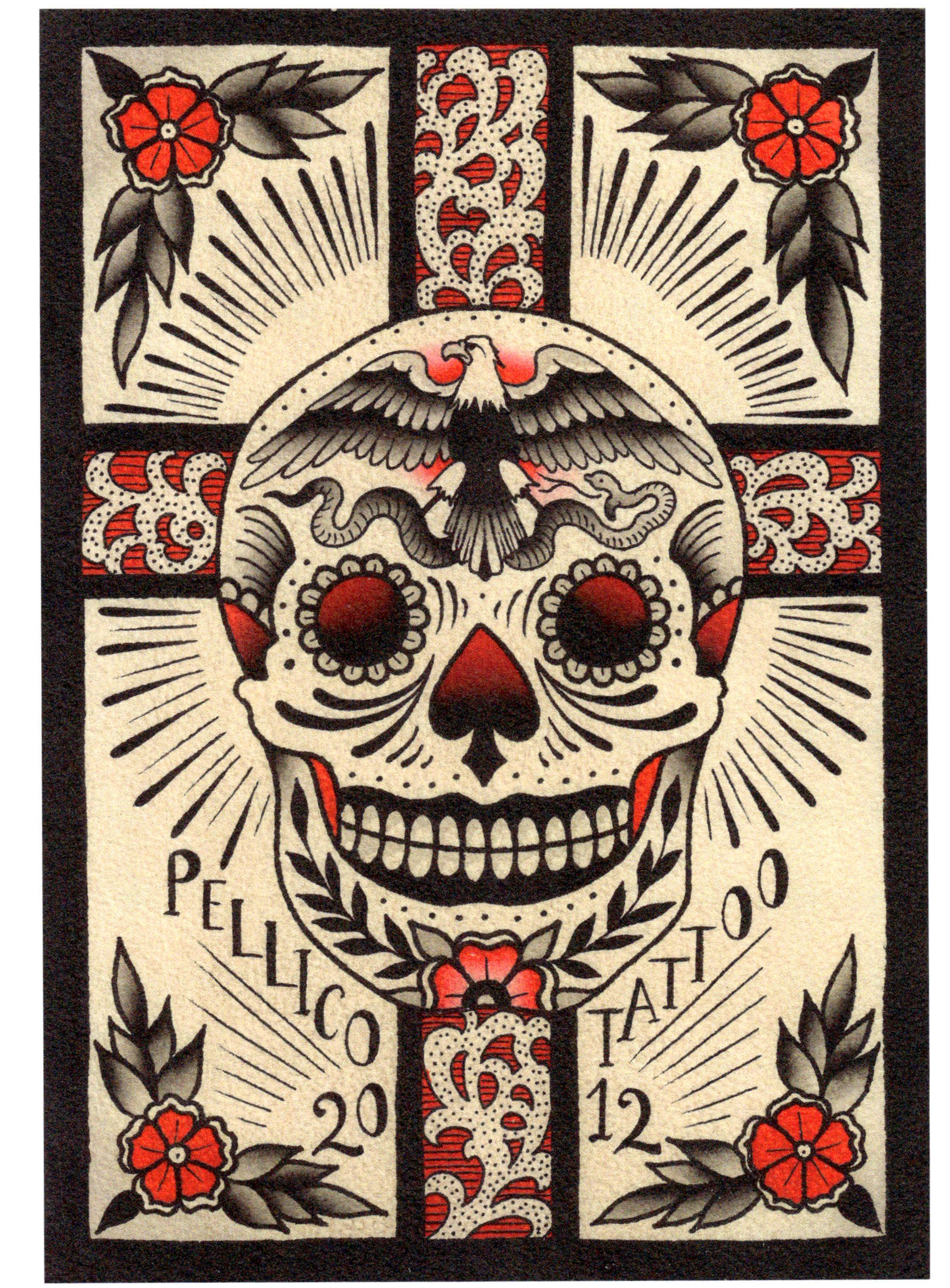
PELLICO TATTOO
20
12

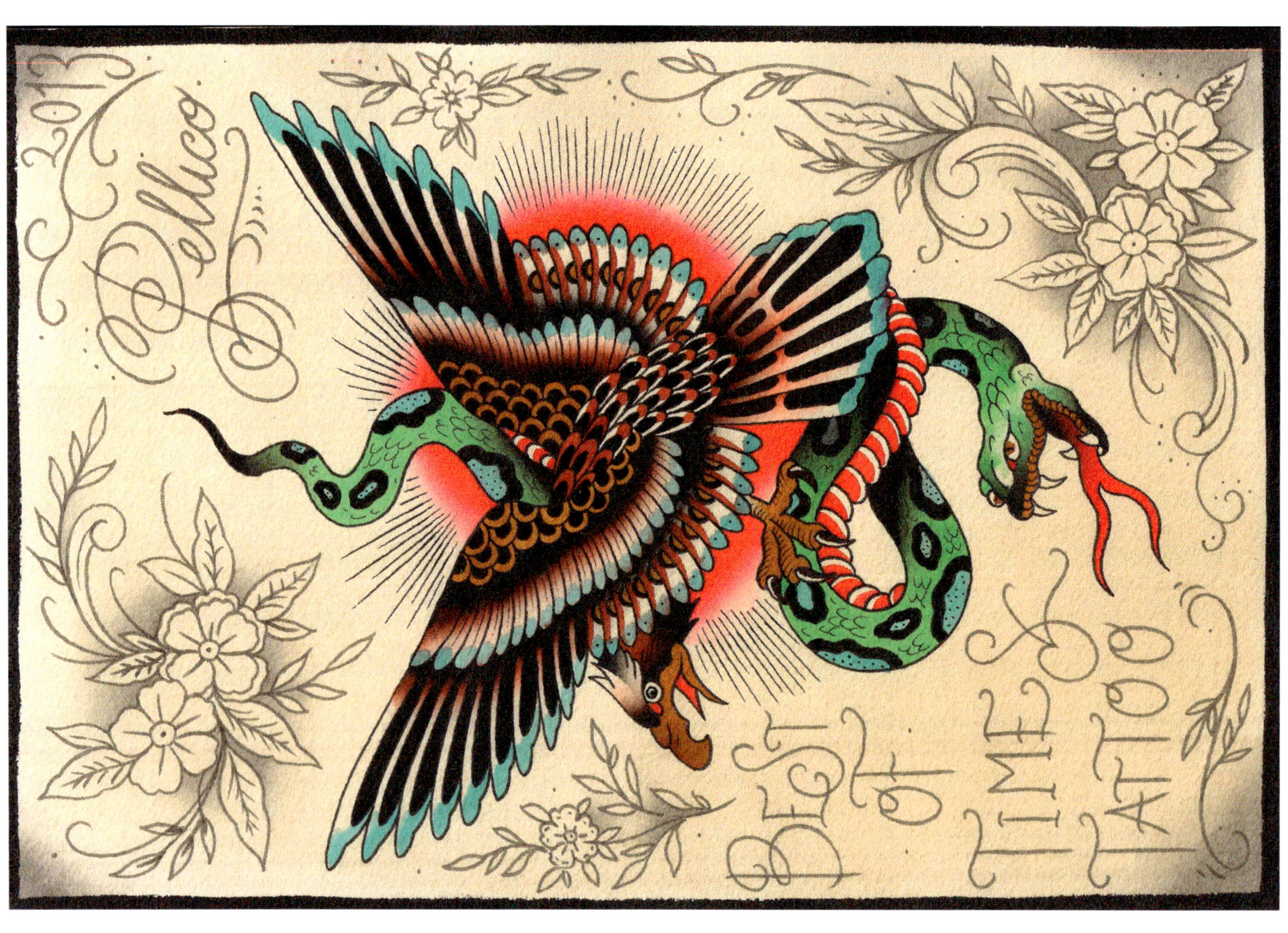
2013
Pellico
BEST OF TIME TATTOO

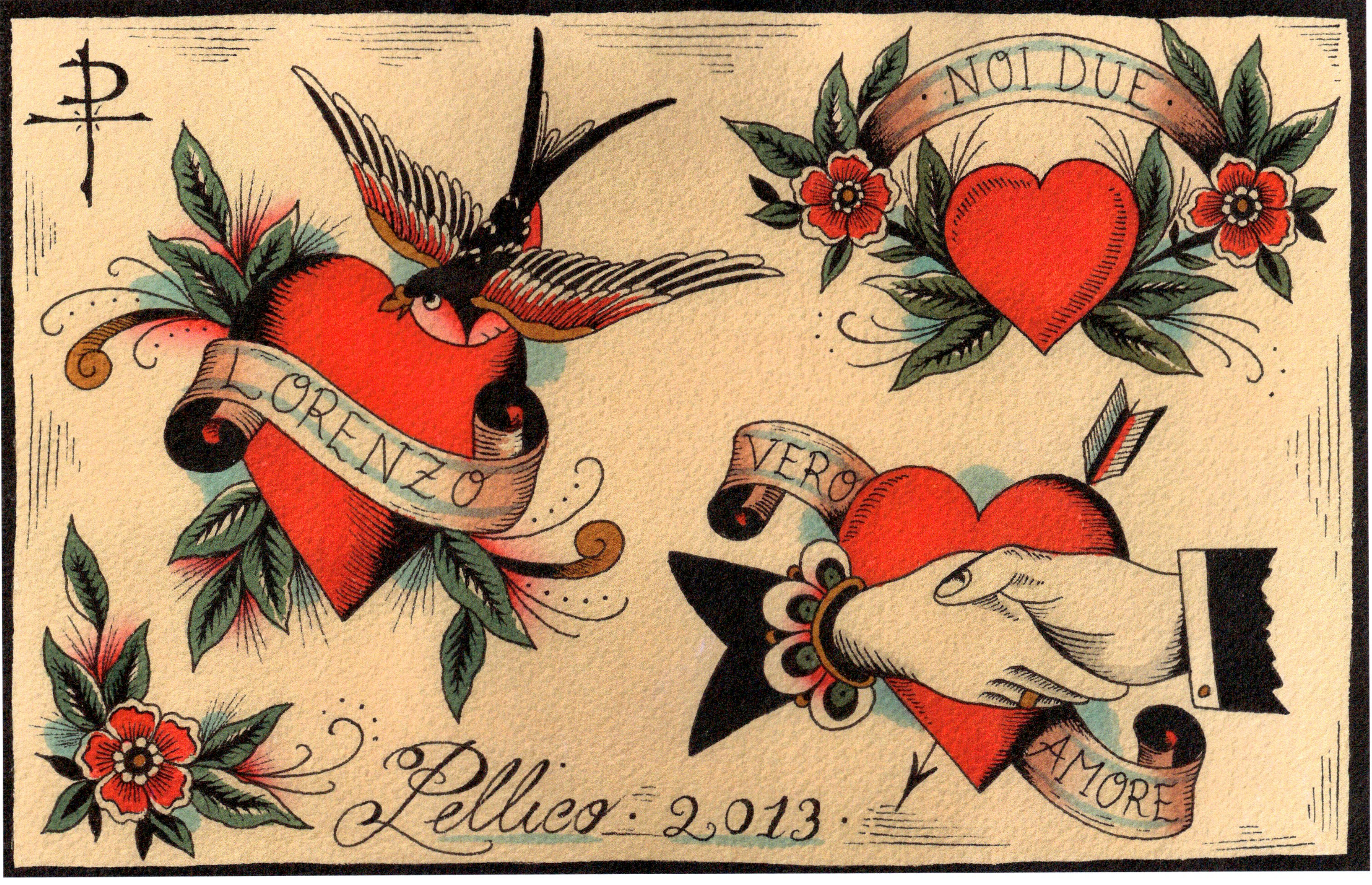
LORENZO
NOI DUE
VERO
AMORE
Pellico. 2013.

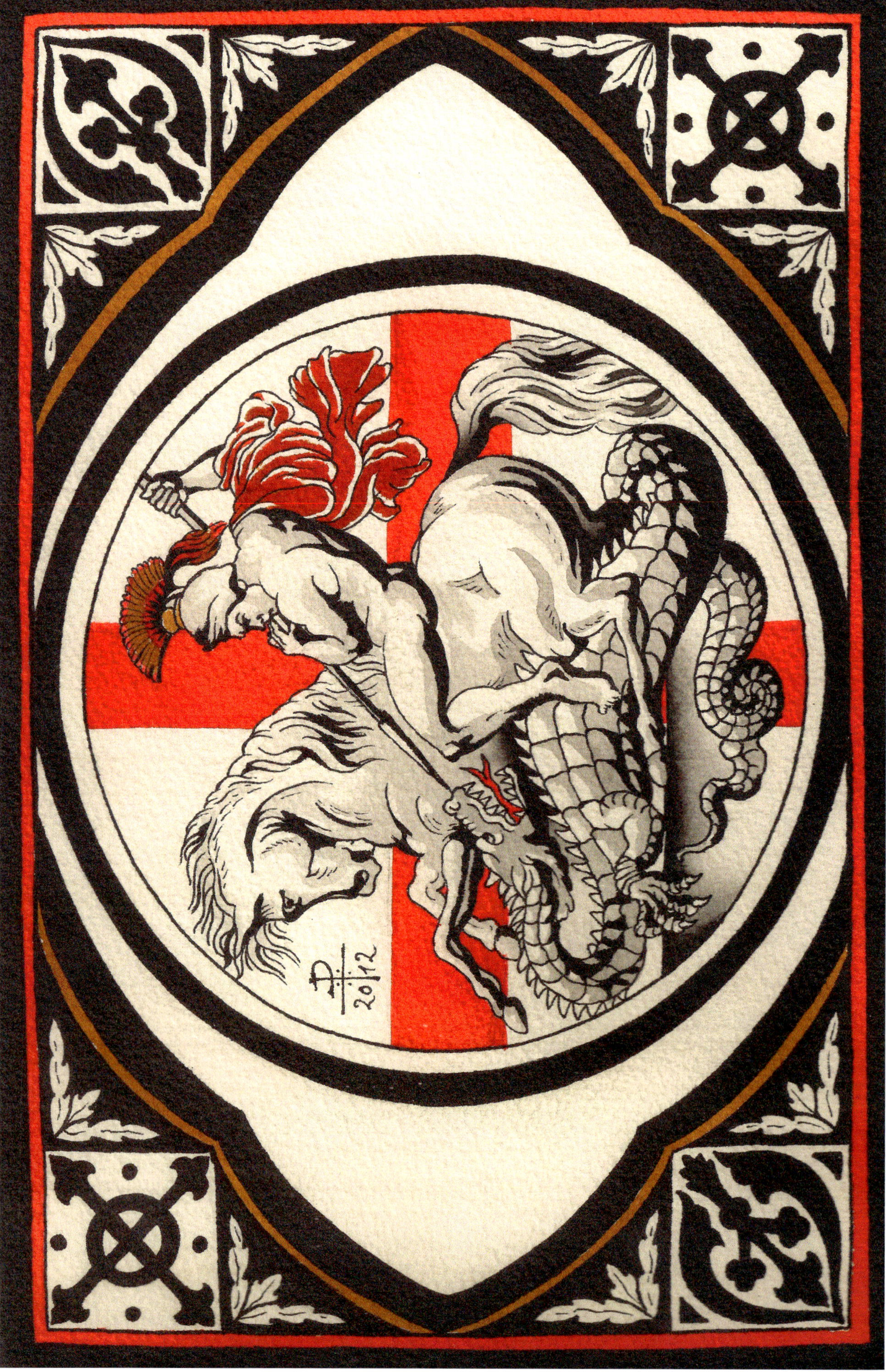

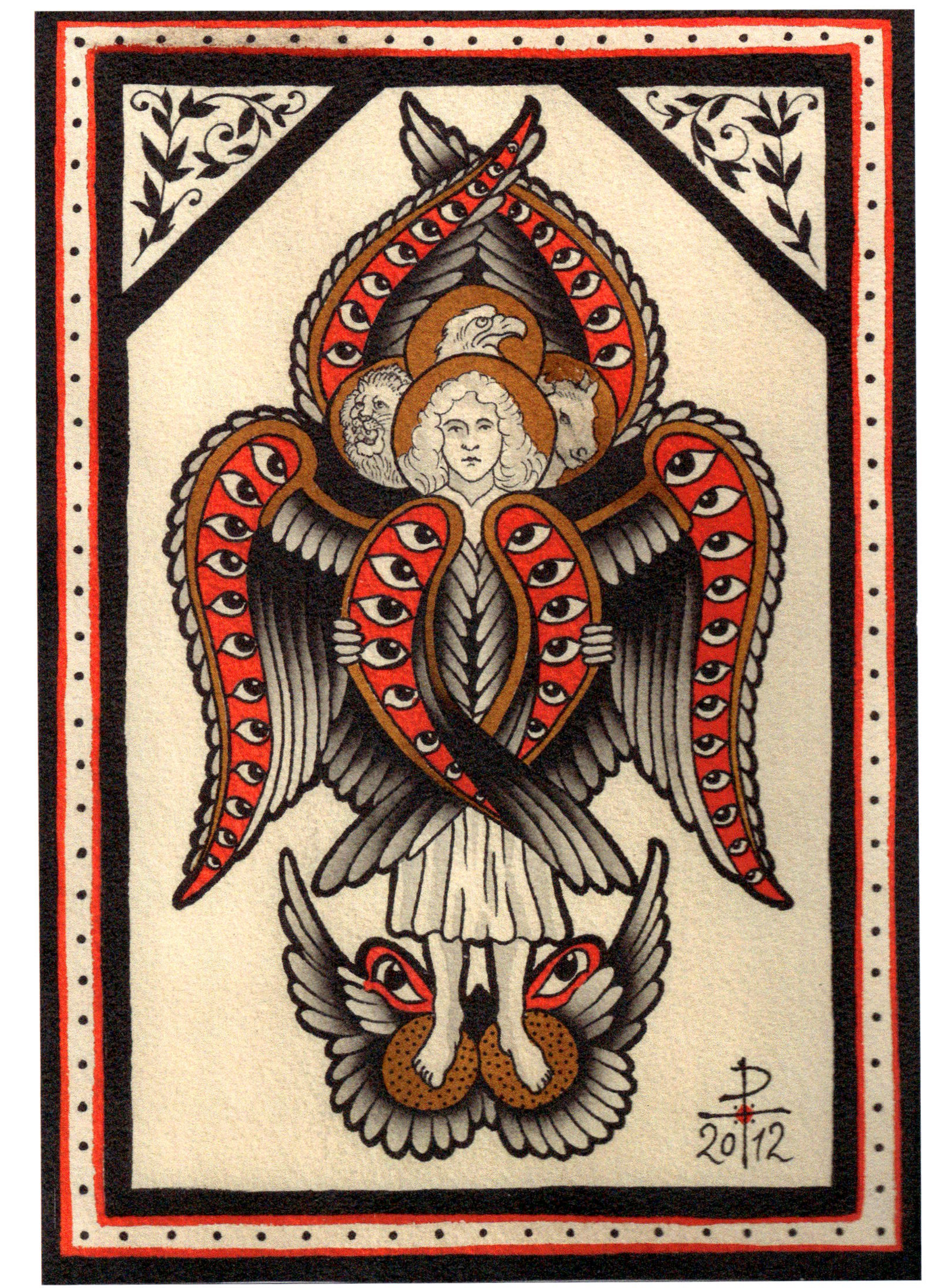

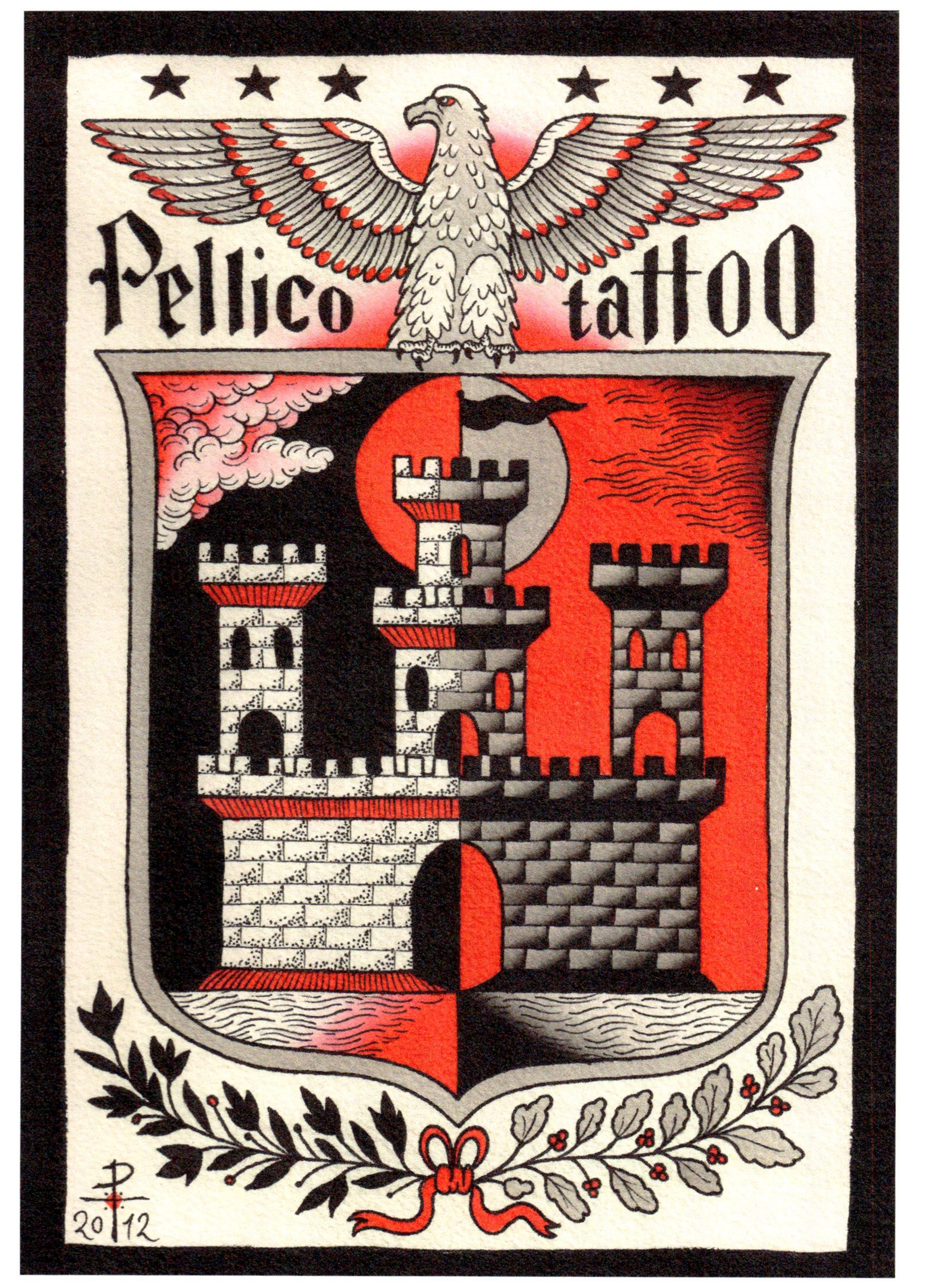
Pellico tattoo
2012

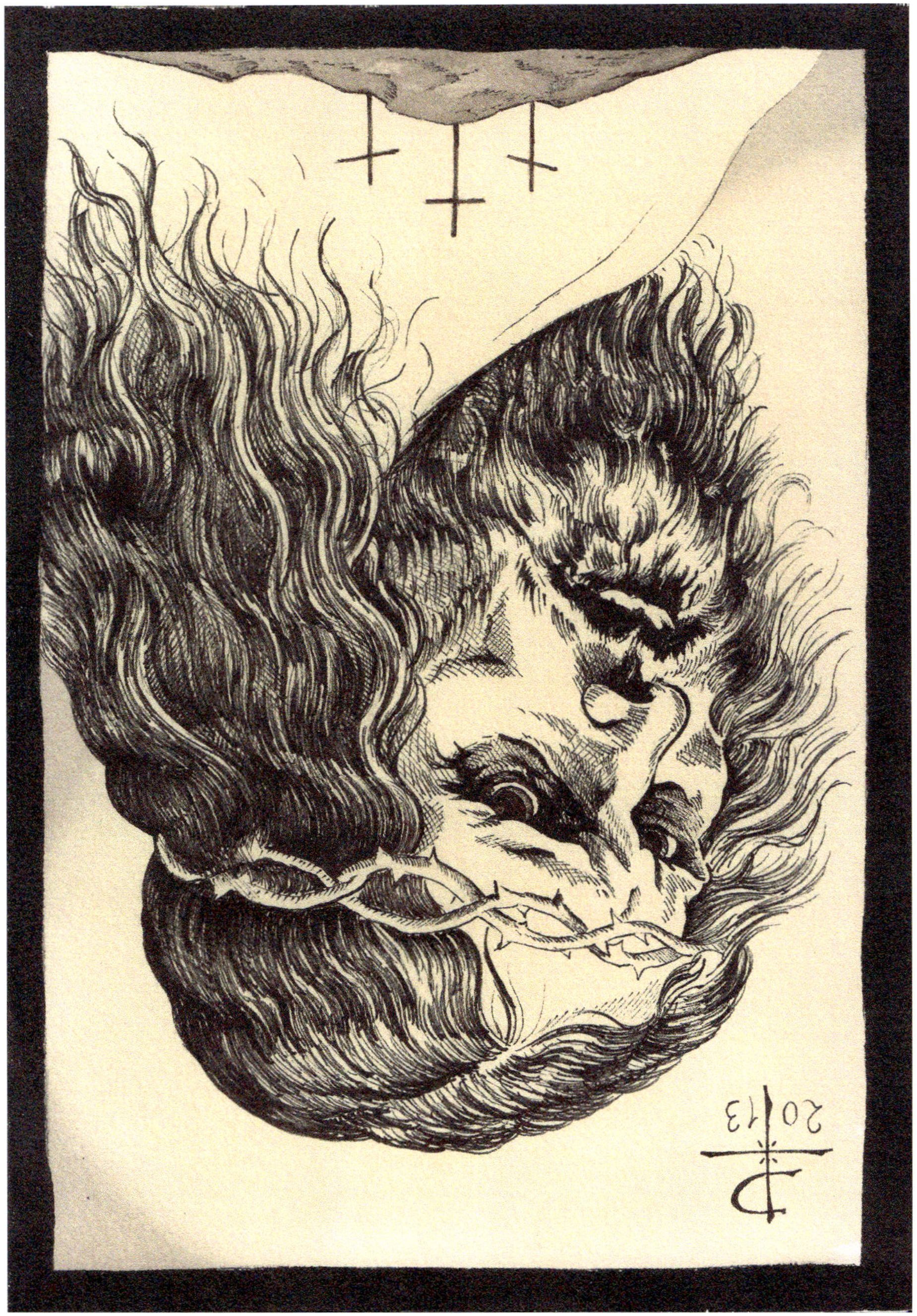

XII

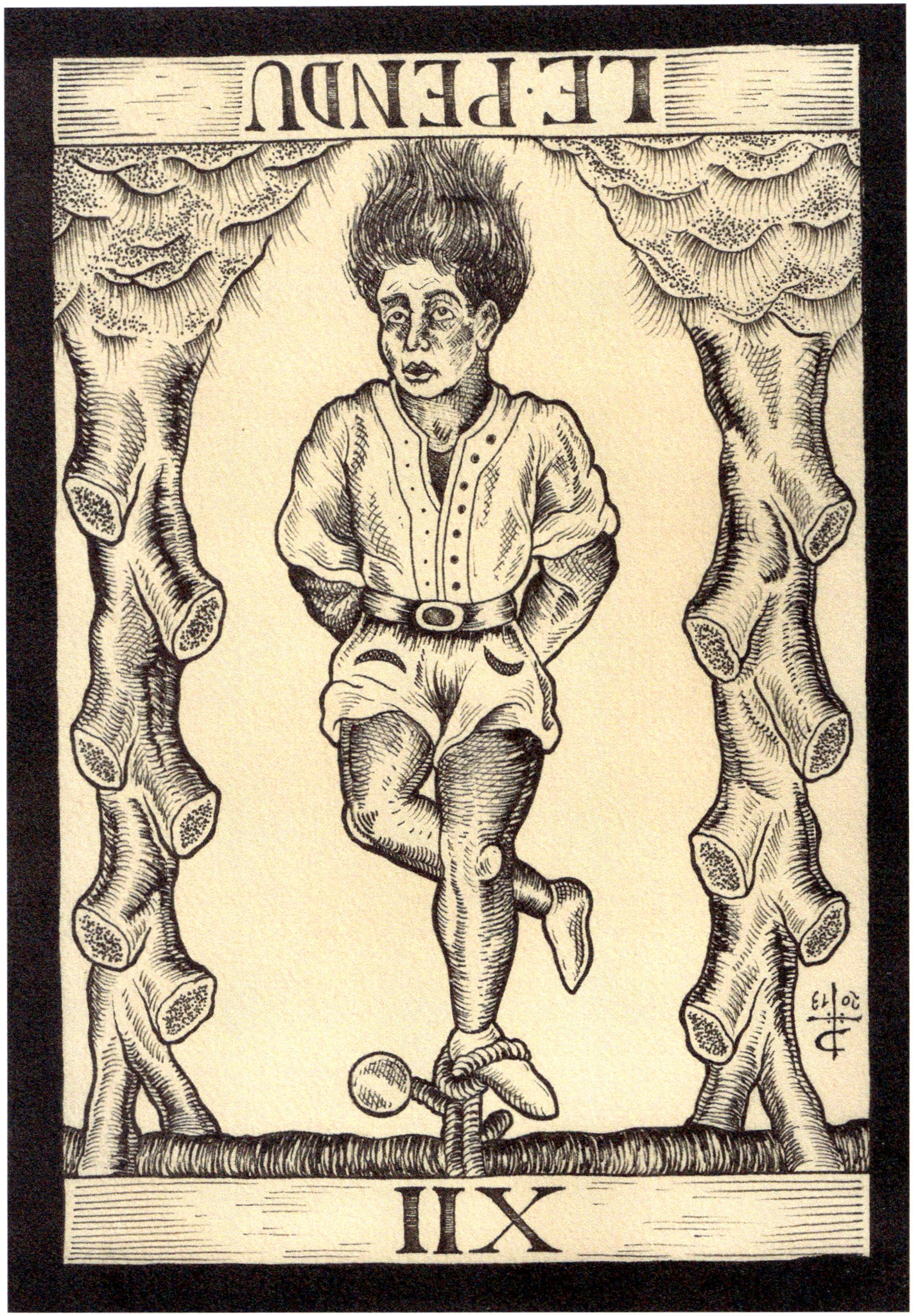

LE·PENDU

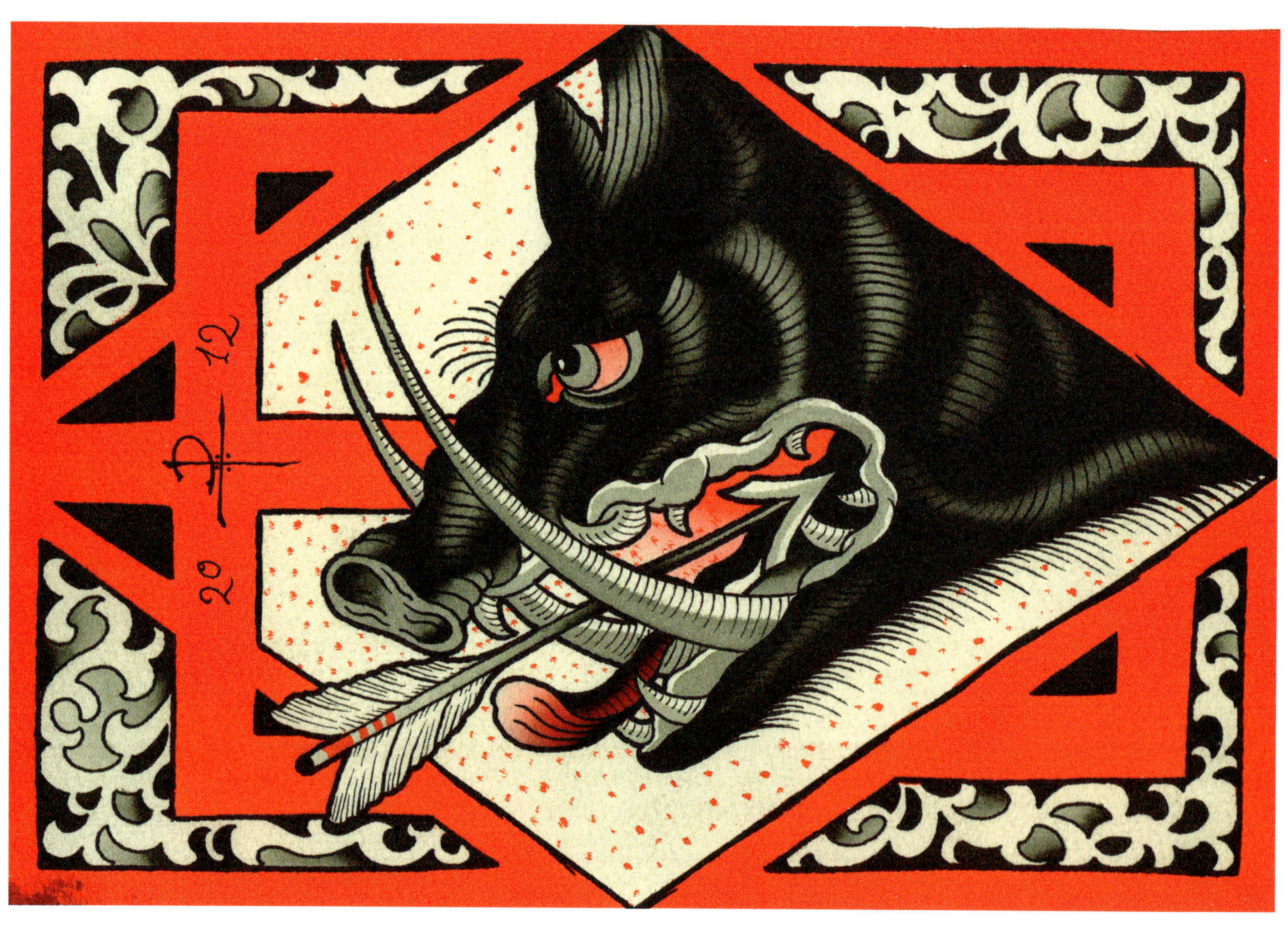

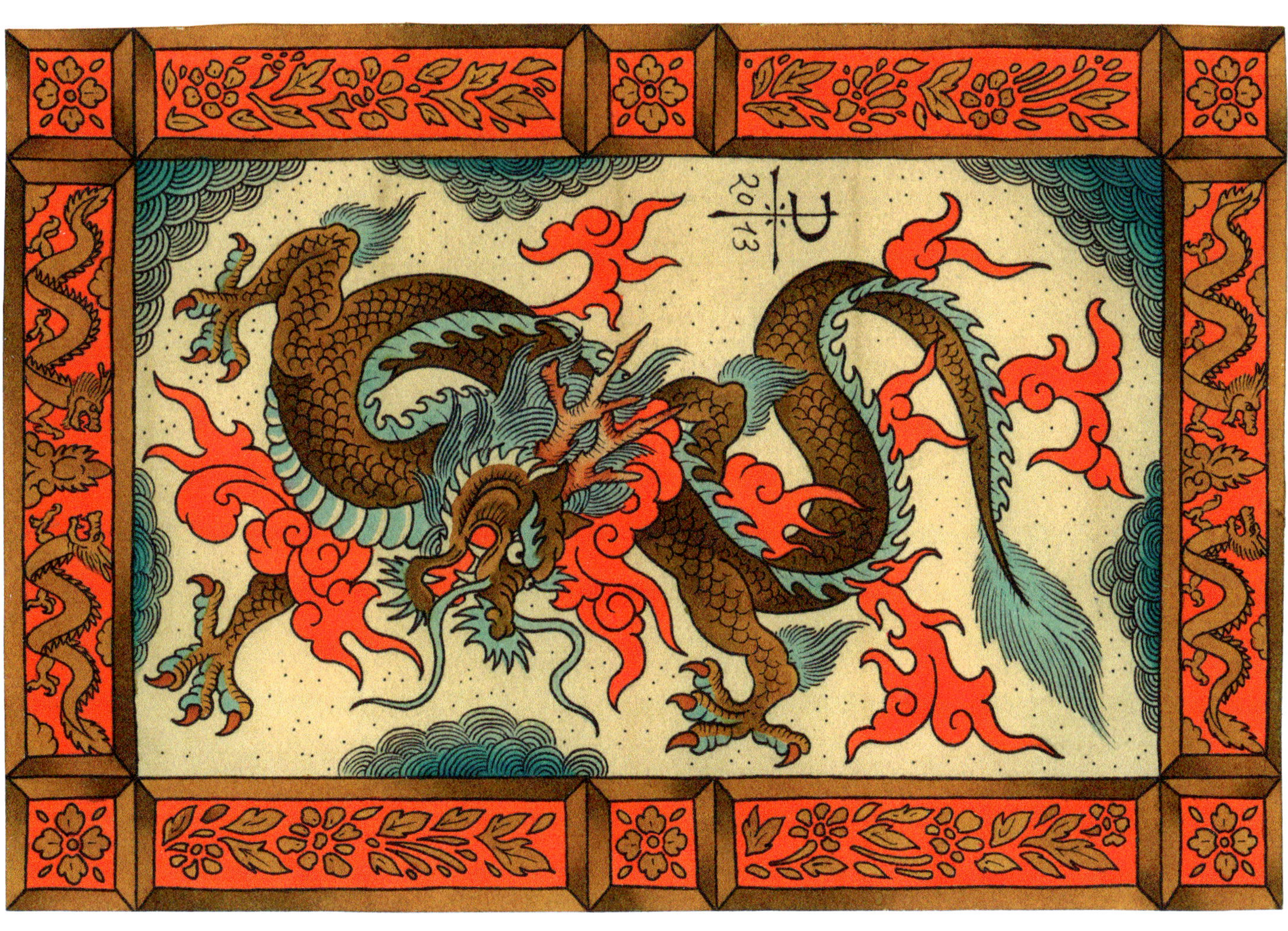
20 13

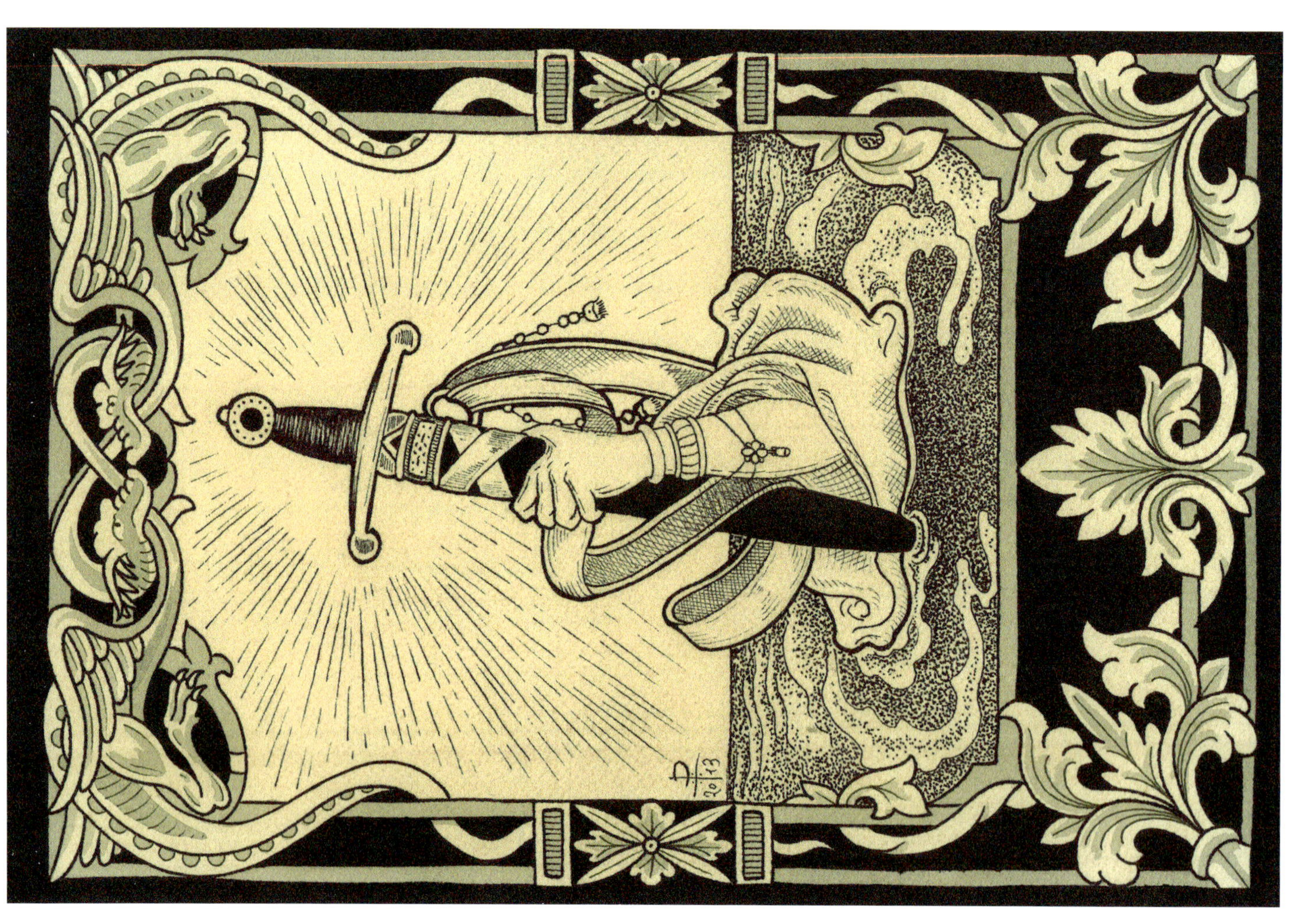

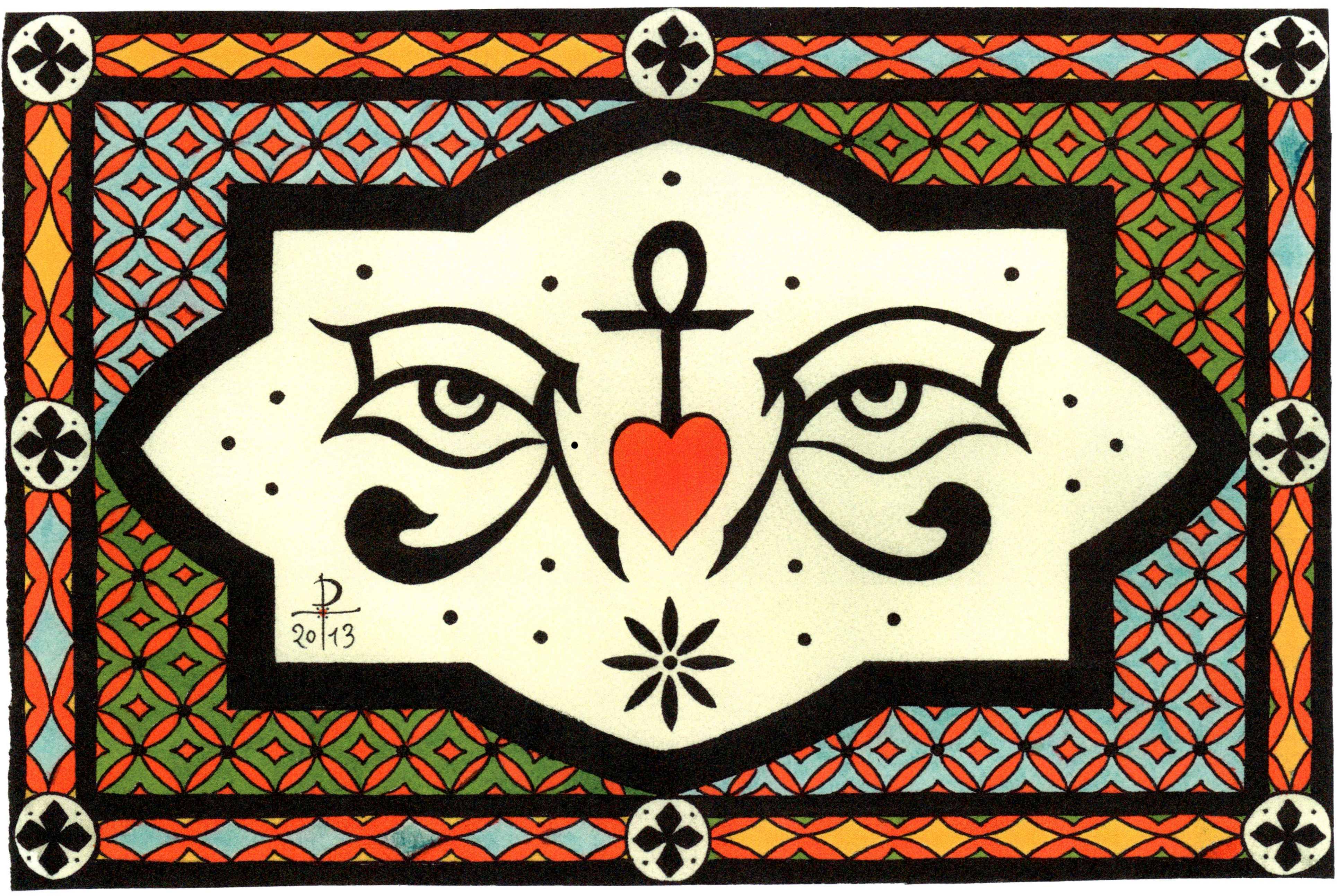
20 13

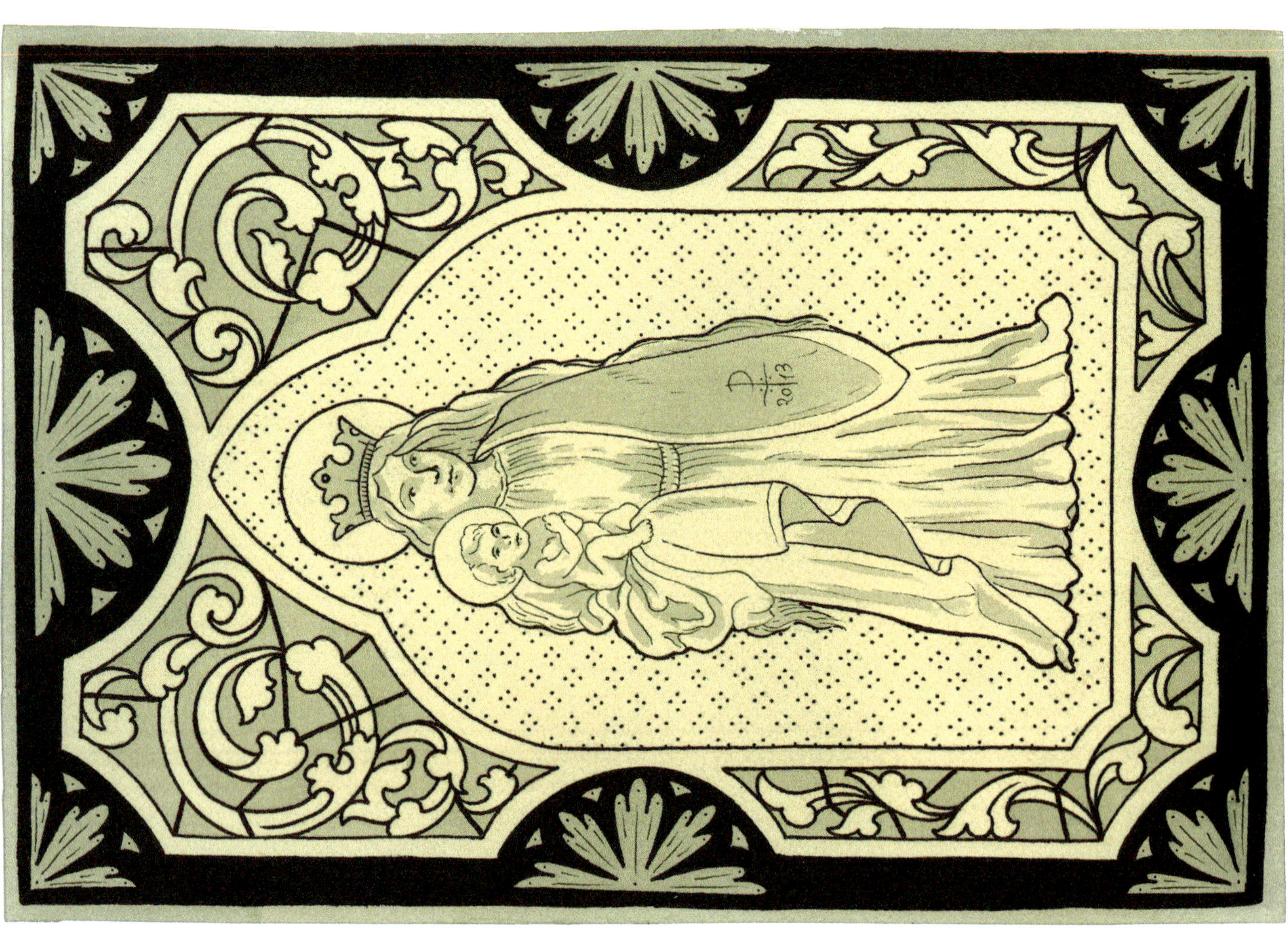

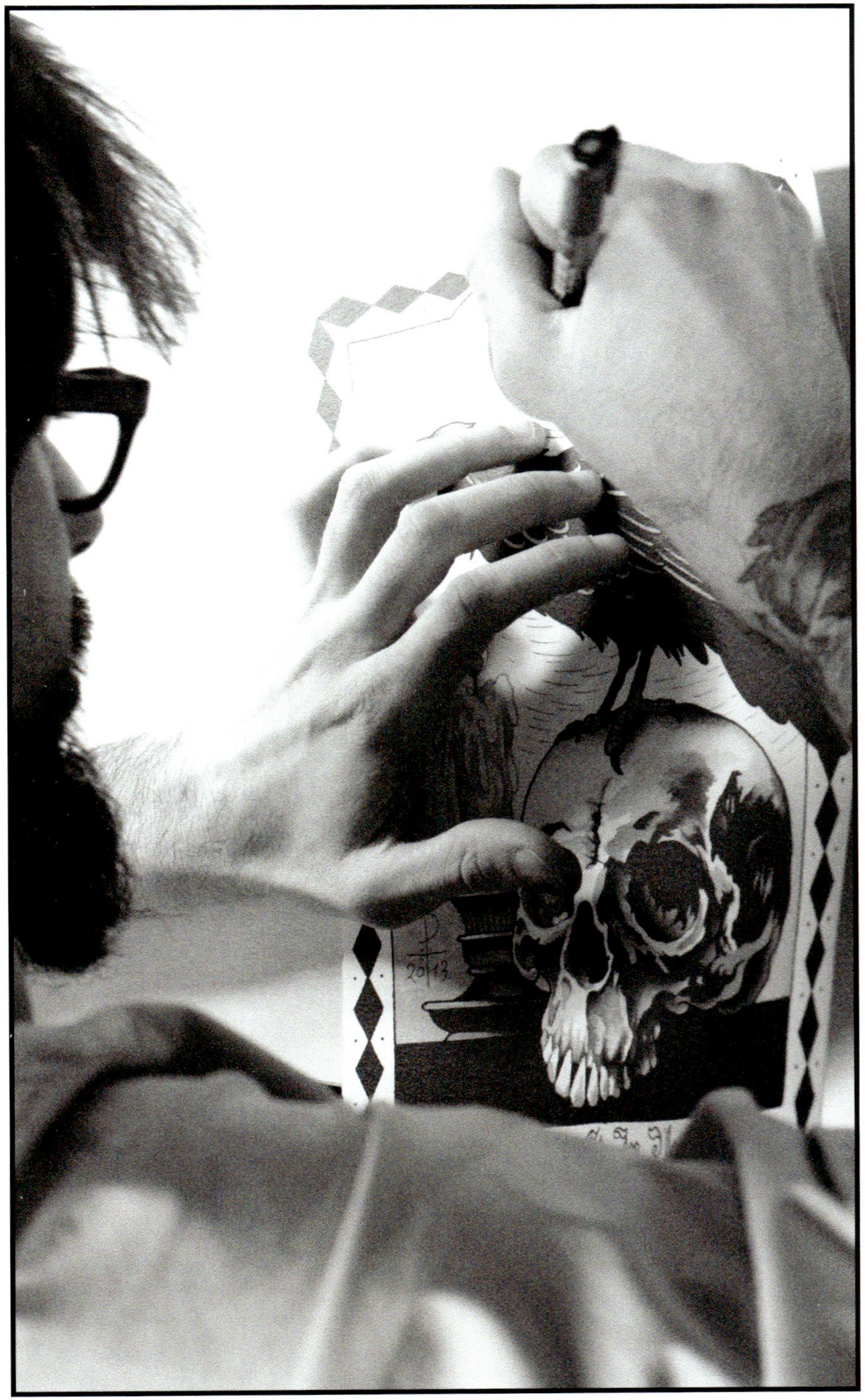

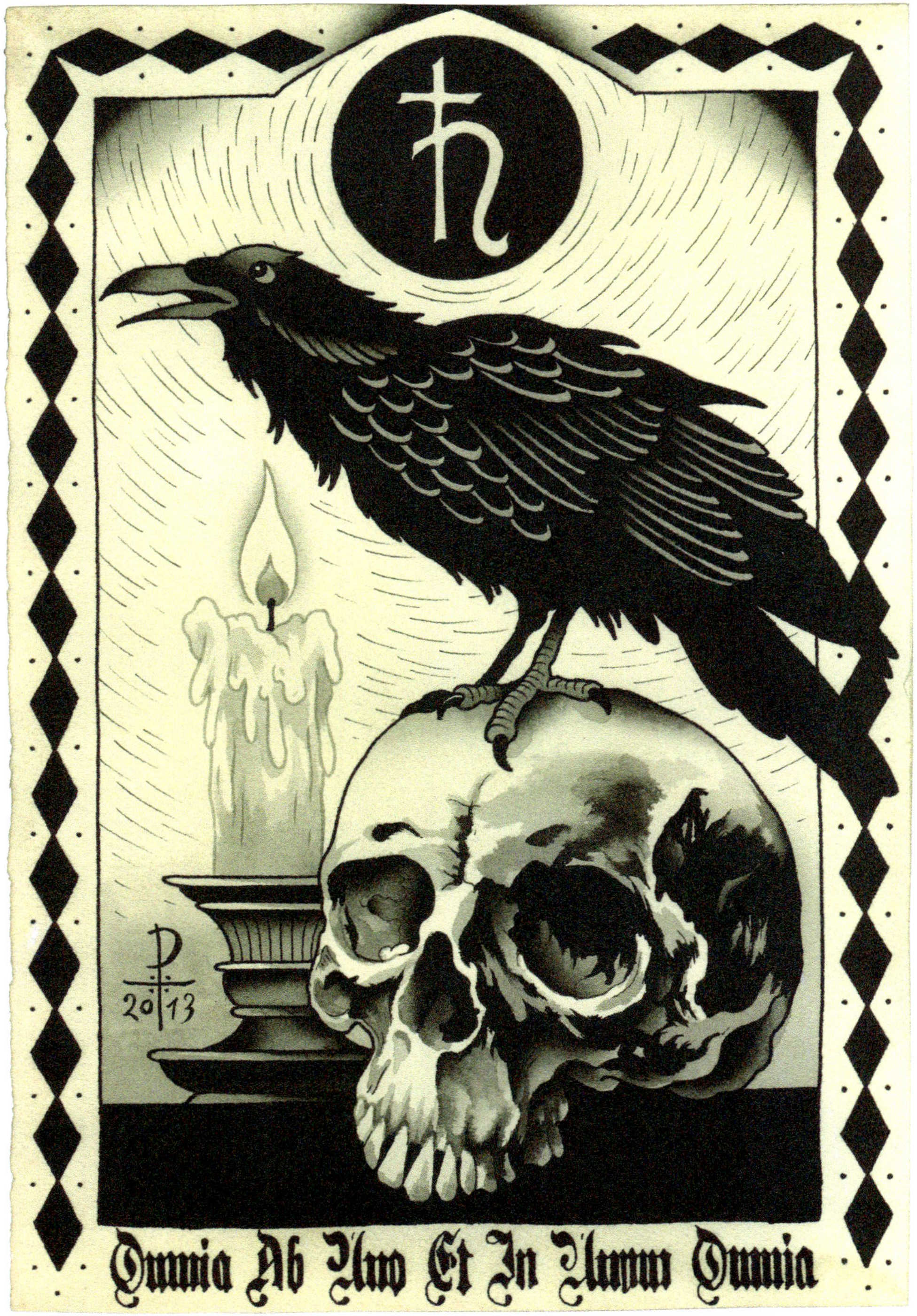

Omnia Ab Uno Et In Unum Omnia

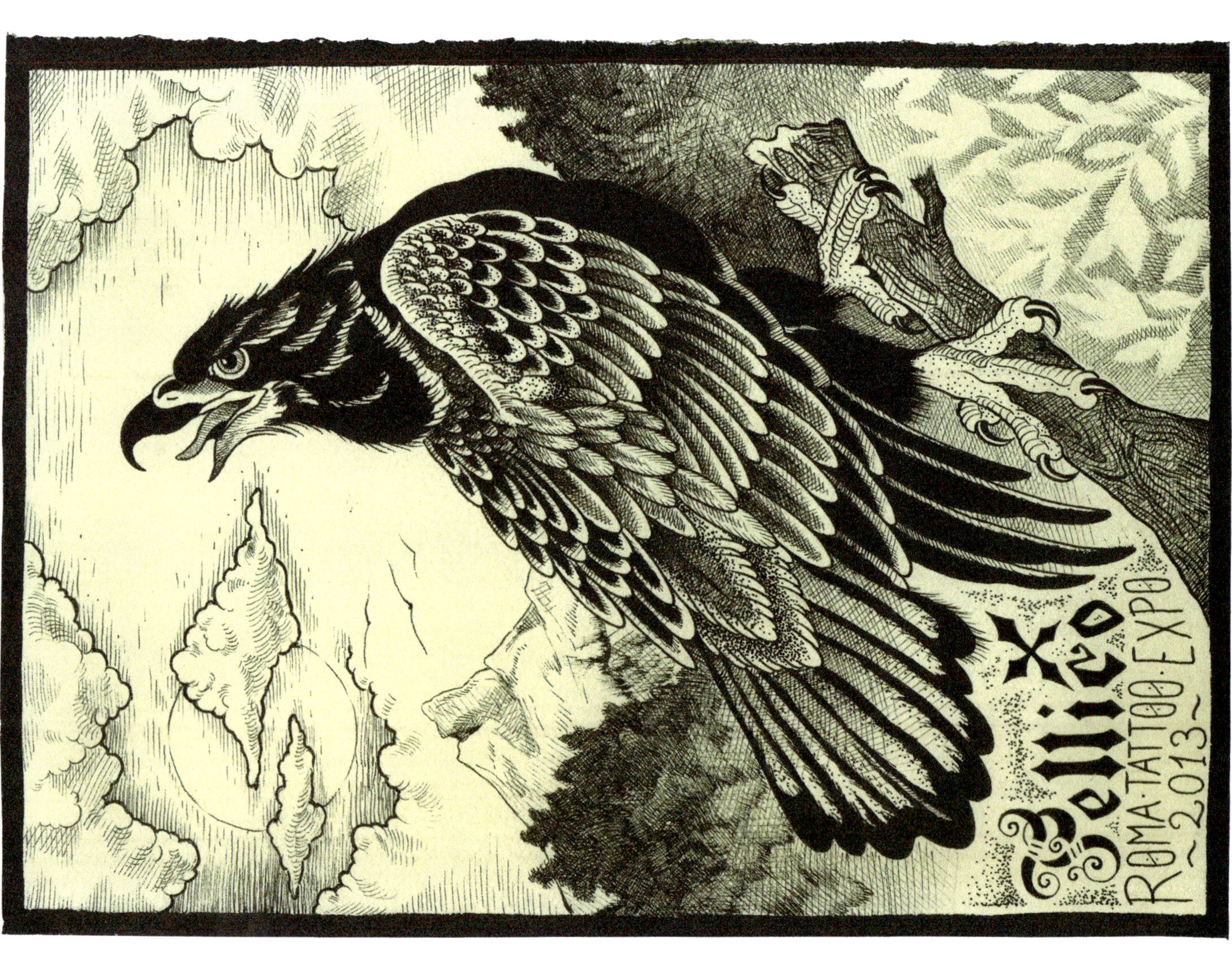
Bellico
ROMA·TATTOO·EXPO
~2013~

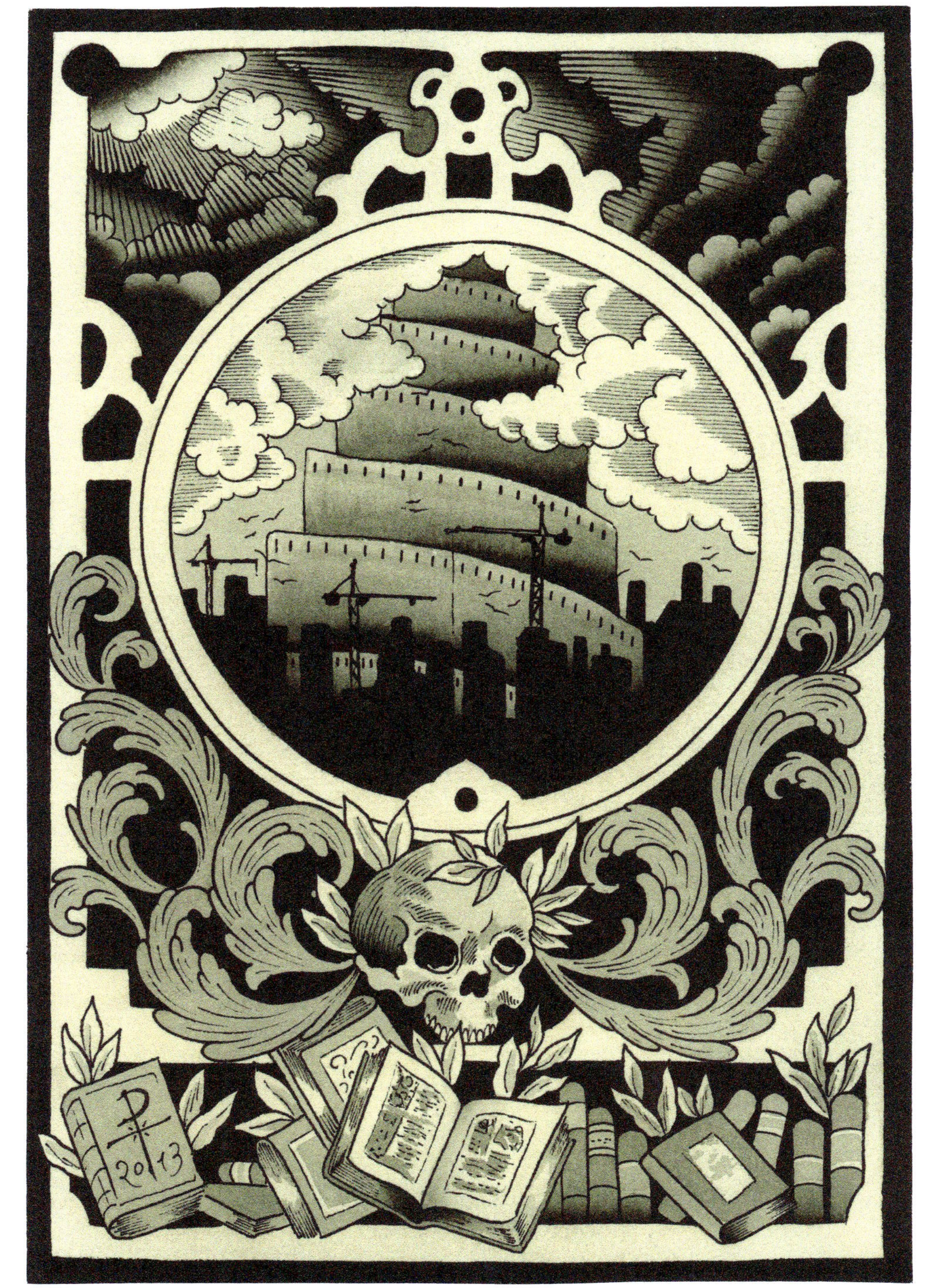
2013

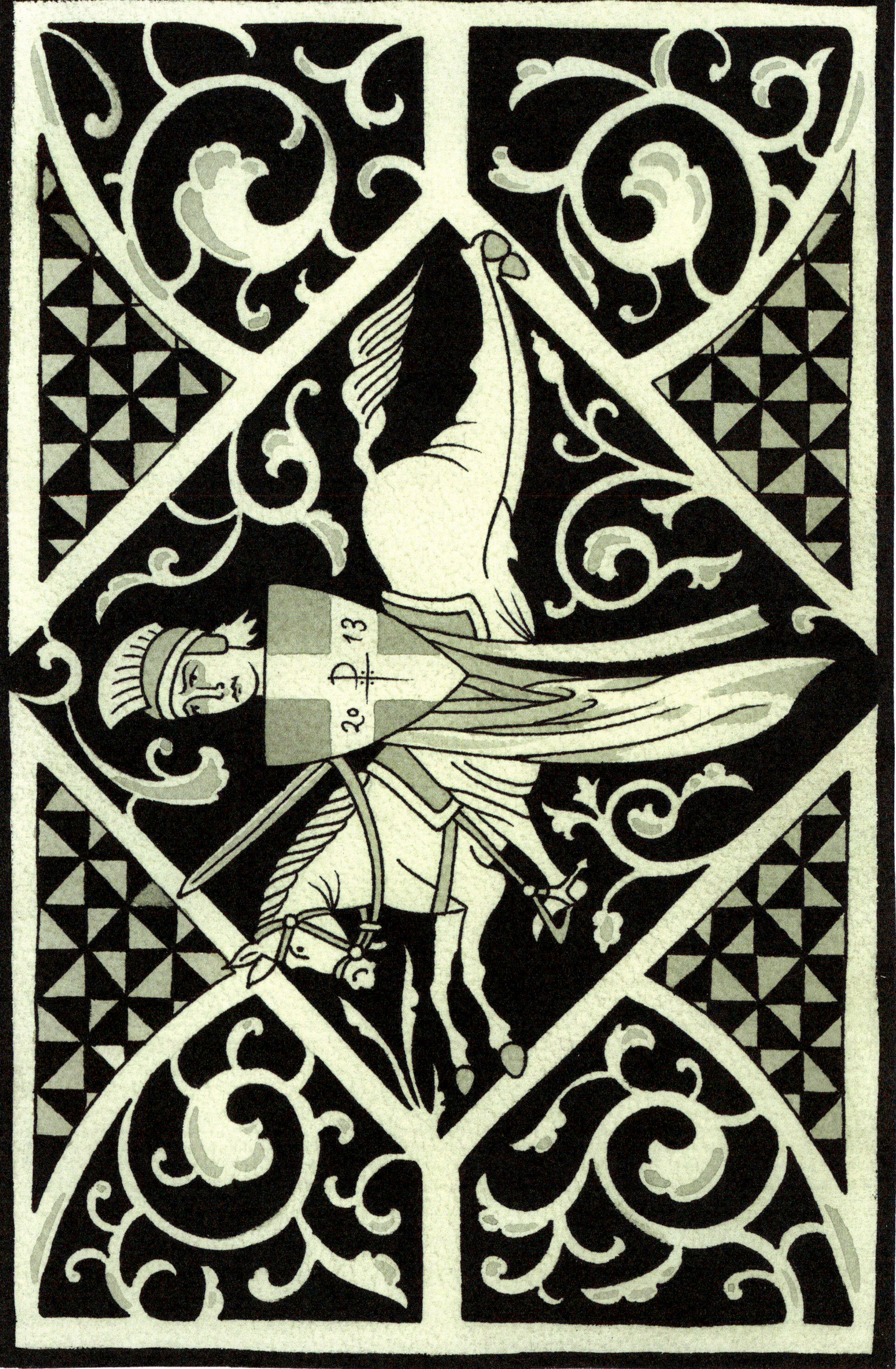

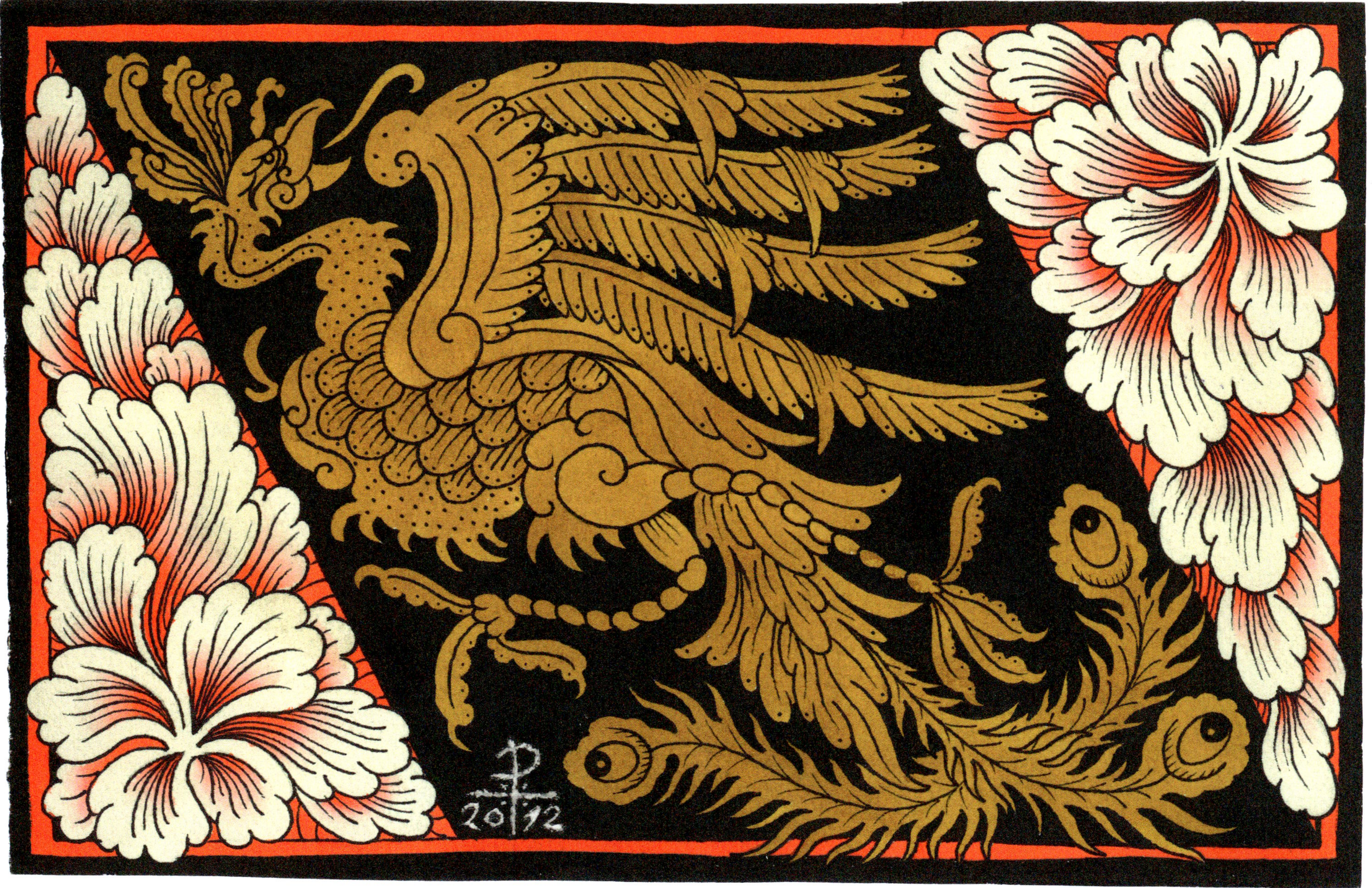

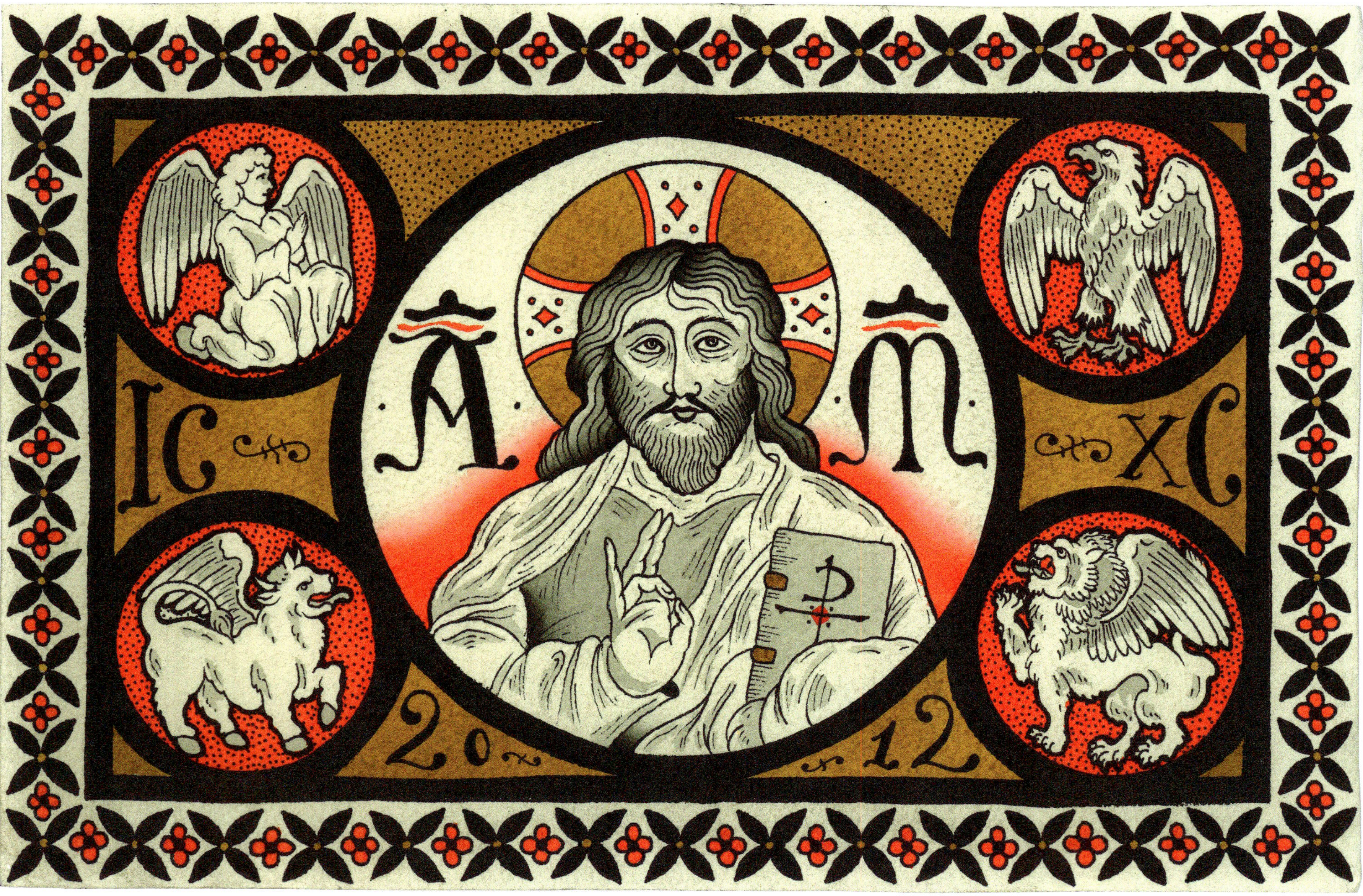
IC
A
M
XC
20 12

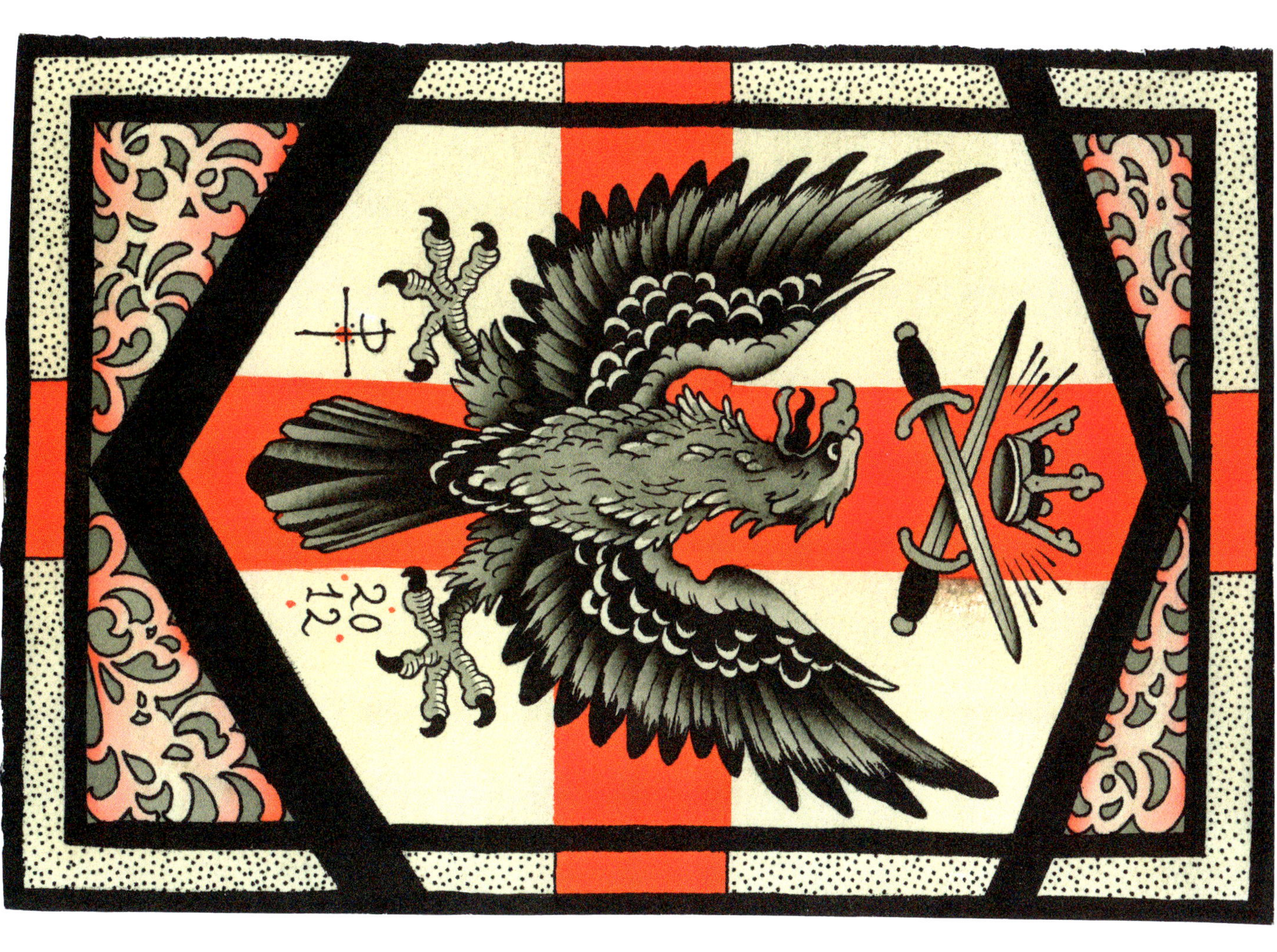

ACKNOWLEDGMENTS

We would like to thank first of all our families. And the following people: Viviana, Giulia B, Martina, Michelangelo, Gianmaurizio Fercioni, Marco Lari, Fabio Tattoo, William Payer, Lupo Horiokami, Miki Vialetto, Rutz, and Katia and Dimitri.

And special thanks from Stizzo to his wife Stefania and his children Lorenzo and Leonardo (true love).

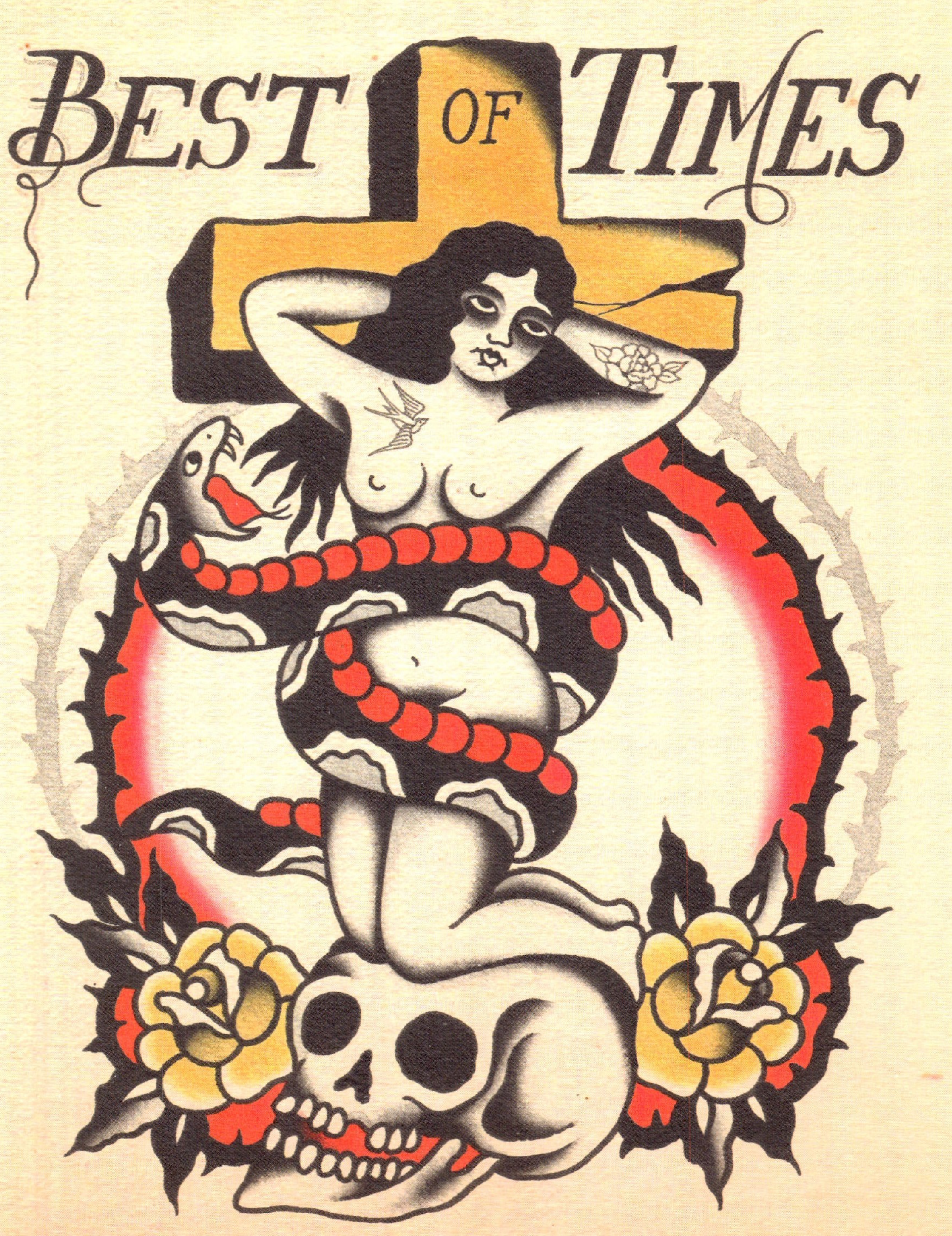
BEST OF TIMES